RENEWALS 458-4574

Aggression, Family Violence and Chemical Dependency

Aggression, Family Violence and Chemical Dependency

Ronald T. Potter-Efron
Patricia S. Potter-Efron
Editors

The Haworth Press
New York • London

Aggression, Family Violence and Chemical Dependency has also been published as *Journal of Chemical Dependency Treatment*, Volume 3, Number 1 1989.

The Haworth Press, Inc. 10 Alice Street, Binghamton, NY 13904-1580
EUROSPAN/Haworth, 3 Henrietta Street, London WC2E 8LU England

Library of Congress Cataloging-in-Publication Data

Aggression, family violence, and chemical dependency / Ronald T. Potter-Efron, Patricia S. Potter-Efron, guest editors.
   p. cm.
   "Has also been published as the Journal of chemical dependency treatment, v. 3, no. 1 1989"—T.p. verso.
   Includes bibliographical references.
   ISBN 0-86656-964-2. — ISBN 0-86656-977-4 (pbk.)
   1. Substance abuse. 2. Aggressiveness (Psychology) 3. Family violence. I. Potter-Efron, Ronald T. II. Potter-Efron, Patricia S.
[DNLM: 1. Child Abuse. 2. Family. 3. Spouse Abuse. 4. Substance Dependence. 5. Violence. W1 J058L v. 3 no. 1 / HQ 809 A266]
RC564.A33   1989
616.85'82—dc20
DnLM/DLC
for Library of Congress   89-24737
                                             CIP

Aggression, Family Violence and Chemical Dependency

CONTENTS

∞   ALL HAWORTH BOOKS & JOURNALS
ARE PRINTED ON CERTIFIED
ACID-FREE PAPER

ABOUT THE EDITORS

Ronald T. Potter-Efron, MSW, PhD, is a clinical psychotherapist for Midelfort Clinic in Eau Claire, Wisconsin. He is the author of *Shame, Guilt, and Alcoholism: Treatment Issues in Clinical Practice* (Haworth, 1989).

Patricia S. Potter-Efron, BA, CADC-III, is a certified alcoholism counselor in private practice in Eau Claire and a consultant to hospitals that have chemical dependency programs.

The Potter-Efrons hold workshops around the country on such topics as the treatment of shame and guilt in alcoholics and on adult children of alcoholics. A primary aspect of their work is the incorporation of Gestalt therapy. They have published articles on family violence and chemical dependency. Ronald and Patricia Potter-Efron are editors of *The Treatment of Shame and Guilt in Alcoholism Counseling* (Haworth, 1988), and authors of *Letting Go of Shame: Understanding How Shame Affects Your Life* (Hazelden/ Harper & Row, 1989), which has been selected by the Psychology Today Book Club as a main selection.

Aggression and Violence Associated with Substance Abuse

Michael M. Miller, MD
Ronald T. Potter-Efron, MSW, PhD

SUMMARY. The complex relationships between aggression, violence and substance abuse are discussed. Specific substances described include alcohol, other sedative hypnotics, stimulants, hallucinogens, opioids, phencyclidine, cannabis, and inhalants. Clinical states associated with substance abuse and aggression include intoxication, withdrawal, paranoid/psychotic phenomena, idiosyncratic intoxication, acute and chronic organic mental disorders (deliriums and dementias), and violence secondary to drug-seeking.

I. INTRODUCTION

Among the repertoire of human emotions and behaviors, anger and violence are among the more complex responses. A number of intrapsychic and environmental variables can influence the quality and intensity of angry and violent reactions. The intent of this article is to explore how drugs of abuse induce states that modify emotional and behavioral responses such that anger or violence can be elicited or intensified. For the purposes of this article, the terms addictive drugs, mind-altering substances, drugs of abuse, and habit-forming chemicals are assumed to refer to the same thing: those compounds which have been demonstrated by animal and human research to be self-reinforcing, and thus preferentially self-administered by people (or by lab animals that serve as models of human behavior) (Pickens and Meisch, 1973). The reinforcing

Michael M. Miller is an addictionologist and psychiatrist at Midelfort Clinic in Eau Claire, WI. Ronald T. Potter-Efron is a clinical psychotherapist at Midelfort Clinic in Eau Claire, WI.

1

qualities of such agents generally involve euphoria or a less intense (but still enjoyable) sense of well-being. Anger and violence are usually not desirable effects of abused drugs, not even desirable to the user: but understanding how such agents can affect behaviors and emotions can aid professionals in their clinical work with chemically dependent clients and their families.

The authors recognize that angry or aggressive behavior can rarely be attributed only to the effects from ingestion of a mood-altering chemical. Usually violence is a result of a combination of the drug, situation, and the personality of the user (Niven, 1986). In fact, the majority of anger and violence episodes associated with substance abuse may well be predicated more upon the psychological traits of the individual (as determined by personality variables — diagnosable psychopathological entities [which are reviewed in Chapter 2 of this volume]) or else to the psychological state of the individual (as determined by enviromental stressors and the individual's response to these stressors) than upon the specific alteration in central nervous physiology induced by drugs of abuse. As Cohen (1985) notes, no chemical is invariably criminogenic. However, the disinhibitory effects of certain drugs of abuse are often pivotal in the violent expression of pent-up anger. Further, certain drugs predictably move individuals toward aggression and these effects cannot be attributed to personality and socio-cultural variables alone. For example, phencyclidine (PCP) has a demonstrated "ability to produce disruption above a certain dosage level [which is] consistent and to some degree free from social determinants and expectations" (Morgan, 1985).

This paper will examine various drugs and the states of intoxication produced by them, with emphasis on how anger and violence are modulated in such states. Chemicals can affect brain function in various ways. Acute ingestion of a chemical can produce a state of *intoxication*, with rather predictable behavioral outcomes. After a state of physical dependency to a drug has been acquired, the *withdrawal* of that chemical from the brain can result in altered brain function, with profound effects on behavior. Additionally, intense or chronic exposure of the organism to intoxicants can result in toxic damage to brain tissue and clinical syndromes called *organic mental disorders* (or, under previous nomenclature, organic brain syndromes). Habitual chemical abuse can also result in shifts of an individual's overall behavioral repertoire, even during intervals when an individual is temporarily "drug-free." Short and long term *psychotic states* can be triggered as well.

We have chosen to organize this paper along two dimensions: (1) that of various drugs of abuse themselves; and, (2) that of clinical syndromes, exploring drug effects in each type of syndrome, and exploring how anger and violence are relevant dimensions of these clinical states.

Table I highlights the covariance of aggression and substance abuse, indicating how chemicals are generally associated with the appearance of aggression under specified conditions. Table II reflects the covariance of substance abuse and the emotional states of anger and irritability.

These relationships will be discussed further both through the literature review that follows this section and in a discussion of the various states noted above.

II. LITERATURE REVIEW

Although violent behaviors may be associated with the use of any drug (Niven, 1986), certain substances appear to be more commonly aggression-stimulating than others. These are alcohol, phencyclidine (PCP), amphetamines, and sedative-hypnotics (Levenson, 1985). The authors would add cocaine to this list.

Cohen (1985) describes succinctly the interactions and mechanisms for drug-violence interactions. Some of his major conclusions are that: (1) specific actions of particular drugs may induce belligerence and hostility; (2) drug-induced aggression varies by dosage, often following a curvilinear path as maximum dosage incapacitates the user (also see Sanchez and Johnson, 1987); (3) aggression is more likely to occur on the ascending limb of the blood drug concentration than on the descending limb; (4) the set and setting of the drug modifies and can even overwhelm the pharmacologic effect of the substance; and (5) there are a number of pathways that drug-induced violence might take, including: (a) the drug might diminish ego controls and release submerged anger; (b) it might impair judgment; (c) it might induce restlessness, irritability and

TABLE I. Covariance of Substance Abuse and the Behavioral States of Aggression and Violence

DRUG NAME OR CATEGORY:	Intoxication	Intoxication Delirium	Withdrawal	Withdrawal Delirium	Idiosyncratic/ Paradoxical Response	Substance Induced Dementia	Chronic Substance Induced Paranoia	Drug-Procuring Violence
Alcohol	c		c	occ	occ	occ	occ	occ
Other Sedative/Hypnotics			c	c	occ	occ*		
Phencyclidine (PCP)	c	c					c	
Cocaine	c						c	occ
Other Stimulants	c						c	occ
Opiates								c
Hallucinogens					occ			
Cannabis							occ	occ
Inhalants		occ						

c = common

occ = occasional

* only gluthethamide

4

TABLE II. Covariance of Substance Abuse and the Emotional/Psychological States Associated with Irritability and Anger

	Production of Irritable "Short-Fused" State	Induction of Acute Paranoid Thoughts and Behavior	Exacerbation of Underlying Paranoid State	Disinhibition of Intrinsic Anger
Alcohol or Sedative Intoxication	2+ - 3+	1+	0 - 2+	3+
Alcohol/Sedative Withdrawal	3+ - 4+	1+ - 2+	1+ - 2+	0
Stimulant Intoxication (includes cocaine)	*3+ - 4+	3+ - 4+	3+ - 4+	0
Stimulant Withdrawal	0	0	0	0
Opiate Intoxication	0	0	0	0
Opiate Withdrawal	3+	0	0 - 1+	0
Hallucinogen Intoxication	0 - 1+	0 - 1+	1+ - 3+	1+
Cannabis Intoxication	0 - 1+	1+ - 3+	2+ - 4+	1+
Phencyclidine Intoxication	2+ - 4+	4+	4+	0

= includes caffeine

5

pulsiveness; (d) it could produce a paranoid thought disorder; (e) an intoxicated or delirious state might result in combativeness, hyperactivity and violence; (f) a user's drug-induced feelings of omnipotence and bravado may promote dangerous behavior; and (g) unpredictable and uncharacteristic behavior may be associated with amnestic and fugue states.

Among delinquents, abusers of cocaine have been found in one study (Simonds and Kashani, 1985) to be most violent, followed by users of amphetamines, barbiturates, PCP, and Valium. Cocaine (and heroin) is also implicated heavily in the criminal activity of incarcerated female felons, although the mean rate of violence was generally low for all groups (Sanchez and Johnson, 1987).

Severely violent outpatients have a higher rate of substance abuse than do less violent patients at a psychiatric clinic (Mungas, 1983). This may be due to a reduction of inhibitions associated with the drug use or because there are common linkages between substance abuse and violence that predispose certain individuals toward both sets of behaviors (Mungas, 1983). There still remains a significant confusion as to whether substances of abuse reinforce, cause or are simply incidental to violent behavior (Simonds and Kashani, 1985).

Alcohol

There is a general consensus that alcohol is the drug most commonly associated with violence (Cohen, 1985). This is probably due to the high base rate of alcohol use in the population rather than to more pronounced anger-inducing effects of ethanol. Alcohol use can trigger aggression during intoxication, withdrawal, and in other specific clinical states. Except at the highest levels of alcohol exposure, when individuals cannot act upon aggressive urges, alcohol is consistently associated with violent behavior.

Individuals with a history of physical abuse score higher on the Michigan Alcoholism Screening Test than do other males in discordant marriages (Van Hassalt et al., 1985) while alcoholics who are not anti-social but have a history of violence drink more per day than other alcoholics, have a higher percentage of alcohol related problems, and have a poorer ability to maintain sobriety after treatment (Schuckit and Russell, 1984).

The aggression associated with alcohol cannot be fully explained through models that rely entirely upon either physiological or sociocultural explanations of that behavior. Laboratory studies indicate that individuals generally become more aggressive when they drink alcohol and that high alcohol use predicts more aggression than does lower use (Taylor and Leonard, 1983). Also, when a placebo is substituted for the alcohol individuals do not become more aggressive, thus indicating that the effect is not entirely environmental or cognitive (Taylor and Leonard, 1983). However, not all alcohol users become aggressive. Taylor and Leonard (1983) note that 32 percent of high dose users did not become aggressive in their study. Cloninger (1987) views links between violence and alcohol use as occurring predominantly in "Type II" alcoholics—those with a kind of alcoholism manifested by an early onset, an ability to abstain, an almost exclusively male membership, and in which arrests and fights are frequent.

Taylor and Leonard conclude that "aggression is a function of the interaction of the pharmacological state induced by alcohol and the cues in the social setting" (Taylor and Leonard, 1983). They suggest that a person who is affected by alcohol is physiologically unable to attend to the complexity of multiple and ambiguous cues that normally mediate behavior. Instead, they notice and act upon only the most immediate cues, which might be aggression instigating. The balance between aggression instigating and inhibiting cues is distorted in this process.

In summary, alcohol use is regularly associated with aggression and this linkage is best viewed as a mixture of personality, social and physiological causes.

Other Sedative-Hypnotics

Withdrawal from sedative-hypnotics, in particular the barbiturates, is strongly associated with both interpersonal violence (Levenson, 1985) and with suicidal intent (Grinspoon and Bakalar, 1985). Cohen (1985) rates these drugs second only to alcohol as contributors to assaultive behavior. Although these chemicals are supposedly sedating, they tend to produce argumentative, irritable behavior, perhaps because the affected individual is released from normal inhibitions as part of the intoxicant effect (Cohen, 1985).

Spotts and Shantz (1984b) conducted an in-depth interview of heavy barbiturate users, seeking to discover how the drug interacts with the ego state of the user. They found that heavy barbiturate ingestors (chronic) developed an increase in irritability and impatience: "The user experiences a welling up of anger, rage and hostility and intense impulses to violence; a need to strike out, hit or attack things or people, to wreck or destroy" (Spotts and Shantz, 1984b, 307). Users suffered paroxysmal outbursts of rage, becoming bellicose, belligerent, quarrelsome, abusive, and they tended to provoke senseless fights with family and others. Their anger had a strong element of self-destruction about it; for example, users would pick fights with stronger individuals and often were badly beaten. Their aggression was not related to the development of paranoid delusions nor was it totally impulsive. Spotts and Shantz believe that the heavy barbiturate user frequently simply wants to find oblivion, to destroy the ego, and that his aggression reflects that basically annihilative, suicidal urge (Spotts and Shantz, 1984b). The possibility exists, however, that the anger and belligerence of some individuals is a physiological response to frequent phenomena of partial withdrawal from sedative drugs (see section III. B. 1).

Phenycyclidine (PCP)

PCP is regularly associated with the appearance of aggression, most commonly among those heavy, chronic users who develop a psychosis that in many ways mimics a schizophrenic episode (Allen, 1980; Peterson and Stillman, 1978). Yago et al. (1981) found that 68 percent of PCP admissions to a psychiatric hospital emergency room had paranoid delusions, hostility and negativism. PCP users may move quickly between the states of sociability and hostility (Grinspoon and Bakalar, 1985). PCP psychosis is characterized by insomnia, tension, hyperactivity and intermittent unexpected aggressive behavior (Luisada and Brown, 1976).

PCP and aggression are not exclusively linked with extended psychotic episodes. Morgan (1985), quoted previously, indicates that PCP appears to produce disruptive effects above a certain level of dosage that are relatively free from social expectations, an indication that the drug does not simply precipitate psychotic responses in those already at high risk for psychosis.

Chronic PCP usage is associated with gradual personality changes, with about one-third of the users at a residential treatment facility reporting that they become more angry, irritable and violent when regularly using PCP (Fauman and Fauman, 1980). While some violence was goal-directed, other aggression was impulsive, bizarre, idiosyncratic or psychotic, suggesting that certain individuals are very prone to extreme reactions to PCP (Fauman and Fauman, 1980).

PCP has a "conspicuous association with those who come into contact with the criminal justice system" (Siegel, 1980). Among 45 persons incarcerated for adult PCP-related violent crimes, 40 percent had had previous violence/PCP episodes. These persons report a high rate of obsessive thoughts, paranoia, and hallucinations during PCP intoxication (Siegel, 1980).

PCP remains one of the most dangerous drugs of abuse currently available with regard to the appearance of aggression and violence.

Cocaine

Cocaine is an extremely volatile substance in that the intoxication state is both intense and short-lived. The cocaine "rush" is sometimes connected with guarded suspiciousness and frank paranoid delusions. Such acute reactions occur after extended bouts of using (Crowley, 1987). Chronic intoxication may also precipitate paranoid psychotic reactions that persist for some days after termination of dosage (Crowley, 1987).

Crowley (1987) found such minor psychological problems as irritability, guardedness and suspiciousness among 99 percent of his subjects, while 43 percent reported more serious symptoms, including hallucinations, delusions, and serious suicidal ideation or attempts. Washton's study of Cocaine Hot Line users (Washton et al., 1984) indicated that 82 percent reported irritability and 65 percent paranoia. Cohen (1983) added that withdrawal from the cocaine "high" may be associated with dysphoria, restlessness and irritability (see also Gawin, 1988).

The mood state described above certainly increases the potential for aggression. However, researchers cite few instances of cocaine related aggression in comparison to other substances of abuse. Grinspoon and Bakalar (1985) conclude that cocaine is probably not as aggression conducive as alcohol, barbiturates or amphetamines. Similarly, Spotts and Shantz (1984) suggest that the chronic cocaine user is more likely to flee, endure the situation or use other drugs to get away from cocaine-induced paranoid feelings than to act against another. Honer et al. (1987), on the other hand, notes that smoking "crack," a more recently appearing method of self-administrating cocaine, seems more likely to trigger significant psychotic symptoms, thoughts or acts of violence, than previous modes of intoxication. Cocaine can definitely not be considered to be a safe drug with regard to agression and violence.

Other Stimulants

"Speed kills" was a popular saying in the 1960s and 1970s. The adverse effects of amphetamines include irritability, hostility and psychosis (Grinspoon and Bakalar, 1985). This psychotic pattern can develop in essentially normal persons (Grinspoon and Bakalar, 1985; Morgan, 1985), even with relatively short term administration of dextroamphetamine (Grinspoon and Balakar, 1985), implying that the drug itself is a causal agent. Amphetamine psychosis arouses a patient's suspiciousness and ideas of reference which may persist for months after the overt psychotic symptoms ease (Grinspoon and Bakalar, 1985).

Cohen (1983) links large doses of amphetamines with hyperactivity, paranoid suspiciousness and impulsivity. Moyer (1976) notes that the tendency toward aggression tends to be cumulative with continuing amphetamine usage and that intravenous use increases the risk for violence. Withdrawal from amphetamines, especially after a "run" of up to two weeks' duration, is also associated with assaultiveness and destructiveness (Moyer, 1976). "Ice" (smokable amphetamines) has recently gained popularity and must be considered very likely to trigger episodes of violence.

Other Substances

Opiates are often associated with criminal behavior in order to procure money to purchase drugs (Cohen, 1983; Jaffe, 1985a). Crime rates for narcotics users are generally high even when these individuals are not actively using drugs, possibly because of the strong positive correlation between heroin abuse and antisocial personality disorder (Potter-Efron, 1989), but they are higher during periods of addictive use (Shaffer et al., 1987). Violence may occur during these criminal pursuits, but it is not the focus of activity. Since all drives are diminished with heroin intoxication, Cohen (1983) suggests that early withdrawal is a more likely time to expect aggression.

Hallucinogens are occasionally linked with violent behavior. Siegel (1980) cites evidence of delusional self-violence as a result of adverse responses to ingestion of LSD, as well as examples of aggression directed toward others. An acute psychotic reaction to LSD is possible which is often accompanied by paranoid ideation (Cohen, 1985). Smith and Seymour (1985) also describe a psychotic break process associated both with visual imagery during early stages of intoxication and with the metaphorical and philosophical wanderings of the mind that accompany later stages. They add that chronic LSD use may contribute to prolonged psychotic reactions and life-threatening depressions. But, as is the case with cannabis/crime associations, the linkage may be more a function of sociopathy or conduct disdorder in the user than a function of the drug itself.

Frequent *cannabis* use is sometimes associated with criminal behavior in youths and adults. For example, one study (Dembo et al., 1987) reports that among youths entering a juvenile detection center, those who screened positive for marijuana had twice as many non-drug related felonies as did others. However, these authors attribute this pattern to the involvement of these youths in a culture and lifestyle in which defiance of societal standards is common, rather than to the effects of the drug itself. Fearfulness, panic and intense aggressive impulses have been attributed to marijuana intoxication (Nicholi, 1983); however, most studies of marijuana use indicate that it is at least as likely to reduce violent impulses as to encourage them. For instance, Taylor and Leonard (1983) found that while high doses of alcohol trigger more aggressiveness than lower dosages, the opposite is true for marijuana: the more marijuana consumed, the less likelihood there was for aggression. Marijuana may act to suppress crime and violence by inducing generalized lethargy (Grinspoon and Bakalar, 1985). Marijuana may exacerbate psychotic tendencies among those who are already endangered in this regard (Grinspoon and Bakalar, 1985). Finally, it should be noted that most studies on the effect of cannabis have been done with relatively minor dosage levels. The increasingly potent quality of marijuana and related drugs now available in the American market might be significantly more aggression-stimulating as well as addiction-promoting.

III. CLINICAL SYNDROMES WITH CASE STUDIES

This section is designed to familiarize the reader with the relationship among aggression, violence and specific clinical syndromes, such as intoxication and withdrawal states across drug categories. Illustrative case studies are provided.

III. A. Intoxication States

Intoxication is a generic term which means — literally — that an organism has been poisoned by a toxin. It is acute poisoning of the brain by the toxin — the intoxicating substance — which produces the behavioral manifestations of the intoxicated state. The effects of intoxicants on behavior are almost always self-limited; as the brain is no longer exposed to the intoxicant, its premorbid function gradually returns. Metabolic derangements of brain functioning can, of course, be induced by a variety of other provocations: physical illnesses, non-addicting medications or head trauma. But the toxic result of all mild brain insults is rather nonspecific; i.e., it is a generalized manifestation of brain dysfunction regardless of the specific etiology of the dysfunction. In colloquial language, people call intoxication "drunkenness," since being "drunk" after alcohol exposure is the most commonly observed form of brain intoxication.

III. A. 1. *Ethyl Alcohol Intoxication*

In low doses and with short-term exposures, ethanol actually serves as a mild stimulant to the brain (Eckardt et al., 1981). It can thus produce enthusiastic or mildly excited states akin to low levels of intoxication with stimulant drugs (see Section III. A. 3 below). This is why alcohol can serve to allay fatigue (hence the classic 5 p.m. "pick-me-up" cocktail prior to dinner). But in general, ethanol serves as a central nervous system depressant. Ethanol also specifically serves as a disinhibitor of ongoing brain activity (Shaw, 1978). This disinhibition is manifested behaviorally by the drinking person doing things while intoxicated that they would otherwise never consider doing while sober. Any individual with intense feelings of anger, from whatever source, that have been suppressed by normal psychological defense mechanisms, can have that anger de-repressed by the disinhibiting effects of ethanol. Thus, the disgruntled spouse, harboring intense but deeply buried resentments, can uncover these and bring them to the conscious level of awareness, and thus, once "in touch with" these feelings, can behave in accordance with those angry affects by becoming loud, confrontive or threatening in word or deed, and can even display physical aggressiveness. This physical aggressiveness can be directed outward if the object of the anger is someone else; the anger can be introjected and the disinhibition of introjected anger can result in violence against the self through self-mutilation or suicide attempts; or intrinsic self-hatred can be displaced onto others and thus "acted out" through destructive behaviors against other persons or property. In these scenarios, the anger (toward self or others) is present prior to the exposure to alcohol, and it is the disinhibiting effect of the ethanol that simply induces the expression of these feelings and associated behaviors. Through these mechanisms, alcohol becomes related to a wide range of violent behaviors in our culture, including fighting, assault, vandalism, sexual violence and suicide. Such de-represessed anger in the hands of the driver of a motor vehicle, in combination with the altered motor behavior of the alcohol-intoxicated state, can result in significant carnage as well. Such outward displays of anger and violence related to disinhibition by ethanol should be considered within the "normal" spectrum of the intoxicating effects of ethanol.

III. A. 2. Sedative-Hypnotic Drug Intoxication

Being a central nervous system depressant, ethanol falls in the broad category of sedative drugs—those that diminish ongoing brain activity both at the cortical level and the level of the reticular activating system in the brain stem. Sedative drugs are generally used pharmacologically to alleviate anxiety or to induce sleep, and with chronic exposure, they have the potential to induce or exacerbate depressive states. Most of these substances, when ingested acutely, will produce a state of intense lethargy or even stupor and coma, with such sedated syndromes having their onset fairly early after exposure if the dose was sufficient to induce them; and this sedated phase often appears without there being much of an intermediate phase of intoxication being observable first (Jaffe, 1985: 546). Further, impaired judgment from barbiturate intoxication can persist after the sluggishness wears off (Grinspoon and Bakalar, 1980: 1623). But so-called recreational use of barbiturates or nonbarbiturate sedative hypnotics (especially methaqualone—trade name Sopor or Quaalude) can induce states of euphoria which are emotionally and behaviorally akin to the drunkenness induced by ethanol intoxication (Khantzian and McKenna, 1979). Thus, an individual who is "soaped out" on methaqualone can act drunk and have the same disinhibitions of anger as are described in the above section on alcohol intoxication (Jaffe, 1985: 546). Hostility and quarrelsomeness can be just as prominent with barbiturate intoxication as can be sadness and stupor (Grinspoon and Bakalar, 1980: 1623).

III. A. 3. Stimulant Drug Intoxication

The primary action of stimulant drugs (Weiner, 1985: 166) is to activate the central nervous system, usually by direct stimulation of the central cortex and possibly the reticular activating system in the brain stem, and by enhancement of neurotransmission at all levels of the nervous system. The basic physiologic responses are qualitatively identical across the spectrum of stimulant agents — from nicotine to caffeine to amphetamine to cocaine.

A behavioral excitation accompanies the physiologic ehancement of blood pressure, cardiac output and temperature. With a drug-induced nervous system stimulation, the patient can have a heightened degree of awareness, with hyperacuity of sensation and hypersensitivity to environmental inputs. Physical hyperactivity is a concomitant sign, often accompanied by behavioral irritability (Khantzian and McKenna, 1979). Thus, the individual is so sensitive to emotional as well as other inputs from his environment that he could be quick to respond in a snappy way, evidencing impatience that can take on qualities of true anger. The tendency toward feistiness and argumentativeness and even verbal assaultiveness, in such irritable patients, is behaviorally akin to the irritability of a hypomanic state of psychopathology (O'Brien et al., 1987). This general picture of physical and emotional hyperactivity and irritability is quite analogous to the clinical picture seen in sedative withdrawal states (see III. B. 1 below).

While qualitatively very similar, the intensity of these reactions certainly varies with the intensity of the pharmacologic effect of the stimulant drug in question. Nicotine is a relatively mild stimulant. Non-chemically-dependent caffeine users are familiar with the irritability that can come with mild overdosage; individuals who abuse caffeine via regular ingestion of caffeine tablets or regular ingestion of several liters of coffee or caffeinated cola per day can also develop significant irritability. Some individuals who seem to be consistently angry can have a marked resolution of their anger outbursts by simply abstaining from these neuroexcitatory agents. The stimulant effects of cocaine are more intense than those of other agents and can produce not only intense euphoria, but also intense excitability, with concomitant anger and violence. This is a pharmacologic effect of the cocaine itself, in distinction to the propensity for general violent behavior that can be part of the complex operations to pursue and obtain cocaine as part of a behavioral addiction to cocaine usage.

III. A. 4. Phencyclidine (PCP) Intoxication

When considering the potential for angry and violent reactions to abusable drugs, phencyclidine almost serves as the archetype. The hallmark of phencyclidine use is symptomatology of a broad range of possibilities, extending from somnolent oversedation to excited hyperactivity. There can be rapid shifts of demeanor, from withdrawn to threatening (Lydiard and Gelenberg, 1982; Kulberg, 1986). Lay people frequently ascribe more violent and criminal potential to states of street drug intoxication than really do occur, but with the case of phencyclidine, almost every "horror story" that can be recounted can indeed fit with the clinical phenomenology of phencyclidine intoxication. Thus, counselors working in detoxification centers, health care personnel working in emergency rooms, ambulance drivers and the police all think of phencyclidine when observing exceptionally agitated and violent behavior in the community. Psychiatrists not well-schooled in addictive diseases also have many misconceptions about the violent potential of abusable drugs, but most psychiatrists are fully aware of the truly violent potential with phencyclidine (Fauman and Fauman, 1980), for patients admitted to acute psychiatric units—especially in large cities—frequently have phencyclidine intoxication as a major precipitant of the clinical picture (Nicholi, 1983).

One of the ways to differentiate phencyclidine intoxication from other forms of agitated behavior or psychosis is to note the unique physiological features of phencyclidine. It is basically an anesthetic. So perceptions of analgesia or numbness and tingling, or blunted tactile sensation (especially in the extremities) can accompany phencyclidine intoxication. Jerky eye movements are also common, especially up and down eye movements or even circular eye movements. Eyelids are sometimes droopy even if the user seems agitated (Lydiard and Gelenberg, 1982). Perceptions of distorted body image are also common, especially perceptions that the arms or legs are ten feet long or more, and serpentine. All emergency medical personnel should be well-acquainted with the manifestations of phencyclidine intoxication in the community, and professionals should think of phencyclidine intoxication in cases of intense violent behavior in the community.

Phencyclidine serves as an adulterant in many street drugs (Rainey and Crowder, 1974; Hart, 1972). People intending to buy LSD, amphetamines or cocaine, or THC, are often buying samples of product diluted with phencyclidine (Lydiard and Gelenberg, 1982; Nicholi, 1983), or samples of inert mediums such as talc, in which the only real active ingredient is phencyclidine. Given the plethora of clinical outcomes possible with phencyclidine, and given the role of suggestion and expectation in the users' subjective response to the drug, it is possible for the users to believe that they are taking an amphetamine when they expect amphetamine, but use phencyclidine instead; to believe they are using an opiate analgesic when they are expecting that; to believe they are using an hallucinogen when they are expecting that; and to believe they are experiencing very intense cannabis intoxication when they are actually having a phencyclidine intoxication (whether or not there is any THC in the crushed leaves they are smoking). It is sometimes said that any chemical ingested off the street has a likelihood of containing phencyclidine, so safety requires the utmost certainty in knowing the source of the product procured. Similarly, any smoker of marijuana is at risk of having bought a sample that was phencyclidine-tainted.

Case Study: Phencyclidine
Intoxication

As a chemical dependency counselor for the Community Corrections Department, you are asked as part of a pre-sentence investigation to do a chemical dependency history on a 19-year-old college student. He is known to have a history of regular marijuana smoking, heavy drinking of alcohol on the weekends, and experimentation with psilocybin mushrooms. He has no criminal history whatsoever, but one night, he broke into a record store, assaulted the clerk, and gathered into his arms a half-shelf full of albums of his favorite "heavy metal" band. Upon questioning the jailer about his behavior the night of his arrest, one learns that he was banging his hands on the walls of the cell, but saying that it didn't hurt, and talking incoherently, with very rapid emotional shifts, sometimes laughing hysterically, other times yelling in intense rage, and saying he felt as if his arms were ten feet long and getting entwined in the bars of the cell.

Discussion

This is a case of intense, otherwise inexplicable, violence in a patient with no past history of criminality. In trying to understand what happened that evening to bring this on, several factors are salient. One is that this young man had a history of drug experimentation. The other is that marijuana was his drug of choice. The other is his unusual behavior at the time of the violent crime, including reports consistent with anesthesia in his extremities and a sense of distortion about the length of his extremities. Such symptoms are consistent with phencyclidine intoxication, which commonly occurs when marijuana has been laced with phencyclidine in an attempt to make inexpensive marijuana seem as potent as the most expensive imported varieties.

III. B. Withdrawal States

III. B. 1. Sedative Withdrawl

Probably the best understood and most frequently seen withdrawal state from drugs of abuse is the sedative withdrawal syndrome. Because the clinical manifestations of withdrawal from alcohol and sedative-hypnotic drugs are so similar, Jaffe has referred to this as the General Depressant Withdrawal Syndrome (Jaffe, 1985b). The most common form of sedative withdrawal is alcohol withdrawal syndrome. This is, of course, because alcohol is the most widely used sedative drug — and in fact, other than possibly caffeine and nicotine, the most widely used mood-altering drug in the world. The phenomenology of the alcohol withdrawal syndrome is quite well-understood and has been divided into four clinical stages for the purposes of clinical description and understanding (Brown, 1982). Stage I alcohol withdrawal syndrome has to do with the acutely altered physiological state of sympathetic nervous system hyperactivity occurring in the first 6 to 96 hours after the last drink. Stage II alcohol withdrawal syndrome includes hallucinosis, appearing most often 24 hours after the last drink. Stage III alcohol withdrawal syndrome includes withdrawal seizures, which occur 6 to 48 hours after the last drink. Stage IV alcohol withdrawal syndrome involves delirium tremens—a full-blown acute organic mental syndrome of delirium—beginning 72 hours or more into withdrawal.

It is widely hypothesized that withdrawal phenomena are manifestations of abstinence from a substance which has been affecting the function of a previously altered central nervous system. Thus, it is presumed that sedative drugs such as alcohol, when steadily presented to central nervous system cells, affect brain function by "down regulating" the activity of those cells, and that the human organism, in an attempt to maintain an equilibrium of function existing prior to the sedative drug exposure, intrinsically "up regulates" itself. This is probably a mechanism of alcohol tolerance. Thus, the reason that an organism can function at a blood alcohol level that is usually intoxicating—if not stupor-inducing—is that the central nervous system has adapted to the chronic alcoholic's drinking by up-regulating the brain—probably at the level of reticular activating system, and then projecting upward into higher midbrain and cortical centers—such that the sedating effects of the alcohol are counter-balanced by the hyper-aroused brain. When the chronic alcoholic thus abstains from alcohol exposure, what is experienced are the metabolic and behavioral states of a hyper-aroused "up-regulated" nervous system. This hyperactive state involves an increased irritability of the nervous system not only manifested in hyperactive deep tendon reflexes, and in fasciculating or tremulous skeletal musculature, but also in behavioral hyperirritability. Thus, the person is in a state akin to amphetamine intoxication (O'Brien et al., 1988). There is an outpouring of sympathetic activity centrally and peripherally.

This is the mechanism of irritability, quick-temperedness, and anger seen in State I alcohol withdrawal syndrome (Brown, 1982). It thus takes not much more than a neutral stimulus to produce snappy, defensive or argumentative responses in an individual undergoing alcohol withdrawal. It is important for professionals who work with alcoholics, especially withdrawing alcoholics in detoxification centers and hospitals, to realize that the crankiness and oppositionality of the withdrawing patient cannot be explained simply as a manifestation of their personality; it is instead a biochemically mediated, well understood and almost predictable pathophysiologic response to the withholding of alcohol or other sedative drugs from the individual who has become tolerant to alcohol or other sedatives. It is incumbent upon all individuals around such a patient to be aware of these processes and to provide a calming environment to decrease the chance of inciting the irrascible individual to aggressive behavior.

Withdrawal syndromes from longer-acting sedatives such as phenobarbital and ethchlorvynol (Placidyl) can be protracted (Garetz, 1969). Professionals should understand that a rather long-term period (several days to a few weeks) of hyperirritability and a lower threshold for anger and violence can exist in patients withdrawing from such substances, and even from benzodiazepines such as diazepam (Valium) (Ayd, 1983; MacKinnon and Parker, 1982). Professionals interacting with such patients should be aware of these processes and monitor their own behavioral interactions with such patients during the span of time that patients are neurochemically at risk for violent behaviors.

Stage II alcohol withdrawal syndrome involves the complicating factor of perceptual disturbances. There can be frank halluncinations, but more commonly, the individual experiences misperceptions. These are visual as well as auditory, such that the sound of an electric motor can be mistinterpreted as being the sound of a hissing snake or a roaring lion, etc. Stage II alcohol withdrawal syndrome is often accompanied by paranoid conclusions that are drawn in response to the hallucinated objects or sounds. It is common for lay people — or even health care personnel — to be humored at times by the alcoholic's report of seeing snakes or bugs or pink elephants during a phase of alcohol withdrawal hallucinosis. But these experiences are rarely humorous to the patient experiencing them (Thompson, 1978) and instead are usually very frightening experiences. Because they are so frightening and often accompanied by paranoid thoughts, individuals can act out very dangerously to defend themselves against presumed threats in their environment. Again, this is neurochemically and behaviorally akin to the aggression seen in response to paranoid thoughts that occur in stimulant intoxication syndromes (O'Brien et al., 1988). It is important that hallucinosis episodes in withdrawing ethanol and other sedative drug dependent patients be appropriately treated with antipsychotic medications, and that the patient experiencing these phenomena be reassured that what is happening to them is an understandable part of their syndrome and will be time-limited. With appropriate chemotherapy for these hallucinatory states, staff can be protected, seclusion and restraining of the patient can usually be avoided, and patients can be made much more comfortable while they're enduring this phase of their withdrawal syndrome.

Because of the commonness of hyperirritable and aggressive phenomena during sedative withdrawal episodes, one should always consider this possibility when one confronts an angry or violent individual in an addictive disease setting. The individual can have a relatively minimal amount of tremulousness and diaphoresis and can have completely logical thought processes, and thus not appear to be psychotic or aberrant in any way except that they are quite angry, and this can all be on the basis of their withdrawal states as opposed to any intrinsic antisocial personality characteristics.

III. B. 2. Cocaine Withdrawal

Fascinating literature is appearing regarding specific phases of the cocaine abstinence syndrome (Gawin, 1988). In general, cocaine withdrawal involves depression or anhedonia. But during the phases of high craving, drug-seeking behavior can be intense, and with this, at times, violent means to attain new drugs can be employed by the addict. This is reviewed in Section III. F. below.

III. B. 3. Opiate Withdrawal

Opiate withdrawal is considered by most nonprofessionals to be the most gruesome and most clinically significant form of drug withdrawal. Stories abound about individuals going "cold turkey," screaming and writhing in pain in jail cells, etc. But several things are important to note for the purposes of this paper. First, opiate withdrawal syndrome is unpleasant to the person experiencing it and can be very anxiety-provoking, but it is, in general, not life-threatening (Morgan, 1985). Further, except for purposive drug-seeking behavior (Lydiard and Gellenberg, Part II, 1982), there is relatively little anger and aggression associated with opiate withdrawal as compared with alcohol withdrawal syndrome.

Case Study: Alcohol Withdrawal

A 44-year-old accountant with a peptic ulcer condition and frequent headaches comes to a family therapist complaining of difficulty tolerating conflicts at home. He says his 16-year-old son is becoming more oppositional, with heightened verbal conflict with mother. The accountant's 41-year-old wife has been drinking more, and despite her attempts to hide this from her husband, he is concernced about her drinking. When he comes home, his wife is often sobbing, complaining of how she just can't control the boy anymore.

But the accountant says that what really upsets him is the amount of fighting in the mornings when they're trying to get the children off to school. He's trying to calmly gather himself for his day ahead, and his wife has intense shouting matches with the son. Her yelling seems to escalate her son's oppositionality, and she's been so irritable lately that there have been times that she's thrown a coffee cup across the kitchen, either trying to hit the boy with it or just crash it against the wall.

Discussion

What may be happening is that, before beginning her daytime drinking again (out of a sense of frustration and exhaustion) after her husband and children have gone off for the day, this woman is experiencing alcohol withdrawal. She drinks throughout the day, will usually have a nightcap after her husband has gone to sleep, but experiences alcohol abstinence in the mornings. She dismisses her tremulousness as nervousness about the family tension, but she is particularly irritable and prone to getting into conflicts with family members because of her hyperaroused central nervous system from her alcohol abstinence syndrome. Ironically, if she were to have had a drink at dawn to abate her withdrawal, mornings around the house would be more peaceful, with less anger and potential for violence — though such breakfast-time conflicts are currently serving as one of the more conspicuous signs of her illness, and thus increases the likelihood that her husband will force an intervention to usher her into treatment.

III. C. Substance-Induced Paranoid Psychotic States

One of the characteristics of chronic stimulant drug exposure is the induction of paranoid psychotic states (Ellingwood, 1967; Snyder, 1973). An individual who regularly uses several doses of amphetamine or similar drug per day, either by oral, nasal or intravenous routes, can develop racing thoughts and delusional beliefs, with a full paranoid picture, including delusions of persecution and auditory and visual hallucinations (Greenblatt and Shader, 1974). This can produce some of the most intensely violent behaviors observable, as an individual — from a drug-induced state — suffers from deranged mental processes that directly parallel those seen in an acute flare-up of chronic paranoid schizophrenia (Bell, 1965; Khantzian and McKenna, 1979). "Speed freaks" and cocaine addicts can thus truly believe that they are being stalked, pursued or threatened, and they can misperceive neutral objects in the environment as being very threatening to them. In an attempt to protect themselves from such perceived assailants, the individual can be very physcially violent (Cohen, 1984), engaging in hand-to-hand combat or use of weapons (Grinspoon and Bakalar, 1980). To the naive observer, it can appear that someone suddenly burst into unprovoked violence; in fact, the violent individual believes that the violence was quite provoked by persons whom they are perceiving to be threatening. Thus, an ambiguous or even neutral facial expression can be interpreted by the paranoid patient as being very hostile, and the paranoid individual can then make a preemptive strike against the presumed assailant. The paranoid individual can also hallucinate voices coming from presumed assailants (Khantzian and McKenna, 1979), threatening voices that challenge the individual to fight or foretell of an assault coming from the presumed assailant. One of the major difficulties in such syndromes is that the thought content and proceses are truly psychotic, such that the individual is unaware of their unreality. Thus, as self-preservation, individuals can honestly believe that they must act in physically aggressive ways to protect themselves from danger.

Paranoid psychotic states can occur from acute intoxication with amphetamine-type products or from cocaine (Cornelius et al., 1984; Roxanas and Spalding, 1977), especially if the acute intoxication has happened repeatedly (such as an individual on a "speed run" who has been regularly dosing himself with amphetamines or cocaine for two or three days in a row). Sleep deprivation can also contribute to these psychotic states. Apart from the acute hallucinations, delirium or other psychiatric states that can be induced by amphetamine or — more commonly — by cocaine intoxication, there is also a chronic, sometimes delayed syndrome, within which an individual who has abused stimulant drugs heavily for a number of months can develop a permanent paranoid disorder in which he/she is perpetually paranoid to greater or lesser degrees, always vigilant, always feeling potentially put upon by hostile forces, or even chronically hallucinating visually or auditorially. Such individuals are then relegated to a life of chronic psychiatric care, and may need to be maintained on antipsychotic medications for the balance of their lives. Even though the syndromes of amphetamine psychosis (Jaffe 1985a; Grinspoon and Bakalar, 1980) and cocaine psychosis (Post, 1975) are well-described in the literature and well-known clinically, they are by no means the only substance-induced psychotic states (see Tables I and II).

One recent comparative report (Wilford, 1987) ranks PCP as the most likely drug associated with the development or precipitation of psychotic states, followed by central nervous system stimulants, central nervous system depressants and marijuana (all grouped at the same level of risk), followed by hallucinogens and solvents. The authors note that LSD hallucinosis is now relatively rare, that marijuana psychosis is rare but more common in areas where large doses are consumed, and that amphetamine, cocaine and PCP psychosis are particularly linked with violence and aggression. Cannabis is particulary well-known (Grinspoon and Bakalar, 1980; Treffert, 1978) to exacerbate pre-existing psychotic states, such as in patients with histories of schizophrenia or psychotic mania.

Case Study: Amphetamine Psychosis

A 31-year-old male security guard has been brought to a chemical dependency counselor by his superiors because of concerns of marijuana use on the job. Superiors report that he is noticeably paranoid, and the other night confronted a new worker in the job with whom he was not familiar. Upon coming around a corner and bumping into this other guard in the dark, the guard grabbed the new worker and began choking him until a third guard came to his aid. When the guard calmed down, he said that he had thought that this new employee was someone who had been sent there to rub him out as part of a Mafia hit. The supervisor says this guard has been a good employee overall, but that he wonders if marijuana use is making him more paranoid.

On collecting the history, one discovers that this man had injected "crystal" methamphetamine daily for two years while in the service ten years ago. Upon discharge from the military, he continued to use oral speed, up to 16 "hits" a day of "white cross" amphetamine tablets for four years. He had been psychiatrically hospitalized for what was reported to be paranoid schizophrenia, and though never rehospitalized, had had continuing paranoid experiences episodically ever since.

Discussion

It's impossible to determine from this data how much the patient's cannabis exposure exacerbated his paranoid state, but the underlying paranoid state is one of residual psychosis, induced by heavy chronic amphetamine exposure. A residual syndrome has been produced, involving paranoid delusions, and a tendency toward excessive suspiciousness — a paranoid condition continuing in the absence of amphetamine exposure. Psychiatric referral may be necessary to place the patient on maintenance antipsychotic agents to treat this chronic amphetamine-induced paranoid state.

III. D. Pathological (Idiosyncratic) Intoxication

Idiosyncratic responses to substances occur when an individual reacts strongly, uncharacteristically, and perhaps violently, to a small dosage of a drug. Alcohol and the barbiturates are most frequently mentioned. Alcohol idiosyncratic intoxication (as described in the DSM-III-R [Diagnostic and Statistical Manual, Revised, 1987], p. 128-190; Perr, 1986), is quite uncommon, and at least some clinicians doubt its existence (Jacoby and Galanter, 1986). The possibility of this behavior pattern should be suspected, for example, if a normally placid person becomes quite hostile after imbibing only one or two standard-size drinks. Violence is not the only idiosyncratic reaction described to occur in this syndrome; deep sleep followed by amnesia for the event is also said to occur after the low-dose exposure to the alcohol or sedative. It is not clear if this amnestic spell is postulated to differ from the standard alcohol blackout.

III. E. Substance-Induced Organic Brain Syndromes

Clinical syndromes that affect the so-called cognitive functions of the brain — orientation, attention span, memory, abstract thinking, arithmetic skills, and the like — are considered organic mental disorders (DSM-III-R), in contrast to the so-called functional psychiatric disorders of complex emotions and behaviors (for instance, major depression, schizophrenia, and the like). As more is learned about the molecular biological derangements and the so-called functional psychoses, the distinction between the organic and the functional is becoming less meaningful. Still, the term organic mental disorder is used to imply a brain dysfunction that is the specific result of some anatomical or metabolic derangement in the brain. Chemically induced changes in brain function are therefore, by definition, "organic," and the substance-induced mental disorders are therefore included with intoxication and withdrawal states in the DSM-III-R, along with other organic mental disorders. In the previous sections of this paper, any substance-induced affective or behavioral change could therefore be considered a type of organic condition—such as substance-induced (or "organic") delusional syndrome induced by cocaine. But it is important to note the more general alterations in brain function that can be induced by drugs of abuse.

III. E. 1. Delirium

An acute alteration in cognitive functioning is called a delirium. Chemical dependency professionals are most familiar with the delirium that occurs in alcohol withdrawal syndrome—delirium tremens (Shaw, 1978). The hallmarks of this syndrome are overactivity of the sympathetic nervous system as seen in alcohol withdrawal (producing elevated pulse, blood pressure, temperature, etc.); marked tremulousness; and a delirious state in which the individual has the classic signs of delirium (DSM-III-R. p. 103) which include an alteration in orientation, memory and level of awareness; an inability to consistently fix attention on appropriate stimuli; disturbance of standard sleep/wake cycles; an alteration in perception, involving misinterpretation of visual and auditory stimuli and sometimes even frank hallucinations; and disorganized thinking with incoherent speech. It is important for all chemical dependency professionals, especially those who work in more medically-oriented settings, to be aware that delirium can be induced from a variety of insults to brain functioning, including virtually any abusable drug, and that the basic features of delirium as listed above, are similar regardless of the etiology. Thus, an individual can ingest enough psychostimulant drug or enough cannabinoid to actually become delirious, via poisonous effects of the chemical on brain function to the extent that general cognitive functions of the brain are interfered with (or even overridden) by the drug intoxication.

Many of the toxic effects of PCP parallel the clinical features of delirium (Liden et al., 1975). Delirium symptoms have been reported for cocaine (Wetli and Fishbain, 1985) and inhalants (Kulberg, 1986). Delirious states generally involve so much confusion on the part of the individual suffering through it that behavior becomes semipurposeful at best, with emitted behaviors being rather random and not goal-directed at all. But one of the classical features of delirium is that the clinical status waxes and wanes, so there are times when the individual can be relatively more lucid, and relatively more directed in his or her behavior. It is at these phases of delirium that aggression and violence can manifest themselves. This is probably the pathophysiologic mechanism behind the dangerousness that accompanies inhalant abuse. Inhalation of hydrocarbon gases such as octane and freon produces a state of low oxygenation of the blood, which can result in delirious symptoms if brain oxygen levels are sufficiently impaired. Behavior can become random, impulsive, with striking out that can be violent in appearance.

We have previously mentioned how an individual withdrawing from alcohol or other sedative drugs can act out violently against perceived threats in his or her environment, with these perceptions based on the false data of a paranoid thought or a hallicinated person. But more generally, patients undergoing delirium can fluctuate between a twilight or even a somnolent state of subdued activity and a rather hyperexcited state involving agitation and random, purposeless striking out. In a clinical setting such as a detoxification center, it is easier to ascribe proper meaning to such behavioral flare-ups, as the staff can compare the individual from one moment in time to another, placing the hyperexcited phase in the context of the overall fluctuating course of the delirium. But when delirium occurs "in the field," a clincial professional, a law enforcement officer or a family member can simply encounter an incoherent, rather wantonly aggressive individual. At times an individual can appear so confused and incoherent that he appears to be psychotic on nonorganic grounds. These concepts are reviewed here with the hope of raising the consciousnes of chemical dependency professionals to the potential for delirious reactions at almost any time and any place when drugs of abuse—which by definition alter brain function—might be used.

Clinically, delirium is seen quite often in the case of sedative withdrawal syndrome. Patients with a sedative withdrawal delirium can go through a very hyperexcited phase appearing not altogether dissimilar from the paroxysmal excitement seen in a psychiatric patient having a phase of catatonic excitement. Such individuals can be very aggressive and violent against others, with their semipurposeful behavior at times seeming quite purposeful and specifically directed against certain individuals in the delirious patient's environment. Again, such a reaction can occur in the community just as well as it can happen in a clinical setting, so clinicians working in emergency intake centers must always be aware of the possibility that a delirium has been involved in the violence of a patient brought in for assessment.

III. E. 2. Dementia

Medical nomenclature uses the term dementia to refer to those long-term aberrations of cognitive function that are in distinction to the short-term aberrations of delirium. Dementia usually does not involve the hyperexcited state seen in some delirious states. Instead, the individual is in general rather subdued, with decrements in a variety of intellectual functions. Ethanol, being a specific neurotoxin, damages neural tissue (both directly and indirectly through metabolic and nutritional derangements) and dementia can result. Alcohol-associated dementia (DSM-III-R, p. 133-134) has clinical characteristics similar to other dementias — a rather long-term deterioration in memory, orientation, concentration and other intellectual functions such as calculations, abstract thinking, etc. The individual can thus have the clinical appearance akin to a patient with the senile degenerative dementia of Alzheimer's disease. The violent behavior that occurs in these cases of dementia basically is a result of disinhibition due to a deterioration in the brain pathways that are involved in good judgment, propriety and prudence, and the inhibition of inappropriate behavioral responses. There are times that demented patients react violently, almost randomly, akin to the way that other brain injured patients or even mentally retarded patients can react. But it is rare for alcohol or sedative abuse alone to produce a dementia severe enough such that a person would regress into randomly aggressive behavior. It is worth noting that one non-barbiturate sedative hypnotic, the chemical glutethamide (trade name Doriden), is documented in literature (Morgan, 1985) to produce a unique glutethamide-induced dementia after chronic usage.

III. E. 3. Brain Injury

Violence is in general considered more prevalent in substance-abusing settings than in non-substance-abusing settings, and violence can, of course, result in injuries to victims, including brain injuries (Marjot, 1982; Pernanen, 1986). Brain trauma — either the result of physical violence or accidents, such as alcohol-related automobile crashes or simply falling-down spells — can alter brain function and induce delirious states acutely or dementiform states chronically. Brain injuries not only involve the potential for disinhibited or otherwise aggressive behavior in their own right, but also leave the individual more susceptible to untoward behavioral effects in the face of drug exposure. It is important to note pathologic intoxications do seem to occur with more prominence in brain-injured individuals (Shaw,1978). Disinhibition, aggression and other poor behavioral control can result in random impulsive aggressiveness in brain-injured individuals. Brain injury, including closed head injury, can result from blunt trauma to the head incurred from motor vehicle or other accidents associated with alcohol or drug intoxication states; from falls incurred while intoxicated with sedatives; or from violence (for instance, via mugging or a barroom brawl) associated with the lifestyle of many heavy users of alcohol or drugs. Epidemiologically, trauma is, of course, quite common in chemically dependent patients, and there is an enhanced risk of serious brain trauma (for instance, from drunk driving accidents) associated with substance abuse.

III. E. 4. Pathological Jealousy

Pathological jealousy is a fascinating syndrome well-reported in the psychiatric literature. It is common and involves a firm but well-subcribed delusional system that one's spouse has been unfaithful. For unknown reasons such a syndrome is epidemiologically linked to chronic alcoholism. It would appear that there is something specific about the chemistry of alcohol that interacts with as yet unspecified loci in the brain that results in this specific form of delusional thought content. Such patients rarely have loose associations or other signs of psychosis. The content of the paranoid delusion is limited to the issue of infidelity. This can be a very distressing syndrome for the patient, and, of course, very unsettling to loved ones, for the delusion has all the classic qualities of delusion—a fixed belief that, though completely false, is incontrovertible in the face of refuting evidence. There have been cases of quite violent behaviors, including murder, as an outgrowth of such a set of delusional beliefs on the part of such afflicted patients. Unfortunately, this is a condition which is chronic, with the fixed delusional system remaining in place even years after the last exposure of an individual to ethanol or other drugs of abuse; it is relatively resistant to amelioration with antipsychotic medications.

III. F. Violence Secondary to Drug-Related Antisocial Behavior

No comprehensive review of substance-related violence would be complete if it did not include the violence of disinhibited alcohol intoxicated individuals whose judgment is impaired during an armed robbery attempt, when the individual is seeking funds to buy more drugs. Intoxication states in general tend to promote criminality in individuals so predisposed. This is, of course, seen more frequently in cases of heroin addicts, who can be quite violent in seeking out illicit sources of funds for subsequent drug procurement. The sociopathic nature of many heroin addicts makes this sequence of events even more likely. But it is important to recognize that in the acute abstinence phase of cocaine withdrawal, drug craving can be quite high, and there can be a whole range of aberrant behaviors involved in seeking out the next dose of cocaine, or the money by which to procure that dose. Other substance abuse related antisocial behaviors, such as family violence (Fitch and Papantonio, 1983; Bard and Zacker, 1974) and a sexual assault (McCaghy, 1968) are reviewed elsewhere in this volume (Flanzer, 1989).

IV. CONCLUSION

Caution is necessary when summarizing the relationship between substances of abuse and aggression. Following the ideas of others, we can state that in general substance-related acts of violence are a combination of the physiological effects of the substances themselves, the underlying personality of the user, and the social setting that favors or disfavors aggression. Still, certain substances are quite regularly associated with the appearance of aggressive patterns of behavior: the clearest evidence is for ethanol, phenycyclidine (PCP) and stimulants including amphetamines and cocaine. Aggression might occur during intoxication or withdrawal, as well as from paranoid/psychotic responses to a drug from the development of organic deliriums or dementias, and from idiosyncratic violent responses under normally benign circumstances. Aggression and violence may also be secondary to the pursuit of money to purchase drugs.

Organic, psychiatric and sociocultural explanations all help explain certain aspects of the aggression/substance abuse linkage. Readers are referred to the next article in this volume (Potter-Efron, 1989) for a discussion of these factors.

REFERENCES

Allen, Loyd. PCP: A Schizophrenomimetic. U.S. Pharmacist, January 1980: 60-66.

American Medical Association. Council on Scientific Affairs. Marijuana: Its Health Hazards and Therapeutic Potentials. Journal of the American Medical Association 246(16), 16 October 1981: 1823-1827.

Ayd, Frank, Benzodiazepine Dependence and Withdrawal. Journal of Psychoactive Drugs 15(2), 1983: 67-68.

Bard, M.; and Zacker, J., Jr. Assaultiveness and Alcohol Use in Family Disputes: Police Perceptions. Criminology (12), 1974: 281-293.

Behnke, Roy H. Recognition and Management of Alcohol Withdrawal Syndrome. Hospital Practice, November 1986: 79-84.

Bell, D.S. Comparison of Amphetamine Psychosis and Schizophrenia. British Journal of Psychiatry (III), 1965: 701-797.

Brown, Charles G. The Alcohol Withdrawal Syndrome. Annals of Emergency Medicine, May 1982: 276-280.

Cloninger, D. Robert. Neurogenetic Adaptive Mechanisms in Alcoholism. Science 236, April 1987: 410-416.

Cohen, Sidney. The Cocaine Problems. Drug Abuse and Alcoholism Newsletter 12(10), 1983.

_____ Recent Developments in the Abuse of Cocaine. Bulletin on Narcotics 36(2), 1984: 3-14.

_____ Aggression: The Role of Drugs. In The Substance Abuse Problems, Vol. 2. New York: The Haworth Press, Inc., 1985.

_____ Marijuana. In The American Psychiatric Association Annual Review,

Vol. 5. Allen Frances and Robert Hales (Eds.). Washington, D.C.: American Psychiatric Press, 1986.

Cornelius, Jack R.; Soloff, Paul H.; and Reynolds III, Charles F. Paranoia, Homicidal Behavior, and Seizures Associated with Phenylpropanolamine. American Journal of Psychiatry 141(1), January 1984: 120-121.

Crowley, Thomas. Clinical Issues in Cocaine Abuse. In Cocaine: Clinical and Behavioral Aspects by Seymour Fisher, Allen Raskin and E.H. Ulenhuth. New York: Oxford University Press, 1987.

Dembo, R.; Washburn, M.; Wish, E.; Yeung, H.; Getreu, A.; Berry, E.; and Blount, W. Heavy Marijuana Use and Crime Among Youths Entering a Juvenile Detention Facility. Journal of Psychoactive Drugs 19(1), 1987.

Diagnostic and Statistical Manual of Mental Disorders. 3d ed., rev. Washington, D.C.: American Psychiatric Association, 1987.

Dipalma, Joseph R. Cocaine Abuse and Toxicity. AFP Clinical Pharmacology 24(5): 236-238.

Eckardt, Michael; Harford, Thomas; Kaelber, Charles; Parker, Elizabeth; Rosenthal, Laura; Ryback, Ralph; Salmoiraghi, Giam; Vanderveen, Ernestine; and Warren, Kenneth. Health Hazards Associated with Alcohol Consumption. Journal of the American Medical Association 246(6), 1981: 648-665.

Ellinwood, Jr., G.H. Amphetamine Psychosis I. Description of the Individuals and Process. The Journal of Nervous and Mental Disease 144(4): 1967, 273-283.

Fauman, Michael; and Fauman, Beverly. Chronic Phenylcyclidine (PCP) Abuse: A Psychiatric Perspective. Journal of Psychedelic Drugs 12(3-4), July-December 1980.

Fitch, Frances; and Papantonio, Andre. Men Who Batter: Some Pertinent Characteristics. Journal of Nervous and Mental Disease 17(3), 1983: 190-192.

Flanzer, Jerry. Alcohol and Family Violence: Then to Now. Who Owns Problem. Journal of Chemical Dependency Treatment 3(1), 1989.

Garetz, Floyd D. Ethchlorvynol (Placidyl) Addiction Hazard. Minnesota Medicine 52(7), 1989: 1131-1133.

Gawin, Frank H. Chronic Neuropharmacology of Cocaine: Progress in Pharmacotherapy. The Journal of Clinical Psychiatry 49, February 1988, Supplement: 11.

Greenblatt, David; and Shader, Ricard. Drug Abuse and the Emergency Room Physician. American Journal of Psychiatry 131(5). 1974: 559-562.

Grinspoon, Lester; and Bakalar, James. Drug Dependence: Non-narcotic Agents. In Comprehensive Textbook of Psychiatry, 3d ed. H.I. Kaplan, A.M. Freedman, and B.J. Sadock. 1980: 1614-1629.

———— Drug Dependence: Nonnarcotic Agents. In Comprehensive Textbook of Psychiatry/IV. Vol. One, 4th ed. Harold Kaplan and Benjamin Sadock (eds.), Baltimore: Williams and Williams, 1985: 1003-1015.

Hart, J.; McChesney, J.C.; Griefi, M., et al. Composition of Illicit Drugs and Use of Drug Analysis and Abuse Abatement. Journal of Psychedelic Drugs 5, 1972: 83-88.

Honer, William; Gewirtz, George; and Turey, Maureen. Psychosis and Violence in Cocaine Smokers. The Lancet. Aug. 27, 1987: 451.

Jacoby, Jacob; and Galanter, Marc. Alcohol Idiosyncratic Intoxication and Other Alcohol-Related States of Acute Behavioral Disinhibition. In Psychopathology and Addictive Disorders. Roger Meyer (ed.). New York: Guilford Press, 1986. 238-259.

Jaffe, Jerome. Opioid Dependence. In Comprehensive Textbook of Psychiatry, Vol. One, 4th ed. Baltimore: Williams and Williams, 1985. 987-1003.

———— Drug Addiction and Drug Abuse. In The Pharmacological Basis of Therapeutics. A.G. Gilman, L.S. Goodman, T.W. Rall, and F. Nurad (eds.). New York: Macmillan, 1985. 532-557.

———— Opioids. In American Psychiatric Association Annual Review. Vol. 5, Allen Frances and Robert Hales (eds.). Washington, D.C.: American Psychiatric Press, 1986. 137-159.

Khantzian, G.J.; and McKenna, G.J. Acute Toxic and Withdrawal Reactions Associated with Drug Use and Abuse. Annals of Internal Medicine 90, 1979: 361-372.

Kulberg, Alan. Substance Abuse: Clinical Indentification and Management. Pediatric Clinics of North America 33(2), 1986: 325-361.

Levenson, James. Dealing with the Violent Patient: Management Strategies to Avoid Common Errors. Postgraduate Medicine 78(5), 1985: 329-335.

Liden, Craig; Lovejoy, F.H.; and Costello, C.E. Phencyclidine: Nine Cases of Poisoning. Journal of the American Medical Association 234(5), Nov. 3, 1975: 513-516.

Luisada, Paul; and Brown, Bernard. Clinical Management of the Phenylcycldine Psychosis. Clinical Toxicology 9(4), 1976: 539-545.

Lydiard, R. Bruce; and Gelenberg, Alan. Treating Substance Abuse, Part I. Drug Therapy Hospital, April 1982: 57-66.

———— Part II. May 1982: 287-294.

Mackinnan, Glenda; and Parker, William A. Benzodiazepine Withdrawal Syndrome: A Literature Review and Evaluation. American Journal of Drug and Alcohol Abuse 9(1), 1982: 19-33.

Marjot, D.H. Alcohol, Aggression and Violence. The Practitioner 226, 1982: 287-294.

McCaghy, C.H. Drinking and Deviants' Disavowal: The Case of Child Molesters. Social Problems 16, 1968: 43-49.

Mendelson, J.H. Biologic Concomitants of Alcoholism. New England Journal of Medicine 283, 1970: 24-32, 71-81.

Morgan, John. Alcohol and Drug Abuse Guide for Pharmacology Faculty. Rockville, Md.: National Institute on Alcohol Abuse and Alcoholism, 1985.

Moyer, K.E. The Psychobiology of Aggression. New York: Harper and Row, 1976.

Mungas, Dan. An Empircal Analysis of Specific Syndromes of Violent Behavior. The Journal of Nervous and Mental Disease. 171(6), 1983: 354-361.

Nicholi, Armand. The Non-therapeutic Use of Psychoactive Drugs. The New England Journal of Medicine 308(16), 1983: 925-933.

Niven, Robert. Adolescent Drug Abuse. Hospital and Community Psychiatry 37(6), 1986: 596-607.

O'Brien, Charles P.; Childress, Anna Rose; Arndt, Isabelle 0.; McLellan, A. Thomas; Woody, George E.; and Maany, Iradj. Pharmacological and Behavioral Treatments of Cocaine Dependence: Controlled Studies. APT Foundation North American Conference. Washington, D.C.: September 16, 1987.

Pernanen, K. Alcohol and Crimes of Violence. In The Biology of Alcoholism: Social Aspects of Alcoholism, Vol. 4. B. Kissin and H. Begleiter (eds.). New York: Plenum Press, Inc., 1986.

Perr, Irwin. Pathological Intoxication and Alcohol Idiosyncratic Intoxication, Part I: Diagnostic and Clinical Aspects. Journal of Forensic Sciences 3(3), 1986: 806-811.

Petersen, R.; and Stillman, R. Phecyclidine (PCP) Abuse: An Appraisal. Rockville, Md.: NIDA, 1978.

Pickens, Roy; and Meisch, Richard. Behavioral Aspects of Drug Dependence. Minnesota Medicine 3, 1973: 183-186.

Post, Robert. Cocaine Psychosis: A Continuum Model. American Journal of Psychiatry 132(3), 1975: 225-231.

Potter-Efron, Ronald. Differential Diagnosis of Physiological, Psychiatric and Sociocultural Conditions Associated with Aggression and Substance Abuse. Journal of Chemical Dependency Treatment 3(2), 1990.

Rainey, Jr., J.H.; and Crowder, Mik. Prevalance of Phencyclidine in Street Drug Preparations. New England Journal of Medicine 290: 1974: 466-487.

Reed, Barbara; and May, Philip. Inhalant Abuse and Juvenile Delinquency: A Controlled Study in Albuquerque, New Mexico. The International Journal of the Addictions 19(2), 1984: 119-151.

Roxanas, M.G.; and Spalding, Jean. Ephedrine Abuse Psychosis. The Medical Journal of Australia. November 5, 1977: 639-640.

Sanchez, Jose; and Johnson, Bruce. Women and the Drugs-Crime Connection: Crime Rates Among Drug Abusing Women at Rikers Island. Journal of Psychoactive Drugs 19(2), 1987.

Schukit, Marc; and Russell, Jon. An Evaluation of Primary Alcoholics with Histories of Violence. Journal of Clinical Psychiatry 14, 1984: 3-6.

Shaffer, John; Nurco, David; Ball, John; Kinlock, Timothy; Duszyrski, Karen; and Langrod, John. The Relationships of Preaddiction Characteristics to the Types and Amounts of Crime Committed by Narcotic Agents. International Journal of the Addictions 22(2), 1987: 153-165.

Shaw, G.K. Alcohol and the Nervous System. Clinics in Endocrinology and Metabolism 7(2), 1978: 385-404.

Siegel, Ronald. PCP and Violent Crime: The People vs. Peace. Journal of Psychedelic Drugs 12(3-4), 1980: 317-330.

Simonds, John; and Kashani, Javad. Specific Drug Use and Violence in Delinquent Boys. American Journal of Drug and Alcohol Abuse 7(3-4), 1985.

Smith, David; and Seymour, Richard. Dream Becomes Nightmare: Adverse Reactions to LSD. Journal of Psychoactive Drugs 17(4), 1985.

Snyder, Solomon H. Amphetamine Psychosis: A "Model" Schizophrenia Mediated by Catecholamines. American Journal of Psychiatry 130(1), 1973: 61-67.

Spotts, James; and Shontz, Franklin. Drug-Induced Ego States. I. Cocaine: Phenomenology and Implications. The International Journal of the Addictions 19(2), 1984: 119-151.

_____ The Phenomenological Structure of Drug-Induced Ego States. II. Barbiturates and Sedative Hypnotics: Phenomenology and Implications. The International Journal of the Addictions 19(3), 1984: 295-326.

Taylor, Stuart; and Leonard, Kenneth. Alcohol and Human Physical Aggression. In Aggression: Theoretical and Empirical Reviews, Vol. 2. Russell Green and Edward Donnerstein, Edward. New York: Academic Press, 1983: 77-111.

Thompson, W. Leigh. Management of Alcohol Withdrawal Syndromes. Archives of Internal Medicine 138, 1978: 278-283.

Treffert, D.A. Marijuana Use in Schizophrenia: A Clear Hazard. American Journal of Psychiatry 135, 1978: 1213-1215.

Van Hassalt, Vincent; Morrison, Randall; and Bellack, Alan. Alcohol Use in Wife Abusers and Their Spouses. Addictive Behaviors 10, 1985: 127-135.

Washton, Arnold; Gold, Mark; and Pottash, A.L.C. Survey of 500 Callers to a National Cocaine Hotline. Psychosomatics 25(10), 1984: 771-775.

Wetli, Charles; and Fishbain, David. Cocaine-Induced Psychosis and Sudden Death in Recreational Cocaine Users. Journal of Forensic Science 30(3), 1985: 873-880.

Weiner, Norman. Norepinephrine/Epinephrine and The Sympathomimetic Amines. In Gilman and Goodman's Pharmacological Basis of Therapeutics, 7th edition. Alfred Gilman, Louis Goodman, Theodore Rall, and Ferid Mund (eds.). New York: Macmillan. 1985: 145-180.

Weiss, Roger D.; Goldenheim, Paul; Mirin, Steven; et al. Pulmonary Dysfunction in Cocaine Smokers 138(8), 1981: 1110-1112.

Wilford, Bonnie (ed.). Review Course Syllabus. New York: American Medical Society on Alcoholism and Other Drug Dependencies, 1987.

Yago, Kate; Pitts, Ferris, Jr.; Burgoyne, Rodney; Aniline, Orm; Yago, Lane; and Pitts, Andrew. The Urban Epidemic of Phencyclidine (PCP) Use: Clinical and Laboratory Evidence from a Public Psychiatric Hospital Emergency Service. Journal of Clinical Psychiatry 42(5), 1981: 193-196.

Differential Diagnosis of Physiological, Psychiatric and Sociocultural Conditions Associated with Aggression and Substance Abuse

Ronald T. Potter-Efron, MSW, PhD

SUMMARY. Aggression has many possible causes. Any individual who regularly performs acts of violence against family or others may be responding to one or several internal or external cues that stimulate that behavior. This article reviews many common conditions associated with violence. These are divided into neurological/systemic conditions, psychiatric conditions, and societal/cultural expectations. Conditions also associated with substance abuse are emphasized.

INTRODUCTION

The chemical dependency counselor concerned with the excessively angry, hostile and physically assaultive behavior of some clients must be able to differentiate among the multiple possible conditions that could promote violence. For example, a client's violence may be directly and primarily associated with his use of alcohol or mood altering chemicals. The "Doctor Jekyll and Mr. Hyde" alcoholic whose normally placid behavior transforms into aggression only when he is intoxicated represents this condition. Only here can the counselor say with any certainty that the client's violence will probably stop if he can achieve and maintain sobriety.

In many situations a client's violence has an independent or parti-

---

Ronald T. Potter-Efron is a clinical psychotherapist at Midelfort Clinic in Eau Claire, WI.

37

ally independent existence. Frequently the person will become *less* violent but not non-violent during periods of abstinence. A recovering alcoholic may "only" shove or restrain his partner instead of hitting her. This considerable improvement should be respected while the counselor recognizes that other factors might still need to be addressed before the violence can be reduced further.

This article is intended as a companion to its predecessor in this volume (Miller and Potter-Efron, 1989) that focuses upon substance-induced forms of violence. Physiological, psychiatric, and social conditions may exist that can help explain a chemically dependent client's anger and aggression. The conditions noted represent a selected group that are encountered relatively often in the field of chemical dependency treatment.

PHYSIOLOGICAL CONDITIONS

No distinct line can be drawn between physiological and psychiatric diagnoses since many conditions traditionally of concern to the mental health field, such as depression, are now known to have a significant physiological component. Therefore the grouping below of physiological and psychiatric problems is relatively arbitrary. Physiological conditions include traumatic brain injuries, seizure related disorders, attention deficit disorder (residual), and premenstrual syndrome. Each of these concerns has been treated primarily by non-psychiatric physicians and individuals with these disorders may seldom be referred to substance abuse counselors or mental health practitioners. Still, these persons often develop or exhibit substance abuse problems that need to be screened and treated.

Organic Mental Disorder: Traumatic Brain Injury

Human aggression is both generated and contained within the brain in a complex interaction between the phylogenetically ancient limbic system and more recently appearing higher cortical functions (Elliot, 1977). Neurological damage due to sudden trauma or disease can drastically affect the ability of an individual to moderate aggressive impulses or to transform them into socially acceptable actions. Several conditions have been identified that increase the potential for the occurence of hostility and aggression against family members or in general.

Chemical dependency counselors frequently encounter patients with past or recent history of brain injuries from vehicular accidents, falls, beatings or suicide attempts. These injuries can cause damage to the frontal lobes and the deeper structures of the brain, producing frontal lobe syndrome, one component of which is an inability to control angry affect. Silver (1987) writes that 70% of patients with traumatic brain injury are known to have periods of aggression and irritability of significant distress to the patients and their families. Explosive rage may be the only sequel to these injuries and might occur months after the accident (Elliot, 1977).

Pathological intoxication is common with brain injured persons (Elliot, 1977). Even a modest drinking bout can trigger pathological rage that appears suddenly and may not stop until much damage has taken place. The counselor will hear from these patients that they are very confused because they used to be able to consume far more without negative consequences. They may never have been warned by their past physicians or counselors about this possibility. Equally possible, they may well have been alerted but have forgotten or ignored these cautions. It is helpful to explain to these patients, in the company of their families, that a single beer (or dose) now may have the effect of a six pack or more and that, furthermore, the effects of consuming even a couple of drinks are now unpredictable and highly dangerous.

Some victims of sudden brain trauma suffer devastating injury that radically alters their life styles. They may find themselves wheelchair bound and devoid of careers, partners, resources and hope. These persons may be extremely attracted to alcohol or other intoxicants that serve to relieve their despair and fill up empty time. If so, they will be strongly resistant to the information presented above. Their families, often guilt-ridden and eager to please the injured individual, may have difficulty confronting the injured person, especially when he or she has a tendency to become irrationally belligerent. The counselor must understand the extent of emotional pain in such families and help them face up to this problem as part of the total picture of brain trauma.

Individuals with traumatic brain injury should take care to avoid alcohol and the barbiturates in particular since these intoxicants are most frequently linked with aggression (Elliot, 1977).

Seizure Related Disorders: Intermittent Explosive Disorder and Epilepsy

Intermittent Explosive Disorder. Individuals with this diagnosis experience ego-dystonic assaultive or destructive episodes in which they can become violent with little or no provocation. Such outbursts are discreet events and the perpetrator normally demonstrates few or no signs of generalized impulsivity or aggression between episodes (Reid and Balis, 1987). The individual, afterwards, may be stunned by his or her behavior (Bolton and Bolton, 1987), as well as deeply remorseful. The period of violence is frequently minimally provoked, poorly focused, carried out in a state of clouded consciousness, and followed by partial amnesia for the violent incident itself (Conn and Lion, 1984). Conn and Lion (1984) state that the rage reactions of the individual with intermittent explosive disorder have been linked with an epileptic mechanism within the limbic system. Although much research needs to be completed in this area, the implications are that control of these violent episodes will depend at least partially upon the use of appropriate medications such as Tegretol (Conn and Lion), lithium (Yudofsky, 1987) or propanolol (Jenkins and Maruta, 1987).

Temporal Lobe Epilepsy. Before modern medicine, temporal lobe epilepsy was commonly associated with seizure-related "Herculean fury" (Madden and Lion, 1976). Currently most attention is paid to the appearance of occasional violence in the "inter-ictal" period between seizures (Silver and Yudofsky, 1987) which is characterized by angry irritability, mood changes, overreaction to specific provocations, and the absence of amnesia about the incident (Blumer, 1976).

A major unanswered question with clients diagnosed with either intermittent explosive disorder or epilepsy is the extent to which they retain some control over their actions. The Boltons (1987) note that "In most family violence cases, the perpetrator's description of being out of control (as a result of a mysterious force) is nothing more than an attempt to deny responsibility" (Bolton and Bolton, 1987: 71), but then acknowledge that the client with intermittent explosive disorder may indeed actually be completely honest in that explanation. Tardiff (1987), reviewing the research on epilepsy, finds that other factors such as low socioeconomic status, sex, age, and problems with early childhood development may be more important than the presence or absence of epilepsy itself. He concludes that "Violent persons with epilepsy have other conditions that are associated with poor impulse control independent of seizure activity" (Tardiff, 1987: 453).

The chemical dependency counselor working with violent patients who are suspected of having intermittent explosive disorder or epilepsy must coordinate his efforts closely with physicians who can consider appropriate medication. The counselor can best augment this attention by helping the client consider the secondary gains that his violence achieves as well as practical ways to protect himself and his family from the worst manifestations of his condition.

Attention Deficit Disorder (Residual)

Attention Deficit Disorder is a problem usually associated with children and adolescents. However, adults are increasingly recognized as carrying a similar pattern of behavior that includes restlessness, emotional lability, "hot temper" and impulsivity (Wender, 1985). *Attention Deficit Disorder, Residual* is the term that is applied to such adults when these individuals do not suffer from schizonhrenia, borderline personality or other significant problems.

Wender (1981) reviews studies that indicate that alcoholics display an increased frequency of the signs and symptoms of childhood hyperactivity. He also notes that the parents of hyperactive children have increased prevalence rates for alcoholism, sociopathy and hysteria. He concludes that some forms of alcoholism and antisocial personality may be genetic "relatives" of Attention Deficit Disorder. It is apparent that chemical dependency counselors working with both adolescents and adults should be watchful for evidence of this concern. A patient's aggressiveness, low tolerance for frustration and temper outbursts may indicate the presence of Attention Deficit Disorder and may escalate into violence (Reid and Balis, 1987) if not treated.

Individuals with Attention Deficit Disorder often respond well to carefully monitored medication, in particular methylphenidrate (Ritalin). Wender (1981) reports a 60% reduction in "hot temperedness" with the use of this medication. He also notes that many persons who are treated in this manner are themselves mostly unaware of their changes, just as they tend to be unaware of the problems their unaltered behavior cause. Chemical dependency counselors treating clients with Attention Deficit Disorder will need to utilize family reports regularly instead of relying upon the client.

Drug addiction counselors should be particularly alert for symptoms of residual Attention Deficit Disorder. Gittelman (1985), in a follow-up study of young men ages 16-23 who had been diagnosed as hyperactive years before, discovered that those men who retained hyperactive symptoms had a much higher rate of drug abuse (not alcohol) than the group whose symptoms diminished.

Premenstrual Syndrome

Irritability is one of the more commonly found symptoms of Premenstrual Syndrome and is often linked with anxiety (Abraham, 1980). Furthermore, such irritability may be connected with a series of other negative affects including depression, loneliness, tension and mood swings (Moos, 1977).

Women with PMS are likely to abuse alcohol and other mood-altering substances. For example, Halliday (1986) found that 51% of women seeking gynecological care for PMS-related problems answered at least one of the four CAGE questions (a screening device for alcohol abuse) positively and that 21% met the criteria for alcohol abuse. She concludes that "Women who seek medical care for PMS are at much greater risk to be alcohol abusers" (Halliday, 1986: 322). Bender (1987) reports that 70% of women treated at a Colorado clinic who drink alcohol develop an increased desire for alcohol during the premenstrual phase and that 57% describe exaggerated effects from alcohol use. These studies confirm earlier efforts by Belfer (1971), who noted that 67% of menstruating alcoholics related their drinking with their menstrual cycle and

Podolsky (1963), who wrote about seven women with severe PMS who utilized alcohol to relieve their symptoms. Alcohol counselors should be aware that alcohol is absorbed more quickly into the blood stream during the premenstrual period (Halliday, 1986), resulting in significantly higher blood alcohol levels and greater intoxication at that time and at ovulation (Jones and Jones, 1976). Other drugs, especially tranquilizers, may also be taken in an effort to alleviate PMS discomfort (Bender, 1987).

Markoff (1984) discusses a denial pattern that is common among women who are burdened with both alcoholism and PMS. She states that these women are not relieved when told that their behavior pattern is related to PMS because they then feel overwhelmed with the enormity of facing this dual disorder. However, denial must be confronted to minimize relapse potential.

The substance abuse counselor can help a recovering client who has PMS deal with her anger in several ways. First, the counselor can give the client relevant information so that she can understand better what is occuring and why she is irritable. The client may need referrals to family physicians, gynecologists, and dieticians during this phase so that symptoms can be minimized and alleviated. Secondly, women with PMS can be encouraged to take time outs, practice relaxation techniques and to develop useful cognitive messages (such as "I'm not really mad at him. This is my PMS acting up"), all of which serve to lessen the damage done during the PMS time. Thirdly, those recovering persons who belong to Alcoholics Anonymous or similar self-help groups should increase their participation in those groups premenstrually; they might also commit themselves to practice the principles of A.A., especially powerlessness, self care, forgiveness, and promptly admitting one's mistakes, at this time. Finally, PMS, just like drug addiction, should never be allowed as an excuse for irresponsible behavior, including excessive anger displays.

PSYCHIATRIC DIAGNOSES

Many psychiatric conditions are associated with both aggression or chronic anger and with substance abuse. Those that will be considered here include the borderline and antisocial personality disorders, bipolar and major depressive disorders, schizophrenia and post-traumatic stress disorder.

Personality Disorders

The Diagnostic and Statistical Manual of Mental Disorders, Revised Third Edition (DSM-III-R, 1987) defines personality disorders as constellations of enduring, inflexible and dysfunctional traits that cause either significant functional impairment or subjective distress (DSM-III-R, 1987: 335). These patterns are usually recognized by adolescence or early adulthood and continue throughout life, sometimes lessening with age. Certain personality disorders are particularly associated with chemical abuse and the presence of excessive anger and/or aggression. The chemical dependency counselor will probably encounter three relevant personality disordered clients: borderline, antisocial and paranoid.

Borderline Personality Disorder

Inappropriate, intense anger or lack of control of anger, marked by such features as frequent displays of temper, constant anger, and recurrent physical fights is one of the eight criteria for diagnosis of borderline personality disorder (DSM-III-R, 1987). The borderline personality may also be characterized by a pattern of intense, unstable relationships; impulsiveness in many areas including substance use and binge eating; affective instability; recurrent suicidal threats and gestures; marked identity disturbance; chronic feelings of emptiness and boredom; and frantic efforts to avoid abandonment (DSM-III-R, 1987).

Borderline personalities seem to have a "bottomless pit" of anger. They are often rageful, particularly at individuals who are perceived to have abandoned them or who might do so in the future. Borderline personality individuals cannot tolerate loss. Faced with the possibility of the end of a relationship, this person may panic and attempt to prevent intolerable feelings of aloneness through violence toward the other person or against the self. The problem is worsened because these individuals engage in a primitive "splitting" process in which others are perceived either as all good or all bad. The formerly idealized lover can quickly become a totally de-valuated "thing" worthy only of contempt and even annihilation.

Alcohol and drug use is found in a number of borderline persons; perhaps as many as 30% of female alcoholics are found to meet the criteria for borderline personality (Vaglum and Vaglum, 1985). Gunderson and Zanarini (1987) explain this tendency by noting that "the borderline attempts to diminish the intolerable experience of aloneness through impulsive actions, such as drug or alcohol abuse . . . that give contact with new persons." They also state that the substance abuse pattern tends to be episodic, without a favored or stable drug preference. However, this pattern does not preclude the development of long-term chemical dependency.

Prodgers (1984) notes that the core characteristics of child abus-ing parents bears a remarkable similarity to the borderline personal-ity syndrome. These characteristics include arrested emotional de-velopment, poor self-image, emotional isolation, depressive loneliness and poorly suppressed anger. He describes anger as the major or only affect in the borderline individual.

Therapy, especially group therapy, is difficult with borderline clients. Baker (1984) suggests that the first stage of therapy gener-ally is one of testing and anger. Counselors must be able to demon-strate a consistent ability to withstand oppositional behavior without falling apart, as well as setting consistent limits. Borderline clients tend to develop strong dependencies upon their therapists, making termination another complex task. The chemical dependency coun-selor must maintain the focus upon the client's irresponsible and often desperate reliance upon alcohol or drugs while at the same time staying on the alert for other dependencies including eating disorders and "male" or "female" dependency. The client must be guided toward learning how to survive in a non-intense, non-crisis atmosphere. Long-term follow-up counseling is certainly advised as the client struggles to make sense out of life while facing feelings of chronic emptiness and boredom. Counselors should be prepared to listen to accounts of sudden and dramatic violence directed either against others or the self. They should be particularly alert toward the possibility of self-mutilation with these individuals. Borderline clients will almost certainly require long-term follow-up care after their initial treatment for chemical dependency.

Antisocial Personality Disorder

Individuals with antisocial personality disorder have a long history of troubling behavior that frequently includes initiating physical fights, forcible sexual activity, destruction of property, irritability and aggressiveness. These behaviors often develop before the individual has ever consumed alcohol and drugs but they may be exacerbated by the use of mood-altering chemicals.

There are some well-documented connections between antisocial personality disorder and alcoholism. For example, Lewis (1986) cites seven different studies all finding elevated rates of alcoholism among personality disordered clients. Furthermore, he states that "Excessive anger appears to be an integral part of the personality of both the alcoholic and the sociopath" (Lewis, 1986: 660). Schuckit (1984) adds that many males who commit acts of violence have primary antisocial personality disorder and secondary alcoholism. He notes, however, that even when only primary alcoholics are studied that those alcoholics who are also violent have higher rates of psychiatric hospitalization and mental health utilization.

The antisocial personality who does become alcoholic seems to do so with a vengeance. Hesselbrock (1986) writes that antisocial individuals "were more likely to have been exposed to heavy drinking, and, once exposed, tended to develop the full alcohol syndrome" (Hesselbrock, 1986: 78). Their general addiction pattern includes relatively early onset, greater severity and a chronic course of consumption.

Alcoholism and antisocial personality also may have an additive effect on the occurrence of violent behavior. Bland and Orn (1986) interviewed 1200 residents of a Canadian city, discovering that when a person combined these two problems the probability for violent behavior was an astonishing 80-93 percent. (Alcoholism combined with depression had equally strong effects.) By contrast, those respondents whose primary diagnosis was only antisocial personality indicated a 54 percent probability for violence.

The chemical dependency counselor who treats clients with antisocial personality disorder may be struck with that individual's consistent dishonesty, manipulativeness, and lack of remorse. Bolton (1987) suggests that the counselor must balance authority with warmth with the clinician remaining in control of the interaction. His goals with antisocial clients are the increased use of appropriate reason, the development of fairness and the use of rational expectations of others. I would add that the antisocial personality needs to develop, accept, and live by a set of socially responsible values. This means that the chemically dependent adult will have to learn from others how to live a lifestyle characterized by honesty, fairness, etc. Alcoholics Anonymous represents an excellent opportunity for antisocial personalities to graft these values onto their lives.

Therapists should be particularly alert with antisocial personalities for the presence of instrumental violence. Instrumental violence has a specific goal, such as the control of another family member. It does not result simply from a need to express feelings. Counselors can confront the individual's use of violence as just one part of that person's belief that he can do anything he wants to get what he wants. The counselor should emphasize the long-term negative consequences of such behavior while expecting the client to take responsibility for that behavior.

Other Personality Disorders

Several other personality disorders are associated with at least occasional violence, although only the borderline and antisocial personalities include violence in their diagnostic criteria. Nor are the remaining personality disorders as closely associated with chemical abuse or dependency as the two above. Nevertheless, the chemical dependency counselor can benefit from knowledge of the aggressive potentiality of other personality disorders.

Individuals with *Paranoid Personality Disorder* have a "pervasive and unwarranted tendency . . . to interpret the actions of people as deliberately demeaning or threatening" (DSM-III-R, 1987). These persons expect to be exploited by others, bear longstanding grudges, are easily slighted and are quick to react with anger or to counterattack those whom they mistakenly believe are attacking them. Paranoid individuals continually search for and locate evidence that others are plotting against them, dangerous, and secretive. They in turn tend to become secretive and cunning. The paranoid client who is in a period of temporary decompensation is especially likely to become violent (Reid and Balis, 1987).

Any use of alcohol or drugs may increase the paranoid's already strong belief that he lives in a menacing world. For instance, the intoxicated paranoid may become convinced that his spouse wants him to leave the house only because she is having sexual relations with someone else. He may then feel totally justified in harming his wife, her alleged paramour, or himself.

The client with *Narcissistic Personality Disorder* has a "pervasive pattern of grandiosity . . . lack of empathy, and hypersensitivity to the evaluation of others" (DSM-III-R). These persons have an inflated but fragile sense of self worth. They require constant reinforcement of their "specialness," expecting continuing attention and admiration from others. They have a sense of "entitlement," which means that they have an unreasonable expectation of receiving favorable treatment even when they have done nothing exceptional.

The narcissistic personality has little interest in others except to gain their praise. His nurturing ability is severly limited (Bolton, 1987). When others fail to acknowledge or meet the narcissistic person's omnipotent needs and goals that individual may respond with "narcissistic rage" and aggression (Svrakic, 1986). During these rages others are verbally and physically assaulted in order to devaluate and destroy them. This easily activated destructiveness and ruthlessness feels perfectly justified to the narcissistic personality who places no limits on his desire to redress the grievance of being abandoned (Russell, 1985). The rage of the narcissist relates to his basic feelings of inferiority (Svrakic, 1986).

Narcissists may appear to do well in therapy as long as their need to be the center of attention is not disputed. They tend to seek out therapists after groups for important conferences, implying that what they have to say is too unique to share with average group members. They will look bored and distracted while others are speaking. They are attracted to drugs that enhance their sense of superiority, such as cocaine. Cocaine addiction specialists note that it may be unwise to challenge those feelings immediately; rather, the client may be drawn into treatment through the promise of gaining special attention and care (Schulman, 1987).

Conn and Lion (1984) mention several other personality disorders at least occasionally connected with aggression. They note that *Compulsive Personality Disorder*ed persons, who are driven by the need for order and perfection, may strike out against others when that need is frustrated. The *Histrionic* individual is prone to emotional lability which can lead to dramatic shows of violence. Even the *Passive-Aggressive Personality*, whose *forte* is a generalized refusal to respond, may be prone to irrational outbursts. The chemical dependency counselor working with these and other personality disorders will need to intervene upon their clients' repetitive crises, steer these individuals regularly toward reality, confront destructive and violent behaviors, and help them develop a positive environment (Bolton, 1987). Since all personality disordered persons cling precariously to emotional stability they must be persistently and insistently directed away from any mind altering intoxicant.

One final note on personality disorders: the DSM-III-R includes two *proposed* new personality disorders that would clearly be relevant for this paper. One is *Sadistic Personality Disorder*, characterized by a pattern involving the use of physical cruelty or violence for the purpose of establishing dominance in a relationship, control through intimidation, restricting the autonomy of others, and several other aggression related criteria. The other is *Self-defeating Personality Disorder*, a pervasive pattern of behavior which could include choosing situations that lead to mistreatment and inciting angry responses from others. Correlations between these categories and chemical dependency or codependent patterns could be expected to be positive.

Mood Disorders

Mood disorders have in common the essential feature of disturbance of mood, accompanied by a full or partial Manic or Depressive Syndrome, that is not due to any other physical or mental disorder (DSM-III-R). Mood here refers to a prolonged emotional state that colors the entire psychic life of the individual and generally involves either depression or elation (DSM-III-R). Two mood disorders that may be associated with violence are Bipolar Disorder and Major Depressive Disorder.

Bipolar Disorder

Individuals diagnosed with this condition regularly alternate between a depressive phase, in which they experience a markedly diminished interest in their usual activities, insomnia or hypersomnia, loss of energy, feelings of worthlessness, possible suicidal ideation and other related symptoms (DSM-III-R), and a manic phase characterized by a distinct period of abnormally and persistently elevated, expansive or irritable mood. During the manic phase individuals become more energetic and talkative than usual, may be easily distractable, often develop an inflated sense of self-esteem, and are more likely to become involved in pleasurable activities which lead to negative consequences. Conn and Lion (1984) note that manic behavior may be characterized by lability, excitability, belligerence, intrusiveness and outright assaultiveness. Even those Bipolar Disordered persons who appear to be completely happy in their state of heightened excitation can find themselves quickly becoming irritable and argumentative when their wishes are thwarted. Clients with Bipolar Disorder are generally treated with lithium, a salt that is effective in controlling manic episodes.

Major Depressive Disorder

Individuals with this condition experience a general and persistent dysphoria as described above, with no intervening manic phases. Major depressions usually last at least six months but can continue indefintely, may appear only once or several times during the life of an individual, and are found far more frequently with women than men.

Many studies have traced the relationship between depressive symptoms and alcoholism. For example, Bedi and Halikas (1985) discovered that female inpatient alcoholics between ages 20-30 had a 60% chance to meet the criteria for depressive disorder. Deykin (1987) found that depression was associated both with alcohol and drug abuse among an adolescent population. Symptoms of Major Depressive Disorder preceded the substance abuse pattern with these adolescents, suggesting the possibility that they may have turned to intoxicants as a form of self-medication. Both Overall (1985) and Jaffe and Ciraulo (1986) note that in general the number of depressive symptoms drops quickly during inpatient treatment but not with all clients. Overall links continuing depressive symptomatology with the loss of social support (such as marriages) with some depressed clients. Jaffe and Ciraulo discovered a subset of alcoholic clients who retain persistent but subclinical levels of "hypophoria" (joylessness, sense of defeat) long after the completion of treatment and even if these persons attend Alcoholics Anonymous. This last finding suggests that certain abstaining alcoholics whose lives remain bleak long after treatment should be examined for the presence not only of Major Depressive Disorder but also for *Dysthymic Disorder*, a less dramatic but long-lasting mood disorder.

The possibility for violence against self and others by depressed clients is often underestimated by clinicians (Rada, 1981). Increased dysphoria might predict assaultive behavior (Rada, 1981). The author, who facilitates an anger management group mostly attended by recovering alcoholics and chemically dependent clients, regularly enrolls clients with mood disorders (including Major Depressive Disorder, Atypical Disorder and Dysthymic Disorder) in that group. These clients report that their anger and aggression was worse when they used intoxicants but that it continued after abstinence. They also indicate that because of their depressions (often undiagnosed) they did not achieve any sense of serenity despite regular attendance in self-help groups and other efforts to "work" their programs. Their failure to feel good added guilt to their lives, probably only increasing their tendencies toward angry outbursts.

Chemical dependency counselors, especially those whose assignments include aftercare or other opportunities to observe their clients over time, should be alert for the subtly depressed client who cannot achieve serenity or whose peace of mind gradually diminishes into despair, guilt and feelings of worthlessness. *Depressive symptomatology is a major predictor of relapse* (Pickens, 1985). Renewed reports of family arguments and violence may be a key indicator that the abstinent individual is heading into depression.

Short-term chemical dependency counselors can be effective by informing their clients that depressive features are commonly noticed among early-stage recovering persons and that the client can reasonably hope that many of those features will decline quickly with continuing sobriety. Clients should be informed of the major indicators for depression so that they can monitor their changes. They do need to be told that not all clients completely eliminate depression with abstinence, just as not all clients can maintain consistently non-violent behavior.

Schizophrenia

Schizophrenia will be mentioned briefly because most chemical dependency counselors have little expertise in this area and because the connections between this disorder, aggression, and subtance abuse are not clear at this time. Daley (1987) indicates that between two to fifteen percent of hospitalized alcoholics may also be schizophrenic, but these numbers are admittedly speculative. Schizophrenics who harbor paranoid delusive beliefs are most dangerous to others; these individuals may present symptoms of anger, argumentativeness, and violence (Daley, 1987). The schizophrenic individual may turn to mood-altering substances both for relief from symptoms and for socialization. Use of these substances may well exacerbate delusional thinking and could lead toward an increased probability of violence. In particular, schizophrenic patients should be careful not to use PCP; at least one research study (Yesavage and Zarcone, 1983) links PCP usage with inpatient assaultiveness by these patients. These authors also linked assaultiveness with a patient history of alcoholic blackouts.

Post-Traumatic Stress Disorder

Post-Traumatic Stress Disorder (PTSD) is an anxiety disorder that occurs after an individual has been exposed to a strong stressor that would evoke significant symptoms of distress in most persons. Symptoms include regular reexperiencing of the traumatic event, reduced involvement with the world, and the possibility of sleep disturbance, exaggerated startle response, survivor guilt and several other problems. Although neither substance abuse nor chronic anger or aggression are defining components of PTSD, both have been cited as occurring frequently with this population (Daley, 1987; Keane, 1985). Keane notes that anger and drug abuse can be conceptualized as "behavior patterns that are functionally reinforced by their capacity to reduce aversive feelings" (Keane, 1985: 267) among Vietnam-era veterans. He recommends a thorough screening of PTSD clients in both areas with a focus upon the client's impulsivity, irritability and emotional lability. Keane also describes a therapy program that includes relaxation, cognitive restructuring and anger control methods that help PTSD clients manage excessive anger. Pynoos and Eth (1985) add that many adolescents appear to use drugs to relieve trauma-induced dysphoria.

The applicability of the PTSD diagnosis has gradually been expanded since its introduction. For example, one study (Wilson, 1985) compares eight different "survivor groups": Vietnam veterans; victims of rape, battering, and child abuse; victims of serious life threats; persons divorced; serious near-fatal illness of loved one; family trauma (including the effects of alcoholism); death of a significant other; and victims of multiple traumas. All of these groups reported significantly greater rage/anger than did a control group. Interestingly, the family trauma group, which included family alcoholism, reported more anger than several other groups, although the Vietnam veterans group was by far most rageful.

Counseling the PTSD/chemically dependent client with regard to anger difficulties is a delicate task. Daley (1987) suggests that some individuals might benefit from dual treatment in conjunction with a PTSD support group so that the client can focus appropriately on each issue. He also suggests that the counselor must be particularly careful to mix caring with confrontation since PTSD clients tend to be highly sensitive while occasionally using their PTSD as an excuse for irresponsibility.

SOCIOCULTURAL FACTORS THAT INFLUENCE THE RELATIONSHIP BETWEEN FAMILY VIOLENCE AND SUBSTANCE USE

Social learning is a crucial intervening variable that comes between the ingestion of mood altering substances and violent family interactions. For example, the husband who becomes intoxicated at a bar and then goes home to attack his wife or children somehow seems to understand that: (1) his state of intoxication is special in that he can be violent as part of being drunk; (2) the proper target of his aggression is a family member; and (3) he can later attribute his action to the chemicals inside him rather than take full responsibility for the damage he has done.

The alcohol and substance abuse counselor must be careful never to argue that the dependent individual's use of alcohol or drugs alone caused that person to aggress. Rather, the use of these substances must be placed in the context of a complicated situation in which clients and sometimes entire families must quit taking intoxicants as part of a much larger recovery process.

Two sociocultural areas that will be discussed in this section are the general cultural expectations that surround chemical usage and family violence in American society and more specific family connections with regard to family process and structure among chemically dependent and violent families.

General Cultural Expectations

American society seems to take a decidely ambivalent approach toward alcohol and drug usage. It might be said that usage is promoted heavily until users become chronically dependent and their behavior becomes problematic. This confusion is particularly noticeable regarding aggression that is associated with the consumption of mood-altering substances. Although such aggression is deplored the society as a whole still adheres to the disinhibition model in which individuals are excused from their behavior because they are intoxicated. Responsibility for normally inappropriate actions is given to the drug rather than the individual, in effect allowing him a "time-out" (MacAndrew and Edgerton, 1969) from normal expectations. The disinhibition model is certainly inaccurate, a crude simplification that does not appear to be an accurate characterization of the behavioral effects of drinking (Collins, 1983). Authors writing from a family violence perspective (Gelles, 1972; Coleman and Straus, 1979) deplore the use of intoxication as an excuse for violence. Family violence counselors, with some justification, argue that chemical dependency counselors have accepted the disinhibition model too naively and in so doing have failed to insist that their clients accept full responsibility for their supposedly "drunken" or "stoned" behavior.

Intrafamilial Processes

Students of families in which violence is present make several important points: (1) members in these families are often mutually antagonistic, in effect "training" each other to escalate misunderstandings and disagreements into physical aggression (Patterson, 1985); (2) persons who live in these families learn how to be both "victims" and "victimizers" (Wise, 1989); (3) power, and hence the probability of being a victim or a victimizer within a specific family or group, flows downward (Finkelhor,1983); (4) physically aggressive persons tend to be relatively poorly skilled in the area of interpersonal communications and therefore tend to utilize aggression to stay in control (Bolton and Bolton, 1987); and (5) chemically dependent families and incestuous or physically assaultive families share many structural similarities, such as an acceptance of loss of control as a way of coping with the world and the existence of rigid role expectations (Potter-Efron and Potter-Efron, 1985; Bernard, 1989).

The counselor who works with a chemically dependent client who is either a perpetrator or victim of violence should be alert to how that individual and his family interprets his behavior. The helper must be particularly alert to signals indicating that the family or substance abuser explain and excuse aggression "because I got drunk and couldn't help it." The connection between chemical use and violence is primarily learned within families, peer groups and larger societal units. That connection can and should be challenged regularly within a chemical dependency treatment setting.

DISCUSSION

The relationship between the consumption of alcohol and other mood-altering chemicals and the appearance of aggression is complex. The chemical dependency counselor will need to differentiate among four categories of concern: (1) the effects of the drug itself upon the individual; (2) neurological/physiological conditions that interact with alcohol and drugs to increase the risk for violence; (3) psychiatric diagnoses that are frequently associated with both aggression and substance abuse; and (4) sociocultural expectations about the relationship between intoxicants and aggression that affect substance users, physical and sexual abusers, and their families. This article discusses the latter three categories while its predecessor in this volume (Miller and Potter-Efron, 1989) describes the first variable.

A chemically dependent person might need attention in all four areas. For example, a woman with Premenstrual Syndrome may also become depressed, might turn to alcohol for symptom relief only to find her susceptibility to its effects greatly enhanced during the premenstrual week, and might excuse her aggressive behavior toward others either because she had PMS or because she was intoxicated.

Neurological/physiological conditions described in this article include traumatic brain injuries, intermittent explosive disorder, attention deficit disorder and premenstrual syndrome. Psychiatric diagnoses include antisocial and borderline personality disorders, bipolar and major depressive disorders, and post-traumatic stress disorder. Sociocultural factors were general cultural expectations and selected intrafamilial processes.

REFERENCES

Abraham, G.E. Premenstrual Tension. Current Problems in Obstetrics and Gynecology. 1980, 3(12): 1-38.

Blumer, Dietrich. Epilepsy and Violence. In Madden, Denis and Lion, John (eds.), *Rage, Hate, Assault and Other Forms of Violence*. New York: Spectrum Books, 1976, 207-220.

Baker, Patricia. A Comprehensive Model of Practice for Borderline Adolescents. Clinical Social Work Journal. 1984, 12(4): 320-331.

Bedi, Ashok and Halikas, James. Alcoholism and Affective Disorder. Alcoholism: Clinical and Experimental Research. 1985, 9(2): 133-134.

Belfer, M. Alcoholism in Women. Archives of General Psychiatry. 1971, 25: 540-544.

Bender, Stephanie DeGraff. PMS and Chemical Dependence. PMS Access. 1987, 14.

Bernard, Charles. Alcoholism and Sex Abuse in the Family: Incest and Marital Rape. Journal of Chemical Dependency Treatment. 1989, 3(1).

Bland, Roger and Orn, Helene. Family Violence and Psychiatric Disorder. Canadian Journal of Psychiatry. 1986, 31: 129-137.

Bolton, Frank and Bolton, Susan. *Working with Violent Families*. Newbury Park: Sage Publications, 1987.

Coleman, Diane and Straus, Murray. Alcohol Abuse and Family Violence. In Gottheil, Edward; Druley, Keith; Skoloda, Thomas; and Waxman, Howard (eds.), *Alcohol, Drug Abuse and Aggression*. Springfield, Ill.: Ch. Thomas, 1983.

Collins, James. Alcohol Use and Expressive Interpersonal Violence: A Proposed Explanatory Model. In Gottheil, Edward; Druley, Keith; Skoloda, Thomas; and Waxman, Howard (eds.), *Alcohol, Drug Use and Aggression*. Springfield, Ill.: Ch. Thomas, 1983.

Conn, Lois and Lion, John. Pharmacologic Approaches to Violence. Psychiatric Clinics of North America. 1984, 7(4): 879-886.

Daley, Dennis; Moss, Howard; and Cambell, Frances. *Dual Disorders*. Centre City, Mn.: Hazelden Press, 1987.

Deykin, E.Y.; Levy, J.C.; and Wells, V. Adolescent Depression, Alcohol and Drug Abuse. American Journal of Public Health. 1987, 77(2): 178-182.

———. *Diagnostic and Statistical Manual of Mental Disorders, Third Edition*. Washington, D.C.: American Psychiatric Association: 987.

Elliot, Frank. Neurological Causes and Cures of Explosive Rage. Medical Opinion. 1977, (Feb.): 34-46.

Finkelhor, David. *The Dark Side of Families: Current Family Violence Research*. Beverly Hills: Sage Publications, 1983.

Gelles, Richard. *The Violent Home: A Study of Physical Aggression between Husbands and Wives*. Beverly Hills: Sage Publications, 1972.

Gittelman, Rachel; Mannuzza, Salvatore; Shenker, Ronald; and Bonagura, Noreen. Hyperactive Boys Almost Grown Up. Archives of General Psychiatry. 1985, 42: 937-947.

Gunderson, John and Zanarini, Mary. Current Overview of the Borderline Diagnosis. Journal of Clinical Psychiatry. 1987, 48(8): 5-35.

Hesselbrock, Michie. Childhood Behavior Problems and Adult Antisocial Personality Disorder in Alcoholism. In Meyer, Roger (ed.), *Psychopathology and Addictive Disorders*. New York: Guilford, 1986, 78-93.

Halliday, Andrea; Bush, Booker; Cleary, Paul; Aronson, Mark; and Delbanco, Thomas. Alcohol Abuse in Women Seeking Gynecologic Care. Obstetrics and Gynecology. 1986, 68(3): 322-326.

Jaffe, Jerome and Ciraulo, Domenic. Alcoholism and Depression. In Meyer, Roger (ed.). *Psychopathology and Addictive Disorders*. New York: Guilford Press, 1986.

Jenkins, Susan and Maruta, Toshihiko. Therapeutic Use of Propanolol for Intermittent Explosive Disorder. Mayo Clinical Process. 1987, 62: 204-214.

Jones, B.W. and Jones, M.D. Women and Alcohol: Intoxication, Metabolism and the Menstrual Cycle. In Greenblatt and Schukit (eds.), *Alcoholism Problems in Women and Children*. New York: Grune and Stratton, 1976.

Keane, Terence; Fairbank, John; Caddell, Juesta; Zimering, Rose and Bender, Mary. A Behavioral Approach to Assessing and Treating Post-Traumatic Stress Disorder in Vietnam Veterans. In Figley, Charles (ed.), *Trauma and Its Wake*. New York: Brunner/Mazel, 1985, 257-294.

Lewis, Collins; Rice, John; Andreasen, Nancy; Endicott, Jean; and Hartman, Ann. Clinical and Family Correlates of Alcoholism in Men with Unipolar Depression. Alcoholism: Clinical and Experimental Research. 1986, 10(6): 657-662.

MacAndrew, C. and Edgerton, R. *Drunken Comportment: A Social Explanation*. Chicago: Aldine Publishing, 1969.

Markoff, Connie. Cited in PMS and Alcohol Abuse: Cocktail Hour Becomes Cocktail Daze. PMS Connection. PMS Action, Irvine, Cal. 1984.

Miller, Michael M. and Potter-Efron, R.T. Differential Diagnosis of Substance Induced Anger and Violence. Journal of Chemical Dependency Treatment, 1989.

Moos, R.H. Typology of Menstrual Cycle Symptoms. American Journal of Obstetrics and Gynecology. 1969, 103(3): 390-402.

Overall, John; Reilly, Edward; Kelley, James; and Hollister, Leo. Persistence of Depression in Detoxified Alcoholics. Alcoholism: Clinical and Experimental Research. 1985, 9(4): 331-333.

Patterson, G.R. A Microsocial Analysis of Anger and Irritable Behavior. In Chesney, Margaret and Rosenman, Ray (eds.), *Anger and Hostility in Cardiovascular and Behavioral Disorders*. New York: Hemisphere Publishing, 1985: 83-100.

Pickens, Roy; Hatsukami, Dorothy; Spicer, Jerry; and Svikis, Dace. Relapse by Alcohol Abusers. Alcoholism: Clinical and Experimental Research. 1985, 9(3): 244-247.

Podolsky, E. The Woman Alcoholic and Premenstrual Tension. Journal of the American Med. Wom. Association. 1963, 18: 816-818.

Potter-Efron, Ronald and Potter-Efron, Patricia. Family Violence as a Treatment Issue with Chemically Dependent Adolescents. Alcoholism Treatment Quarterly. 1985, 2(2): 1-15.

Prodgers, Alan. Psychopathology of the Physically Abusing Parent: A Comparison With the Borderline Syndrome. Child Abuse and Neglect. 1984, 8: 411-424.

Pynoos, Robert and Eth, Spencer. Developmental Perspective on Psychic Trauma in Childhood. In Figley, Charles (ed.), *Trauma and Its Wake*. New York: Brunner-Mazel, 1985: 36-52.

Rada, Richard. The Violent Patient: Rapid Assessment and Management. Psychosomatics. 1981, 22(2): 101-109.

Reid, William and Balis, George. Evaluation of the Violent Patient. In Frances, Allen and Hales, Robert (eds.), *American Psychiatric Association Annual Review. Vol. 5*. Washington, D.C.: American Psychiatric Press, 1986: 491-509.

Russell, Gillian. Narcissism and the Narcissistic Personality Disorder: A Comparison of the Theories of Kernberg and Kohut. British Journal of Medical Psychology. 1985, 58: 137-148.

Schukit, Mark and Russell, Jon. An Evaluation of Primary Alcoholics with Histories of Violence. Journal of Clinical Psychiatry. 1984, 45: 3-6.

Schulman, Gerald. Alcoholism and Cocaine Addiction. ARCircular. 1987, 4(1): 2-15.

Silver, Jonathon and Yudolfsky, Stuart. Aggressive Behavior in Patients with Neuropsychiatric Disorders. Psychiatric Annals. 1987, 17(6): 367-370.

Svrakic, Dragan. The Real Self of Narcissistic Personalities. The American Journal of Psychoanalysis. 1986, 46(3): 219-229.

Tardiff, Kenneth. Determinants of Human Violence. In Frances, Allen and Hales, Robert (eds.), *American Psychiatric Association Annual Review, Vol. 5.* Washington, D.C.: American Psychitric Press, 1986: 451-464.

Vaglum, S. and Vaglum, P. Borderline and Other Mental Disorders in Alcoholic Female Alcoholic Psychiatric Patients. Pyschopathology. 1985, 18: 50-60.

Wender, Paul; Reimherr, Frederick; and Wood, David. Attention Deficit Disorder (Minimal Brain Dysfunction) in Adults. Archives of General Psychiatry. 1981, 38: 449-456.

Wender, Paul; Reimherr, Fred; Wood, David; and Ward, Mark. A Controlled Study of Methylphenidate in the Treatment of Attention Deficit Disorder, Residual Type, in Adults. American Journal of Psychiatry. 1985, 142(5): 547-552.

Wilson, John; Smith, W. Ken; and Johnson, Suzanne. A Comparative Analysis of PTSD among Various Survivor Groups. In Figley, Charles (ed.), *Trauma and Its Wake,* New York: Brunner-Mazel, 1985: 142-172.

Wise, Mary Louise. Adult Self-Injury as a Survival Response in Victim-Survivors of Childhood Abuse. Journal of Chemical Dependency Treatment. 1989, 3(1).

Yudolfsky, Stuart; Silver, Jonathon; and Schneider, Steven. Pharmacologic Treatment of Aggression. Psychiatric Annals. 1987, 17(6): 397-404.

Yesavage, Jerome and Zarcone, Vincent. History of Drug Abuse and Dangerous Behavior in Inpatient Schizoprenics. Journal of Clinical Psychiatry. 1983, 44: 259-261.

Alcohol and Family Violence: Then to Now — Who Owns the Problem

Jerry P. Flanzer, DSW

SUMMARY. The complex interconnections between family violence and chemical dependency are examined. A review of the literature is provided. Additionally, the historical involvement of the medical, legal and mental health fields in this topic are examined.

In the Western world, alcohol has long been associated with violence. The family has traditionally been viewed as a source of support and understanding; but also the same family can be an arena of physical aggression, violence and abuse. Yet, intrafamilial violence, exclusive of homicide, has only been recently explored and documented. The presence of alcohol accompanying family violence is rarely noted in the newly burgeoning family violence literature, although popular literature has viewed alcohol as a major contributing factor in all aspects of family abuse. Problem drinking and family violence is surely not new. Our literature and folklore are replete with tales of drunkards who hit their wives and abuse their children. Yet only lately has the association of child abuse or spouse abuse and alcoholism been truly scrutinized.

Family violence has been known, accepted, tolerated and regulated since the recording of the written word. Suddenly, it has emerged as a social-problem discovery of major proportions. Why now? What's new? Why is the media so concerned now? Why the

Jerry P. Flanzer, is Professor, National Catholic School of Social Service, The Catholic University of America, Washington, DC.

rise of anti-family violence organizations and treatment centers? Why is there new legislation concerning violence in families?

This is partly true because our moral standards have changed toward children and women. But it is also true because social problems are created, and a structure develops to support their maintenance. Clinical users of research must question every piece they read, as to where did the drive and press and definition originate that successfully accomplished the particular formulation and funding of this social problem.

A social problem is a "condition affecting a significant number of people in ways considered undesirable, about which it is felt something can be done through collective social action" (Horton et al., p. 2). There is bias implicit in our definitions, because each definition carries implicit assumptions about the causes of the problem and the kinds of policy outcomes that are desirable. For example, child molestation can be defined as a problem of sexual deviation or as a problem of child safety. Most social problems and their prevailing professional definitions are inherently conservative — tending to preserve the major values and institutions of the existing society. This presents a dilemma when different sectors of society, not to mention different professional orientations, hold opposing or varying views on the "rightness" or "wrongness" of intervention into said family. Alcoholism and violence in families are dimensions of forms of deviance that are widely regarded as social problems and the "government has unsuccessfully attempted to stamp them out by making them illegal" (Horton et al., p. 324).

Schneider suggests that policy develops and constituencies are established in a dynamic relationship between the group that presents or labels the problem, the group that legitimates or recognizes the existence of the problem, the media and the government. This represents the natural history, as well as a political history, of a social problem. Social problems also create intellectual, emotional and political interests and martial both fiscal and human resources. Chauncey adds that social problems also may have a social life cycle, an evolution, as they wax and wane in popularity and attention.

The treatment and research experts also represent a source of construction. The general trends of consumerism have moved away from expert control (definition, processing, institutionalizing) toward "victim" control. To deprofessionalize child abuse, for example, it would be necessary to demedicalize it. Sometimes it is the funding agency that defines and brings to public awareness a social problem by legitimating an existing condition. Raising the issue to public perception may be a role performed by the victims themselves. In good consumer/Ralph Nader fashion, adult victims of child abuse have done just that, and demedicalized the problem as well. It is reasonable that children's issues will be constructed by parents, physicians, educators, any group chartered to represent children's interests. And some of the definitional dilemmas children's issues face today are probably the result of the battle of ownership—while any definition of the problem could, for example, aid child sexual abuse victims (or children of alcoholics, or children of divorce, or institutionalized children, foster children, ad infinitum), the bigger issue is who will own the problem, who will become the definers, reap the funding, guide the research, support their professional and disciplinary interests, and reap the rewards of being proclaimed the "solvers" of a particular problem. This process may, in fact, cloak the debate over what the definition actually ought to be.

Gusfield suggests that one social agent can own the problem/ define it and manage the suggestions for corrections while laying the ownership/responsibility to another social agent. The example he uses is alcohol abuse and automobile use. The problem, as defined, assigns the responsibility for the problem to the individual drinker. The definer of the problem remains something of a mystery. Those inclined to see Marxist truth behind every paradox could suggest that the automobile industry has actively ignored its actual and ethical responsibility in order to maintain profitability. This can be achieved by *not* owning the problem and encouraging both the "individualistic definition" of problem creation and the public service/private association ownership of problem solution. Gusfield calls these the "moral" and "public" features of political responsibility (Gusfield, 1975; p. 289); and argues that these have important implications for policy development.

The inability to "cure," or "solve," the alcohol abuse/family violence social problem may rest in part in this structural debate over who owns the problem. Solutions will vary if the problem is defined, owned, or managed by the medical profession or by the legal profession, by social work or psychiatry. But in response to our "new" humanness, this notion of social or within-discipline ownership, and the pressures of the children and women's movements, familial abuse in all forms is less tolerated than ever before.

Increasingly, during the end of the nineteenth century and throughout the twentieth century society has become accustomed to viewing the family as independent, nuclear, and increasingly separate from the extended family such as grandparents, cousins, etc. Suddenly, the nuclear family construct is being challenged, as exhibited by rising divorce rates and alternate family form. The family state is in flux. The tension resulting from this flux has led to scrutinization of the family's successes and failures. A universal search for the means to strengthen the family from within and without can be seen in many forms. All of these efforts have been undertaken to buttress the nuclear family's standing versus societal pressures for disintegration and anomie.

In addition, the mounting trend in western civilization towards sexual equality, particularly in marriage and at work has affected our "acceptance threshold." A slowly growing movement inaugurated perhaps by the eloquent work of John Stuart Mill (1869) has been developing that is primarily aimed at enhancing women's and children's rights in juxtaposition to the needs of capitalism and growing nations. Equal rights means equal rights within the family structure as well. Patriarchal dominance is being challenged in all arenas.

For the last 100-150 years child advocacy and woman's rights have been alternating and often competing against each other for changing national policy and laws. Each consistently fights hard to keep their issues in the limelight. The same may be said for alcohol/substance constituency groups. Beginning to look at the relationship of alcoholism and family violence as a clinical and research entity first had to bridge the hurdle of bringing together vested interests. This is clearly the accomplishment of this last thirty years. This can perhaps best be seen with the child abuse and neglect legislation of the 60s, the spouse abuse legislation of the 70s and corresponding separate development of alcoholism legislation of the 60s and then the creation of the federal government's Alcohol Drug Abuse and Mental Health Administration (ADAMAHA), joining mental health, drug abuse and alcoholism in the 70s and the joint findings and focus on dual diagnoses by ADAMAHA in the mid-80s.

Detailed histories of family violence forms throughout the centuries can be found (Behling, 1971). These histories tend to focus upon the issues of equality of the sexes, upon religious persecution, matriarchal versus patriarchal societies, or upon children as property and the need for cheap laborers. Family violence or violence within families is rarely addressed per se. Child abuse and spouse abuse are, instead, dealt with separately; each seeming independent, as if other forms of family violence did not exist. Not only are they rarely considered together in past research, but they have not been theoretically constructed as facets of the same problem. Single issue proponents find themselves as antagonists; competing for funding for research, theoretical and solution ownership, media coverage and popular support and legitimacy. Looking back over the last century, one finds a see-saw struggle between the championing of the rights of children (child abuse, child labor, and child advocacy laws) and of the rights of women (wife abuse, woman suffrage, and equal pay laws).

In the current literature and practice on family violence, evidence of the same struggle exists. For example, "domestic violence" has become the umbrella term for spouse abuse, particularly wife battering. In no way, does the name change suggest that the children's rights-women's rights issues and struggle for power within the "same pie" is diminished. Even within this seemingly unified label are groups who advocate rescuing the victim and punishing, counseling or separating the abuser, versus those who place blame for the abuse on the interaction and contributing roles of all members of the family in the identified abuse as well as those who seemingly "blame the victim." Yet another contender for definition ownership has recently expanded to unite all forms of violence within the family under a systems approach. Advocates for the systems approach argue that the "blame" should be spread among the entire family system, spotlighting all parties focusing on none; looking instead to the structural balance and internal dynamics for the causes and solutions to the problematic relationships which permit the now problematic behaviors. Family violence, no matter what form and what definition or literature or theory base you employ, is still family violence.

The family, in one form or another, exists in all cultures, and the cross-cultural variation in the definition and the characterization of family violence and abuse is great. In this regard, every type of family violence has occurred in at least one cultural setting as conforming behavior not problematic, including family neglect, incest, wife beating, child molesting, and infanticide (Mohr, 1964). In the United States, laws against cruelty to children are only about one-hundred years old. Even relatively small cultural differentiations (such as those between rural and urban America) or relatively short-term historical changes have been accompanied by significant variations in the definition of family violence. The piously executed woodshed whippings of youths in nineteen-century America are considered differently today, and city dwellers might still regard them differently than country dwellers.

Intrafamily aggressive behavior in the guise of parental responsibility for character development is a common, but by no means a necessary norm. Undoubtedly there are very few of us who have not been the victim, or perpetrator or rescuer (Flanzer, 1981). Many parents have spanked their child harder than they intended; few husbands/wives have not been slapped at least once by a spouse in a moment of rage. These incidents are not considered pathological or dysfunctional unless they are repeated or become a part of a patterned behavior; unless the invisible and ill-defined line of "the harmful act" — the violence line — is crossed. But when alcohol is involved, the chances of overstepping the violence line appears to be greatly increased.

Alcohol abuse incorporates a wide range of imbibing behaviors. Most of our known research centers around alcoholic and frequent drinkers, and there is little knowledge regarding occasional and moderate drinkers. Research regarding the effect of drinking alcohol on everyday, normal (i.e., nonabusive) family life, suprisingly, is sparse and is of little consequence. It is easier to study the captive alcoholic patient and perhaps even the driving-while-intoxicated client than it is the general user of alcohol. Funding awards support this construction of the problem. Increasingly the reports contained documentation of the presence of alcohol and family violence together among clientele of medical or mental health clinics, protective services, and the courts. These reports provide the clinical data linking family violence to the aftermath of incidence of drinking, weekend binges, and the like (Flanzer, 1980; Spieker and Mousakitis, 1976). And findings of what may be a high correlation and probability become the basis for research seeking causative relationships.

"Family violence" is a misnomer. "Violence in families" as the preferred logo for family violence, infers that the cause lies within the family and that it is possible and perhaps expected. Violence in families includes physically, emotionally or sexually harmful behavior through acts of commission or omission by one family member against another that may have its germination inside or outside of the family, hence allowing for the contribution of alcohol abuse to violence in the family, either as a family initiated problem or as an individual's problem affecting the family. The violent behavior within the family includes: family members physically abusing/severely emotionally neglecting another family member, child abuse, spouse abuse (including wife and husband beating and sexual abuse/child molesting), abuse of the elderly, and sibling and teenage abuse. Severe emotional neglect is every bit as damaging as physical abuse and even more likely to be associated with problem drinking (Flanzer, 1982).

Three areas of change and development have heightened and highlighted interest in alcohol *and* family violence among both professionals and the public:

1. Policy. The legitimization of these problem practice arenas for the professional mainstream, greatly influenced by the concommitant concern on the national policy level.
2. Prevalence. The staggering recent findings of high prevalence of alcohol misuse among most forms of family related violence.
3. Portrait. The mounting clinical evidence showing the common portrait and/or behavioral styles of the joint appearance of these two family problems.

POLICY

Policy is generally considered a governmental response to the public perception of a problem. Policy is intended to correct the problem, correct the cause of the problem or alter the responsibility for the solution. If highway repair funds are tied to alcohol consumption laws who can say who owns, in the social construction sense, drunk driving as a social problem? Should the highway department engage in alcohol education or treatment? Actually, they do neither — advertising campaigns are created by National Highway Safety Council, private automobile clubs, "victim" groups (MADD, SADD), and traffic schools belong to the police. If police departments and courts are assigned the detection and protection duties of family violence, how are professional treatment interests (psychiatrists with their individual and medical focus, psychologists with their assessment focus, social workers with their task and function focus, teachers and counselors with prevention interests, self-help groups, clergy and non-professional well-meaning neighbors) going to get into this loop? Policy, the assignment by government interest supported by funding decisions and legislation, sets the parameters for intervention too, by assigning treatment at the direction of the courts.

Is policy ever a response to professional definition? Yes, in that professional "ownership" constructs the definition based on assumptions of correctibility within the limits and interest of that profession. Convincing people that they themselves want help, networking with other professionals, developing areas of expertise and known success, helps correct behaviors defined as problems. Professionals are also most likely to have input in setting future policy — by acting as sources of new information for legislative endeavors.

THE PREVALENCE – THE ASSOCIATION

What is the actual frequency of alcohol involvement in the family violence incidents? What level or amount of drinking is involved? When does the drinking occur in a time relationship to the family violence act? Does the amount of alcohol effect the degree of family violence? Who is the victim? All of these questions address the prevalence of the relationship of alcohol and family violence. Answers to these questions can be found in the exploding research in this area, in light of the historical trends. Differences by type of family violence do exist, but from the family violence system position, the difference may be one only of degree.

Reflective of its criminological research traditional ownership, particularly incest and pedophilia, child molesting literature has had a fairly long history of concern with alcohol-involvement. The criminological findings did not penetrate the mental health and child welfare professional groups until this last decade. As criminologists owned the problem their concern was with detection and punishment, not treatment. Even in this research, however, alcohol is only one of numerous measures considered. But even this literature rarely informed policy beyond the criminal justice field. Explanatory theories of the role of alcohol in child molesting of both psychiatric and criminal perspectives have focused both on the long-term effects of continued and excessive drinking which result in general social and physical deterioration of the offender as well as on the short-term effects of alcohol as a disinhibitor which results in a lessened awareness of socially defined boundaries between acceptable and unacceptable behavior (Gebherd et al., 1965). As early as 1939, Frosh and Bromberg had shown that drunkenness is often used by child molesters as an excuse for the offenses. This excuse allowed the offender to maintain his identity as a normal, non-deviant person, while admitting his crime (McGahy, 1968). This issue of personal responsibility is also linked to social ownership. It does matter, in treatment and personal assessment, who tells you that you have a problem. Is it the police or a social worker? Drawing on convenience samples which skew the findings by the characteristics of the prison populations they study, much of this research finds a wide range of reported alcohol involvement at the time of the offense and in the personal histories of child molesters. They range from 19-49% of offenders drinking at the time, and 7-52% identifiable molesters as alcoholics. Several researchers present comparative data on incest offenders and pedophiles (Frosh and Bromberg, 1939; Apfelberg et al., 1944; Gluek, 1956; Ellis and Brancale, 1956; Gebherd et al., 1965). They indicate that incest offenders are characterized by larger proportions of both offenders who were drinking at the time of the offenses.

Although allusions to violence in alcoholic marriages among U.S. professional 50s-60s literature can be found (e.g., Futterman, 1963), and alcoholism in spouse abuse (e.g., Snell, 1961) and child abuse among opiate-addicted adolescents (Gerard, 1954), the serious early scientific interest of the relationship of alcoholism to family violence (excepting incest/child molestation) was predominantly focused in Europe. Miketic (1972), Grislain (1967), Popisil, Zarricki and Turcin (1968) and Nau (1967) all came to the similar conclusion of a high incidence of alcoholism among child abusing parents. Interestingly, Nau was the first to find that the alcoholic parent often committed the violent act when not intoxicated. Most of these findings are best generalized to populations of young children; for only scant attention in child abuse literature has been paid to the abused adolescent; when it has, it has been primarily related to incest. [See Ramee and Michau (1966) and Virkunnen (1974)]. Chronic brutality and alcoholism are the two most frequently cited complaints of incestuous families. Yet child protective services report a growing significant case load of parents abusing and severely neglecting their children accompanying alcohol use events.

These European findings encouraged other professionals who had heard these findings at international conferences to explore their own and U.S. clinical populations further. And the U.S. researchers began to make similarly striking findings. Fox (1972), Behling (1971), and Goldbetter (1973) reported their association findings at other professional conferences, and the definition began to change. Perhaps, the professionals seemed to say, the joint occurrence is more than a mutual occurrence. Behling, in particular noted:

1. 57% of the abused/neglected children had at least one grandparent who was alcoholic or who abused alcohol.
2. 65% of the suspected child abusers/neglectors were alcoholics or abused alcohol.
3. 84% of the abused or neglected children had at least one parent who was alcoholic or abused alcohol.

Of particular importance were Kempler and Mackinon's 1975 paper at the prestigious American Orthopsychiatry Association Conference and Spieker and Mousakitis's 1976 paper presented at the Alcohol and Drug Problem Association of North America meeting. At the Orthopsychiatry meeting, the child advocacy and mental health movement were "put on their ears" and at the ADPA meeting the alcohol and drug program people noticed a new research issue . . . and ultimately a marketing issue. Kempler and Mackinon's paper legitimated the high rate of association and added some treatment and policy concerns. Spieker and Mousakitis added the issue of the amount of drinking particularly noting that moderate as well as severe drinkers were at high risk to be abusers, thus broadening the association of relationships of drinking to abuse. While these two actual papers were not published until several years later, and in different forms, they were highly circulated and often quoted.

Gebhard (1965), Virkunnen (1974) and Meiselman (1978) report the associational link again of alcoholic perpetrators of incest. Numerous studies have examined the relationship between spouse abuse and alcohol (Eberle, 1982; Gerson, 1978, Labell, 1979; Lehmann and Krup, 1983; Leonard, 1985) Labell, for instance, studying abused women in a shelter found 72% reporting mates with a drinking problem. With wives of alcoholics, Scott (1974) found that 45% had been beaten, and 27% described an assault which was potentially lethal. Caution should be noted, however, because Orme and Rimmer (1981) reviewing 45 studies noted methodological problems in most of the associational data.

Constructing the problem around the perpetrator, similar dynamics and traits between child abuse and alcoholic families have been suggested as providing further evidence of the connection between alcoholism and child abuse (Hindman, 1977; Mayer and Black, 1977). Both abusive and alcoholic families may be characterized by low frustration tolerance, unrealistic expectations of children, role reversals, social isolation, loss of self-esteem and parental childhood histories of abuse. Most studies have concentrated on the offender's drinking behavior as opposed to the victim's drinking behavior. Several studies of women victimized by spousal violence have found some evidence that a subgroup of abused women used alcohol in connection with abusive events (Eberle, 1982; Frieze and Knoble, 1980; Gelles, 1972; Gerson, 1978). The connection between the woman's drinking and the battering is unclear. For example, Gerson (1978) reported that for cases of marital assault, both victim and offender were as likely to be drinking as was the offender only. Frieze and Knoble (1980) reported a positive correlation between drinking in battered women and drinking in their spouses. This finding suggests that battered women may use alcohol more frequently if the partner also drinks.

Various studies have shown that the majority of women were not drinking at the time of the battering (Berk et al., 1983; Walker, 1983), suggesting that drinking may be related to a subgroup of battered women's victimizations. Whether spouse abuse is more prevalent among alcoholic than nonalcoholic women is unknown. Alcoholic women may be at increased risk for spouse abuse due to their drinking, due to differential social response to drinkers and differing feelings of culpability. Decreased self-esteem of alcoholic women may give a husband tacit permission to abuse an alcoholic spouse. But several questions regarding these connections remain.

Flanzer and Sturkie (1986) solidified the evidence on the issue of severity of abuse. Their first finding was that the moderate and severe drinking parents were at higher risk to be battering their children than the alcoholic parents; and then added that the actual severity of abuse to the victim will be greater the greater amount of drinking by the perpetrator. Research on the alcohol involvement in child abuse and neglect usually focuses on the drinking histories and drinking problems of the abusers rather than the timing of the drinking, prior to or during the act. Adding the timing issue actually exploring the timing of drinking to the abuse is the first step towards finding cause and effect. And this represents a significant reconstruction of how researchers can look at the relationship of these two symptomatologies. The few studies that look at the simultaneous drinking and violent act report significantly different associations.

Nau (1967) noted that 44% of the men and 23% of the women in his study of alcoholic parents who abused children were under the influence of alcohol at the time of the event. Flanzer and Sturkie (1987) reported, unexpectedly, among adolescent abusing families, drinking often came after the event rather than before and/or during the actual violent act.

Additional studies on the role of alcohol and child abuse have examined intoxication at the time of the abusive event. Gil (1973) conducted a nationwide survey of reported and confirmed cases of child abuse and found that 12.9% of the abusers were intoxicated at the time of the abusive event. The intoxication and subsequent abuse were often associated with arguments where the child had tried to intervene between the parents. Glazier (1971) working from officially reported instances of child abuse found 13% of the offenders to be intoxicated at the time of the abusive event.

The alcohol literature most closely concerned with wife beating concerns the dynamics of women's response to their alcoholic husbands. Thirty years ago the emphasis was upon the wife's psychodynamics as partly responsible for the husband's condition and a "blame the victim view." The notion now incorporates that wives' behaviors are both responses to and compensations for the husband's alcoholism (Jackson, 1954). Jackson and later Ablon (1976), James and Goldman (1971) confirmed an interactional, sequential response pattern by wives of alcoholics. Police reports as best noted by Bard and Zacker (1974) note the high incidence of alcohol involvement in marital relationship complaint calls. Bard and Zacker found alcohol having been used at the time of the event by 26% of the complaintants and 30% of the non-complaintant/aggressors in these cases. The police officers themselves saw alcohol to be responsible for 14% of these same cases.

Gelles (1972) found alcohol to be an excuse for violent behaviors between husbands and wives. Drinking was reported by one or another of the spouses in 48% of the instances of marital violence. Dobash (1977) found similar excuses in a Scottish study. Researchers focusing on drinking histories and drinking problems of parents of abused children report a wide range of findings. American researchers found that less than one-third of abusive parents had histories of drinking of problems, while foreign studies have consistently reported substantially higher figures. Cultural variations are apparent.

Downs and Miller (1986) have further explored this timing relationship particularly with a spouse abuse population. They first noted the relationship of substance abuse to various forms of child abuse and have since begun to link the relationship of this early childhood experience to later adult life functioning, particularly to study a new generation of adults who are abusing alcohol and battering their spouses and children. Alcoholic women were found much more likely than nonalcoholic women to have been sexually abused, have had a greater number of sexual abuse experiences, and have been abused over a longer period of time. Kaplan and others (1988) have begun to take the research to the next step to show the relationship of these issues to subsequent psychiatric disorder. Similar work is now also focusing on dual diagnoses issues as the two problems are recognized as having a deep and non-trivial relationship.

The literature does not yet reflect this new clinical construction of violence and alcohol abuse. Two sets of literature currently exist; literature targeted at alcoholism, and literature targeted at family violence. The alcoholism construction focuses on studies noting family effects and indirectly family violence. They were begun in the 50s and continued into the early-70s. They included the landmark studies of the children of alcoholics (Chafetz et al., 1971; Cork, 1969); of the relationship of alcoholism to the defaulting of various family statuses and functions as breadwinning, homemaking, sexual performance; and of spousal responses to alcoholism (Jackson, 1954; Lemert, 1960; Edwards et al., 1973). Even genetic studies, constructing the problems of alcoholism inheritability, indirectly supply data on the environmental implications for children of alcoholic parents (Goodwin et al., 1974). Reports comparing alcohol abusers and child abusers which concentrated either on discovering the social-psychological similarities of the two groups of abusers or on finding the extent to which these two groups overlap each other. To this day, however, family problems found in the alcohol literature are constructed around chronic conditions and role impairments, rather than the occurrence of specific events such as family violence and where events are noted or measured, they are often regarded merely as symptoms of a condition.

Regardless of the construction and ownership of the family violence and alcoholism connection, the research suffers from some methodological weaknesses. Samples in research on child abuse are usually selected from hospitals, social service agencies and court cases. With the exception of Gil's (1978) and Strauss et al.'s (1980) population survey, all research has been limited to these often biased samples (Friedman, 1976). Several problems with this type of research limit its generalizability. One of the major problems is the relatively small sample size of most studies. Another is the absence of adequate control groups. Third, as a result of including only officially reported cases of child abuse in their samples, the studies cannot take into account the great number of undetected cases. Since little is known yet concerning the ratio of reported to unreported incidents or of factors associated with reporting versus failure to report, it is impossible to generalize from this data. Last, there are problems encountered in the use of existing case material. Since the data are entered into the records by many different workers, the information recorded is often inconsistent. Much of this information (especially alcohol involvement variables) is based on general observations and impressions of the worker, and thus it is difficult to determine the accuracy of the material.

A further difficulty in recent studies which focus on the similarities of alcohol abusers and child abusers is the intrusion of normative assumptions that drinking and good parenting cannot go together. Thus, Helfer and Kempe (1976) warn of an inherent flaw in this comparative clinical profile research. Problems cannot be solved without accepting that problems are a normal part of our social arrangements, and problems arise not from "bad" people, but from "bad" arrangements. It may be that they cannot be thoroughly solved without "major changes in present social institutions and practices" (Horton et al., 1988), regardless of who owns the problem.

One final set of questions regarding alcohol abuse and family violence — is the knowledge base, both theory and practice, for this social problem to be found in the literature on each? Is the best definition and treatment approach likely to be a straightforward additive combination of knowledge about alcohol and optimal treatment of alcohol abusers with knowledge about family violence and treatments of choice for that problem? The evidence suggests that this is not the best definition of the problem, nor the most likely-to-succeed treatment approach. In the interplay of these two clinical assessments there lies a more complex relationship best treated and understood within the system of the family. The relationship is becoming more well defined with each piece of research, less tolerated with each newspaper article, and its victims are beginning to actively participate in their own treatment and prevention plans. What awaits is the professional research to support these ownership efforts, and document their successes.

REFERENCES

Ablon, J. (1976). Family structure and behavior in alcoholism: A review of the literature. In B. Kissen and H. Begleiter, (Eds.). *The Biology of Alcoholism, Vol. 4.* New York: Plenum Press.

Apfelberg, B., Sugar, C., and Pfeiffer, A.Z. (1944). A psychiatric study of 250 sex offenders. *American Journal of Psychiatry, 100* (May), 762-770.

Bard, M., and Zacker, J. (1971). The prevention of family violence: Dilemmas of community intervention. *Journal of Marriage and the Family, 32*(4), 677-682.

Behling, D.W. (1971). History of alcohol abuse in child-abuse cases reported at Naval Regional Medical Center. Paper presented at the meeting of National Child Abuse Forum, Long Beach, California, June.

Benward, J., and Densen-Gerber, J. (1975). Incest as a causative factor in antisocial behavior: An exploratory study. Paper presented at the American Academy of Forensic Sciences, February.

Black, R., and Mayer, J. (1980). Parents with special problems: Alcoholism and opiate addiction. In C.H. Kempe and R.E. Helfer, (Eds.), *The Battered Child*. Chicago: University of Chicago Press.

Byles, John A. (1978). Violence, alcoholic problems and other problems is disintegrating families. *Journal of Studies on Alcohol, 39* (551-553).

Chafetz, M.E., Blane, H.T., and Hill, M.J. (1971). Children of alcoholics: Observations in a child guidance clinic. *Quarterly Journal of Studies on Alcohol, 32,* 687-698.

Chauncey, Robert L. 1980. New careers for moral entrepreneurs: Teenage drinking. *Journal of Drug Issues, 10*(winter), 45-70.

Coleman, Diane and Strauss, Murray (1983). Alcohol abuse and family violence. In Edward Gottheil, Keith A. Druley, Thomas E. Skoloda and Howard Waxman (Eds.), *Alcohol, Drug Abuse and Aggression*, pp. 104-124. Springfield, IL: Charles C Thomas.

Cork, R.M. (1969). *The Forgotten Child*. Toronto: Paperjacks.

Dobash, R.E. and Dobash, R. (1979). *Violence Against Wives*. New York: Free Press.

Downs, W., and Miller, B. (1986). *Childhood abuse and alcohol histories*. Paper presented at the American Society on Criminology Annual Conference, Atlanta.

Eberle, Patricia (1980). Alcohol abusers and nonusers: A discriminant analysis of differences between two subgroups of batterers. Paper presented at the annual meeting of the Society for the Study of Social Problems, Toronto.

Edwards, P., Harvey, C., and Whitehead, P.C. (1973). Wives of alcoholics: A critical review and analysis. *Journal of Studies on Alcohol, 34*(1), 112-132.

Ellis, A., and Brancale, R. (1956). *The Psychology of Sex Offenders*. Springfield, IL: Charles C. Thomas Press.

Flanzer, J.P. (1980). Alcohol-abusing parents and their battered adolescents. In M. Galanter, (Ed.). *Currents in Alcoholism, Vol. III*. New York: Grune and Stratton.

Flanzer, J.P. (1981). The vicious circle of alcoholism and family violence, *Alcoholism* (January-February), 30-32.

Flanzer, Jerry P. (1982). *The Many Faces of Family Violence*. Springfield, IL: Charles C. Thomas Press.

Flanzer, J.P., and Sturkie, D.K. (1987). *Alcohol and Adolescent Abuse*. Holmes Beach, FL: Learning Publications.

Fox, R. (1972). *The Effect of Alcoholism on Children*. New York: National Council on Alcoholism.

Friedman, R.M. (1976). Child abuse: A review of the psychosocial research. In Herner and Co., *Four Perspectives on the Status of Child Abuse and Neglect Research*. Prepared for the National Center on Child Abuse and Neglect, U.S. Department of Commerce, report number PB-250 852, Washington, DC.

Frosh, J., and Bromberg, W. (1939). The sex offender—a psychiatric study. *American Journal of Orthopsychiatry, 9*(4), 761-776.

Futterman, S. (1953). Personality trends in wives of alcoholics. *Journal of Psychiatric Social Work, 23*, (October), 37-41.

Gebhard, P.H, et al. (1965). *Sex Offenders*. New York: Harper and Row.

Geller, M., and Ford-Somma, L. (1984). *Violent Homes, Violent Children: A Study of Violence in the Families of Juvenile Offenders*. NJ: Department of Corrections, Division of Juvenile Services.

Gelles, R.J. (1972). *The Violent Home*. Beverly Hills: Sage.

Gerard, D., and Kornetsky, C. (1954). A social and psychiatric study of adolescent and opiate addicts. *Psychiatric Quarterly, 28*, 113-125.

Gil, D. (1973). *Violence Against Children: Physical Child Abuse in the United States*. Cambridge: Harvard University Press.

Glazier, A.E. (1971). *Child Abuse: A Community Challenge*. Buffalo: Henry Stewart, Inc.

Golbetti, G. (1973). Alcohol: A family affair. A paper presented at the St. Louis Congress of Parents and Teachers.

Gusfield, Joseph. 1975. Categories of ownership and responsibility in social issues: alcohol use and automobile use. *Journal of Drug Issues, 5*, 285-303.

Helfer, R.E. and C.H. Kempe (1976). *Child Abuse and Neglect: The Family and the Community*. Cambridge, MA: Ballinger.

Hindman, M. (1977). Child abuse and neglect: The alcohol connection. *Alcohol Health and Research World, 1*(3), 2-7.

Horton, P.B., Leslie, G.R., and Larson, R.F. (1988). *The Sociology of Social Problems* (9th ed.). Englewood Cliffs, NJ: Prentice-Hall.

Jackson, J.K. (1954). The adjustment of the family to the crisis of alcoholism. *Quarterly Journal of Studies on Alcoholism, 15*(4), 562-586.

James, J.E., and Goldman, M. (1971). Behavioral trends of wives and alcoholics. *Quarterly Journal of Studies on Alcoholism, 32*(2), 373-381.

Kantor, Glensa Kaufman and Straus, Murray A. (1987). The drunken bum theory of wife beating. *Social Problems, 34*(3), June.

Kempler, H., and McKennon, P. (1975). Clinical observations and belief family therapy of drug abusing adolescents and their families. Paper presented at the 52nd meeting of the American Orthopsychiatric Association, Washington, DC.

Labell, Linda S. (1977). Wife abuse: a sociological study of battered women and their mates. *Victimology, 4*, 258-267.

Lemert, E.M. (1960). The occurrence and sequence of events in the adjustment of families to alcoholism. *Quarterly Journal of Studies on Alcohol, 21*(4), 679-697.

Leonard, Kenneth E. (1984). Alcohol consumption and escalatory aggression in intoxicated and sober dyads. *Journal of Studies of Alcohol, 45*, 75-80.

Mayer, J., and Black, R. (1977). Child abuse and neglect in families with an alcohol or opiate addicted parent. *Child Abuse and Neglect, 1*, 85-98.

McCaghy, C.H. (1968). Drinking and deviance disavowal: The case of child molesters. *Social Problems, 16*(1), 43-49.

Meiselman, K.C. (1978). *A Psychological Study of Causes and Effects of Child Sexual Abuse with Treatment Recommendations.* San Francisco: Jossey-Bass.

Miketic, B. (1972). The influence of parental alcoholism in the development disturbance in children. *Alcoholism, 8*, 135-139.

Mill, J.S. (1869). *The Subjection of Women.* Cambridge, MA: MIT Press (reprinted in 1970).

Miller, Brenda, et al. (1986). Childhood sexual abuse incidents for alcoholic women versus a random household sample. Presented at the 38th Annual Meeting of the American Society of Criminology, Atlanta.

Morgan, Patricia (1982). Alcohol and family violence: A review of the literature. In *Alcohol Consumption and Related Problems, Alcohol and Health Monograph 1*, DHHS Publication (ADM) 82-1190, 223-259. Washington, DC: US Government Printing Office.

Popisil, Z., Turcin, K., and Turcin, R. (1968). Alkolizam, i.e.196. KZzolstavljante i Zapustarye malolgetnika (Alcoholism and Article 196 of criminal law abuse and neglect of minors). *New Ossihijatriija*, Zagreb, *16*, 49-53.

Nau, E. (1967). Kindesmishandlung (child abuse). *Mschr. Kinderheilk, 115*, 192-194.

Ramee, F., and Michau, P. (1966). De onelques aspects de la delinquance secuell dans un department de i-onset de la France (Some aspects of sexual offenses in a province in western France). *Acta Med Leq Soc, 19*, 79-85.

Rist, K. (1979). Incest: Theoretical and clinical review. *American Journal of Orthopsychiatry*, *49*, 704-708.

Schneider, Joseph W. 1985. Social problems theory: The constructionist view. *Annual Review of Sociology*, *11*, 209-229.

Snell, et al. (1964). The wifebeater's wife: a study of family interactions. *Arch. Gen. Psychiatry*. *11*, 107-112.

Spieker, G., and Mousakitas, C.M. (1976). Alcohol abuse and child abuse and neglect. Paper presented at the Alcohol and Drug Problems Association of North America, 27th Annual Meeting, New Orleans, Louisiana, September.

Straus, M.A., Gelles, R.J., and Steinmetz, S.K. (1980). *Behind Closed Doors: Violence in the American Family*. Garden City: Anchor Books.

Virkkunen, M. (1974). Incest offenses and alcoholism. *Medicine Science and Law*, *14*(2), 124-128.

Walker, Lenore (1980). *The Battered Women Syndrome*. New York: Springer.

Spouse Battering
and Chemical Dependency:
Dynamics, Treatment,
and Service Delivery

Alan J. Levy, DSW, ACSW
John S. Brekke, PhD

SUMMARY. Similarities and differences between the chemical dependence and spouse battering populations are noted. Treatment models and practices are also compared. One major difference is that chemical dependency programs emphasize the concept of powerlessness while family violence programs focus upon the need for control and empowerment. Suggestions are presented that could help integrate these two services.

This article serves to familiarize chemical dependency clinicians with the needs of clients who are both chemically dependent and spouse abusers, and to provide them with the conceptual tools to perform assessments and interventions that address both conditions. Family violence is a crucial but often overlooked issue for the chemical dependency clinician.

With the increasing awareness of the relationship between family functioning and the recovery of chemically dependent clients, practitioners in the field have recently recognized the need for intervening in relationships that involve battering among their clients. However, many chemical dependency professionals feel powerless when confronted with clients who are both chemically dependent and who batter or are battered by their spouses. It is common for

Alan J. Levy and John S. Brekke are Assistant Professors, University of Southern California, School of Social Work.

clients who are involved in chemical dependency and battering to be mishandled by agencies and programs that are designed to treat one condition or the other. Therefore the issue of an integrated assessment and treatment plan is critical. Key dynamics related to one condition or the other are frequently omitted from treatment to the detriment of clients and their families.

OVERLAPPING POPULATION INCIDENCE

Information concerning clients who are both chemically dependent and who batter or are battered is still sparse and the guidelines for clinical management are by no means clear. This creates puzzling problems and dilemmas for the chemical dependency professional. In order to clarify matters, this article will review literature concerning this population, and outline the similarities and differences between the dynamics of chemical dependency and spouse battering. Guidelines for the assessment and treatment of spouse battering will be reviewed and applied to clients who are dual substance and spouse abusers. The difficulties in coordinating services for chemical dependency and spouse battering will then be discussed and coordination strategies will be presented.

Research has demonstrated an association between chemical dependency and spouse battering. Eberle (1982) found that victims of alcohol abusing batterers were themselves more likely to abuse alcohol than were victims of batterers who did not abuse alcohol. There was also some indication that batterers who abuse alcohol were a more physically violent group than non-alcohol abusing batterers. Another study by Byles (1978) examined the relationship between alcohol abuse and spouse battering in 139 persons who appeared in family court. A significant association between alcohol abuse and spouse abuse was established.

In studying self-reports concerning the causes of divorce, Cleek and Pearson (1985) found that the alcohol abuse of a spouse was associated with spouse battering. Another study (McKay, 1961) found that adolescents who were considered to be "problem drinkers" reported that they were children of alcoholics and that violent arguments between their parents were common. In a small scale study and a literature review by Wilson and Orford (1978), the relationship between alcohol abuse and battering was also noted. Stewart and DeBlois (1981) found that physically abused mothers of boys who attended a child psychiatry clinic tended to be married to men who were diagnosed as having a substance abuse disorder, antisocial personality disorder, or both. The researchers further noted that these women tended to be adult children of alcoholics or of antisocial men.

Goodman et al. (1986) studied the relationship between alcohol use and homicide in over 4,000 homicide cases in Los Angeles. They found that 46 percent of these victims had a blood alcohol concentration of .1% or higher. They also noted that intoxicated victims were more likely to have known the alleged murderer than were non-intoxicated victims. While not all of these cases involved spouse battering or substance abuse, it provides evidence that there is a strong relationship between substance use and interpersonal violence, especially if victims and perpetrators were acquainted. Although the literature tends to focus upon alcohol and not on other drugs, one could still conclude that there is a clear relationship between chemical dependency in general and spouse battering.

SIMILARITIES IN INDIVIDUAL DYNAMICS

The association between chemical dependency and spouse battering is not surprising if one considers the similarities between these two conditions. Both conditions are quite prevalent and they affect virtually all socioeconomic groups. Denial is a major characteristic of both substance abuse and spouse abuse. Family members are frequently parties to the conspiracy of silence which surrounds both forms of abuse. Indeed, helping professionals are themselves often silent partners in the denial system.

Many chemical dependency specialists are familiar with the progression in the use of chemicals until it reaches the dimensions of abuse. Most are unaware, however, that spouse abuse progresses in a similar fashion from psychological harassment to physical violence. Thus, both forms of abuse tend to increase in frequency and severity. Spouse abuse also may change form, much like the pattern of chemical abuse will change form as the abuse progresses. Both types of abuser were likely to have been exposed to either or both forms of abuse as children. Thus, patterns of abuse were acquired early in their lives. As adults, both spouse abusers and substance abusers tend to manipulate others as they struggle to maintain their homeostasis even as their behavior becomes increasingly dysfunctional. They may swear off abusive behavior, and make other unsuccessful attempts at controlling their behavior. They often minimize their abusive behavior and the effects that were caused by the abuse.

SIMILARITIES IN FAMILY DYNAMICS

The family relationships of substance abusers and spouse abusers also have many common features. As mentioned earlier, both types of families tend to deny the existence of these conditions and attempt to live with an abusing member without directly acknowledging the problem. The abusive behavior tends to be rationalized and minimized while the effects of the abuse tend to be misattributed to other factors. Since the condition is not recognized, the development of effective coping skills is impaired. This impairs family members' capacities to cope effectively with the abuser and his behavior. Such denial thus tends to breed depression and anger. These affects are prevalent and strong in both types of families.

Family members frequently depersonalize their experiences in response to the abuse. They often feel that they are outside of themselves, particularly during periods of abuse. However, despite their lack of control over the abuse, family members often erroneously believe that they have some control over the abuse. Such misperceptions are due to a variety of factors. Family members find the abusive behavior scary and the thought that they cannot control the abuser is even more frightening to them. Also, it is a severe injury to their self-esteem to find that their wishes have little effect on the people they love. In addition, with insight comes responsibility. Admitting that the condition exists places those who are living with the abuser in the position of making some very difficult choices, often with very limited information about the nature of the abuse, or of the options and resources available to them. Such misperceptions thus become alternatives to direct confrontation of the problem.

The energy expended to maintain the system of denial along with the unpredictability of both forms of abuse leads family members to feel as though they are "walking on eggshells." The communication within abusive families is therefore distorted as each member struggles to maintain the denial. Intimacy is lost and roles become rigidified through unsuccessful attempts to maintain a sense of normality in very difficult situations. However, spouses in both types of families are more likely to take action to directly alter the abuse if their children are clearly and seriously threatened with abuse. It appears that spouses' thresholds for tolerance of abuse are lower when the welfare of children is involved.

Relationships in both types of abusive families are characterized by intense conflict (directly or indirectly expressed) and a non-egalitarian approach to decision making. Regardless of the relationship between the spouses prior to the onset of abuse, their relationship suffers as a consequence of it. The lack of intimacy between spouses as a result of the abuse often feeds further conflict between them as couples argue about the perceived shortcomings in their relationship. These conflicts frequently serve to maintain the denial system of the family since the abuse itself is obscured as the couple deals with other "reasons" for the abuse rather than the abuse itself.

DIFFERENCES IN INDIVIDUAL DYNAMICS

While these similarities are striking, differences should be listed. First and foremost, the pathways of the abuse are different. Chemical dependency is distinct from spouse battering because there is a physical agent involved: the drug(s) of abuse. Thus, substance abusers' moods, reactions, and behaviors are often the direct effect of the drug. Substance abusers often experience serious medical consequences of drug abuse. Substance abuse often involves physical addiction and drug withdrawal. Following withdrawal, abusers must learn to tolerate the intense craving for the drug. They deal with the knowledge that they are unable to control themselves because a foreign substance is in control of their lives.

Spouse abusers rarely have physical sequelae to their abuse. They have no easily identifiable agent that causes deleterious consequences. While they too may need to live their lives one day at a time, it is not as easy for batterers to recognize the people, places, and things that may trigger a violent episode. Once denial lifts, spouse abusers must deal with the fact that the abuse is consciously directed at those who are more socially and physically powerless than they. Substance abuse also has serious deleterious consequences for significant others, but much of it occurs because of the effect of the substance. In this sense, the interpersonal consequences of substance abuse may be a by-product of the substance, whereas abuse of a spouse is the goal.

DIFFERENCES IN FAMILY DYNAMICS

A spouse of a substance abuser must deal with the fact that the person that she loves is more involved with a chemical than he is with her. This is a traumatic realization in its own right. Spouses of substance abusers often have the illusion that they are in charge of the family. Indeed, they often have some modicum of independence. Despite this, substance abuse disrupts family functioning and spouses are usually unable to compensate in an adaptive manner. Spouses of batterers are terrorized and thus rarely have any area of their lives in which they can exercise a sense of autonomy. Thus, the interpersonal effects of substance abuse is usually more subtle than are those of spouse abuse. Spouse abusers often have highly patriarchal attitudes and feel victimized by women. This is not necessarily the case with substance abusers. An abused spouse must deal with the fact that the man she loves hurts her by design. Thus, an abused spouse must deal with daily conjugal terrorism. This often involves dealing with the abuser's jealousy, systematic attempts at isolating the spouse from social supports or potential supports, and attempts at brainwashing the spouse in order to keep her dependent upon the abuser.

Thus, the power disparities between the abuser and the abused are integral to spouse abuse. It is the abuse of this power that results in this condition. Therefore, one must be acutely aware of and sensitive to sexism in relationship to family life and to the larger society. Chemical dependency specialists, while understanding the power of chemicals in lives of abusers and co-dependents, need to understand the nature of sexism and its psychosocial sequelae, as well as to examine their own attitudes regarding women and men. Without this, clinicians will be unable to comprehend the fundamental dynamic of spouse abuse.

Another difference in the family dynamics between chemical dependency and spouse battering concerns the cycle of violence that usually occurs in cases of spouse battering. Walker (1979), as well as other observers, have noted that many abused women report a cyclic pattern to the physical abuse. This pattern is comprised of three phases. The first is the tension building phase which can either consist of icy silence, or escalating conflict and verbal abuse on the part of the perpetrator. This phase is followed by the violent eruption itself, the duration of which might last as little as a few minutes to as much as several days. The final phase consists of loving contrition. Abusers pledge to end their violence, are extremely solicitous of the abused partners, and beg for forgiveness. This contrition ends when the tension building pahse begins once again, and the cycle repeats itself.

This cycle appears to be entrenched in the lives of battered women, and can confound the identification of abuse and its treatment. For example, during the tension building and violent phases, abused women may initially reach out for help. This can quickly turn to denial during the loving contrition phase, however. Alternatively, abusers might pledge to seek help during the loving contrition phase, while also seeking to reinforce their spouses' denial. This is thought to occur in order to avoid taking action to end the violence. Therefore, practitioners should be aware that help seeking behavior on the part of abusers and abused partners is usually inconsistent.

Chemical dependency specialists may find this pattern similar to episodic chemical dependency. However, since this is only one of several possible patterns of chemical dependency, the practitioner will encounter more variation in the family patterns associated with this condition. Thus, these cases will manifest various patterns of chemical dependency concurrent with the cycle of violence. The specific nature of the relationship of the cycle of violence to the different patterns of chemical dependency merits further research.

One of the premises of this discussion is that while there are similarities in the clinical features of spouse abuse and chemical dependency, the causal pathways are distinct. Therefore, while the chemically dependent person who is also a victim or perpetrator of spouse abuse might not appear distinct to the chemical dependency clinician, they are in need of treatment that focuses on altering or recovering from violent behavior. This means that the clinician must have a way to detect the problem, as well as knowledge of appropriate treatment strategies so that they can make informed referrals or coordinate further intervention.

Before beginning a discussion of detection and treatment strategies for spouse abuse, it is important to assert that the overall treatment strategy is based upon the notion that if one sobers up an angry drunk man, one has an angry man. Similarly, if one sobers up a drunk battered woman, one has a sober victim. In both cases complete recovery will depend upon how well both problems are treated. What follows is a discussion of clinical indicators of spouse abuse, as well as an overview of treatment approaches for battered women and the battering male.

DETECTION

Clinical indicators as well as a treatment strategy for detecting spouse (and child) abuse in clinical settings are presented in Brekke (1987). His analysis discusses the contexts of detection as well as clinical signposts that suggest the need for detection. For the purposes of this discussion, the indicators for battered women and the batterer will be summarized. The technique for detection, called funneling, is illustrated in detail in Brekke (1987), and is considered essential for detecting and assessing the extent of the problem.

Several clinical signs suggest that a woman may be the victim of spouse abuse: (1) evidence of physical injuries and an unwillingness to discuss them; (2) depression; (3) fear of emotional expression; (4) depersonalization; (5) passivity; (6) violence in family of origin; (7) fear of sexual intimacy; (8) hostility towards partner or others in family; (9) self-deprecation; (10) overconcern for the safety of children; (11) suicide attempts; and (12) mistrust of mental health professionals.

The indicators that suggest that a man might be a spouse abuser are as follows: (1) general hostility or passivity with the clinician, family members, or others outside the family; (2) rigid sex-role perceptions; (3) patriarchal attitudes; (4) history of abuse in his family of origin, either as a victim or witness; (5) feelings of being victimized by women; (6) isolation from relationships outside the family; (7) extreme jealousy; (8) inability to discriminate emotional states other than anger or frustration; and (9) extreme dependence upon the partner to satisfy emotional needs.

Taken alone, none of these indices should be considered indicative of abuse. The clinician must look for consistent patterns. When working in a conjoint context, the interactive patterns that suggest the need for detection of spouse abuse are: (1) any interaction of the indicators for the abusive man and/or abused woman, e.g., hostile man/passive woman, passive man/hostile woman; (2) rigid patterns of interaction; (3) male dominance of the psychological atmosphere of the relationship or the conjoint sessions; and (4) extreme conflict in the relationship, or little or no conflict.

Detection, however, is the beginning of a process that must involve assessment and treatment. The following section discusses approaches to treatment for battered women and batterers.

TREATMENT APPROACHES TO SPOUSE ABUSE

There are two different models for treating domestic violence: the family systems model and the individual recovery model. They are based upon very dissimilar causal frameworks and offer distinct intervention strategies. The family systems approach is based upon these notions: (1) spouse abuse is a result of a dysfunctional relationship; (2) that while violence is learned, the causes of violence are reciprocal; and (3) the fundamental treatment unit, or client, is the interacting partners.

Numerous dyadic treatment models have been offered (Neidig and Friedman 1984; Margolin 1979; Taylor 1984) that consist of conjoint treatment sessions focusing upon learning new interactive and problem solving skills. The treatments described are generally structured, task oriented, and time limited. This approach has been criticized, however, on clinical, conceptual, and ideological grounds (Bograd 1982; Saunders 1986; Brekke 1987). While it is not the purpose of this analysis to resolve these issues, the present bias, based upon work with over 100 batterers, is that the individual recovery approach is preferred for ending battering and facilitating victim recovery. Family systems approaches are advocated in later stages of treatment when the batterer has gained the necessary self-control and the battered woman has begun substantial recovery, or when the interventive focus is solely preventive.

The individual recovery approach is based upon the following notions: (1) spouse abuse is the result of a perpetrator who uses violence expressively or instrumentally, in other words, as a way to deal with frustration or other emotions, or as a way to dominate others and resolve conflict; (2) it is learned and can be replaced by other learned behavior; (3) existing dyadic dysfunction, for the most part, is a result of battering rather than a cause of it; and (4) treatment must focus upon the perpetrator and victim separately, and the dynamics of recovery are distinct for each partner.

Concerning the battered woman, service models, treatment approaches, and knowledge to aid in understanding are available (Walker 1979; Pagelow 1984; Martin 1977). These sources will help the clinician avoid common pitfalls in work with battered women, as well as understand the ideological, political, and clinical issues that surround her experience and treatment. Successful treatment usually involves group methods that focus upon empowerment, consciousness raising, and recovery from victimization.

The individual recovery approach for the perpetrator has been described in depth (Edelson 1984; Saunders 1986) and results from clinical research can be found in Saunders and Hanusa (1986), and Edelson and Grusznski (in press). Treatment consists of structured group methods based upon cognitive-learning principles and strategies. This approach is time limited but may consist of ongoing support groups that the men remain in for unspecified periods of time. The treatment modules usually involve assertiveness training, relaxation skills, cognitive anger control methods and consciousness raising. A semi-structured orientation group method for engaging batterers in treatment and preparing them for subsequent cognitive behavioral intervention is described in Brekke (1989).

While the sources above describe entire treatment packages for batterers, (see also Star 1983) strategies for crisis intervention or beginning phases of treatment can be found in Brekke (in press) and in Saunders (1982, 1984). Clearly, the chemical dependency clinician can become sensitized and versed in beginning skills that will assist them in engaging the victim and/or perpetrator and in coordinating subsequent treatment in this area as needed. The chemical dependency program that wishes to offer more in-depth treatment options could consider implementing entire group modules focusing upon recovering from spouse abuse. In either case it is essential that the family systems or individual recovery approaches are understood and used in a noncontradictory fashion. It is recommended that this be done with the help of male and female clinicians who are experienced in the area of spouse abuse.

The final treatment issues concern systemic factors that cause and sustain spouse abuse (Carlson 1984). Early analyses from within the battered women's movement stressed the importance of political and legal factors in eradicating wife abuse (Dobash and Dobash 1979; Martin 1977). There is recent empirical evidence to substantiate the critical role that arrest, police and legal response plays in ending spouse abuse (Sherman and Berk 1985; Bowker 1983) and in successfully treating the batterer (Edelson and Grusznski, in press). While the use of legal coercion might not be foreign to the chemical dependency clinician, it is considered an integral part of intervention in the area of spouse abuse.

Treatment Similarities

There are many similarities in the treatment of both chemical dependency and spouse battering. Both emphasize the necessity to break the denial system before any other treatment can occur. In addition, treatment approaches to either form of abuse will not tolerate abusive behavior while treatment is occurring. Treatment of spouse abuse and chemical dependency both require that clients learn new social and psychological skills to replace abusive behavior. Thus, techniques such as anger management for abusers, learning to recognize and avoid situations that elicit abusive behavior, use of support systems, and those that facilitate the verbal expression of affect are essential components to treatment, particularly in the early phases. Education of clients about the nature and dynamics of abuse is a crucial form of treatment for both conditions. Both stress the importance of group treatment consisting of members with the same condition for support and treatment. Last, both forms of treatment work to permit clients to focus on themselves and their needs, rather than perceiving their needs as emanating from another person.

Treatment Differences

The treatment philosophies of substance abuse and spouse abuse also diverge in several ways. While most of these differences will be discussed later, it is important to note two major differences here. First, while substance abuse treatment emphasizes clients' powerlessness over the drug, spouse abuse treatment emphasizes self-control and empowerment of clients. Thus, while much substance abuse treatment is devoted to helping clients to recognize and accept the fact that they cannot control their dependence, spouse abuse treatment works toward helping clients to take control of their behavior. Of course, once substance abusers accept their powerlessness over drugs, then treatment emphasizes control over important areas of their lives. Second, treatment of spouse abuse often occurs in a legal context, as court intervention is frequently required to protect the spouse from further injury. Substance abusers, although frequently involved with the legal system, are not as likely to be involved with it in this manner.

TOWARD INTEGRATED TREATMENT

Given this review, how can practice with clients who are either chemically dependent and who batter or those who are chemically dependent and who are battered be integrated? The essential point is that both issues must be confronted at the beginning of treatment. The relegation of one condition or the other to secondary status fosters denial and ultimately impedes the recovery of clients. First and foremost, chemical dependency clinicians should screen all clients to determine whether they batter or are battered by others. If this is the case, immediate steps should be taken to prevent further abuse. No one benefits from abusive behavior and failure to immediately intervene in battering will almost certainly result in injury to abused clients and/or family members. Therefore, failure to screen and intervene may constitute professional negligence on the part of the clinician.

Specific steps to be taken upon intake should include constructive confrontation of the abuser with both conditions. Attempts to rationalize spouse abuse may be treated in the same way as attempts to rationalize substance abuse. Clients need to be clearly and directly presented with their behavior and with its consequences. In addition, treatment plans need to reflect both conditions. It is counter-therapeutic to confront clients with their behavior and not provide them with assistance in altering it.

While it is preferable to refer chemically dependent spouse abusers to groups designed to treat both conditions, this frequently is not available to most clients. In such cases, chemical dependency clinicians should refer these clients to services specifically geared to treatment of spouse abuse. The authors thus advocate that chemical dependency and spouse abuse services be provided concurrently. In order to integrate these services, the clinician should then collaborate with these service providers.

Similarly, it is preferable to treat abused spouses in groups with members who are dealing with both problems. In the likely event that such groups are not available, concurrent treatment in both chemical dependency and spouse abuse treatment programs is necessary. The key point in these cases is to take necessary steps to protect these clients. It is suggested that chemical dependency professionals immediately consult with spouse abuse specialists when treating these clients as the battering spouse may attempt to interfere with treatment. For example, an abusive spouse might attempt to talk a client into signing herself out of a detoxification unit in order to maintain his dominance over her. Discharge from in-patient and rehabilitation programs may thus be more complicated in these cases, as these clients decide whether they will be discharged to a battered women's shelter, to her spouse, or to other relatives. If the dual issue of chemical dependency and spouse battering is not addressed, these clients are vulnerable to further abuse.

TREATMENT CULTURES

Despite the contention that there are striking similarities between chemical dependency and spouse battering, the treatment cultures of the respective service delivery systems are quite different. The term "treatment culture" refers to the dominant values, norms, and belief systems of treatment agencies and service providers. The perception of client case conditions, problems, and service needs on the part of administrators, supervisors, and line clinicians will vary with regard to the nature of their treatment culture. The treatment culture of domestic violence programs is generally characterized by a feminist perspective of battering. Thus, the culture is acutely aware of the power disparities that are inherent in relationships between men and women, and the political nature of these relationships. Domestic violence personnel are clear that the battered spouse (who usually is female) is the victim and that the batterer (who is usually male) is the perpetrator. Domestic violence services are often focussed in this way and most services are directed to empower the abused spouse. In contrast, chemical dependency professionals are aware of the powerlessness of substance abusers over chemicals and understand how this condition results in profound personality and behavioral changes. Most chemical dependency clients are men. Thus, in contrast to domestic violence clinicians, chemical dependency specialists tend to view males as powerless. Treatment tends to be focussed upon helping substance abusers to accept their powerlessness before they can begin to take control of their lives.

A debate exists as to whether substance abusers are responsible for their actions while under the influence of drugs. There is perhaps no area where the debate is strongest as in cases that involve both chemical dependency and domestic violence. A discussion of the relative merits of each position is out of the scope of this paper. Nonetheless, chemical dependency clinicians should take pains to clarify their own attitudes about this issue as they will inevitably be confronted with them. Despite the myriad legal and ethical implications that are engendered by this issue, the authors' clinical position should be clear: clinicians must do everything possible to prevent the occurrence of violence while also affording substance abusing individuals and their families every opportunity to engage in chemical dependency treatment.

Differences in treatment cultures can result in impaired service coordination for populations that are dually affected by chemical dependency and spouse battering. It is not atypical for chemical dependency and domestic violence clinicians to characterize their contacts as "speaking different languages" or that the other specialist "just doesn't understand the case." The point is that there is validity to both cultures. Each addresses different elements of the case. It therefore is incumbent upon chemical dependency and domestic violence specialists to understand and respect both treatment cultures. In order to span the gulf between them, chemical dependency clinicians are advised to focus upon the common goals of both cultures: the termination of both forms of abuse, as well as the recovery and growth of all who have been affected by substance abuse and spouse battering. The point that this can only be accomplished by concurrent, integrated treatment of both conditions must be stressed throughout the course of treatment. Both sets of clinicians should be open to learning the perspective of the other in addition to communicating their own. Thus, an open, pragmatic, non-dogmatic style is essential.

PROGRAMMATIC INITIATIVES

It is suggested that chemical dependency programs identify their domestic violence counterparts in the community. Joint meetings of administrators are strongly recommended to develop protocols for the treatment of dually affected populations. Administrative problems such as confidentiality must be addressed in these meetings. Services arising from such meetings may include the use of treatment staffs to provide mutual consultation on these cases.

It may also prove beneficial to have designated liaison staff members to facilitate coordination of services. Chemical dependency programs are advised to have female staff members serve as liaisons with programs which serve battered women, if possible. Cooperative training arrangements should be developed so that staff members of each program become more adept at addressing the needs of these populations. Chemical dependency programs should consider developing on-site groups to specifically address the needs of battering, drug dependent males. Likewise, groups designed to assist chemically dependent women must be developed. These groups should provide education about spouse battering and encourage their members to recognize the condition and to empower them to take the steps necessary to protect themselves.

Integrated treatment would be best served if chemical dependency programs provide services for co-dependents that are well integrated with other substance abuse services, since spouse battering also occurs in a family context. Thus, programs that have already addressed the issue of integrating services dealing with codependence would be in the best position to serve the needs of those who are affected by battering and chemical dependency.

CONCLUSION

The authors have asserted that attention to both spouse battering and chemical dependency must be integrated and concurrent if true progress is to be made in treatment. While there are some striking similarities between chemical dependency and spouse battering, it is clear that there are also serious differences in the treatment cultures of systems that are designed to treat these conditions. Given the apparent prevalence of battering among populations who are chemically dependent or are affected by substance abusers, efforts need to be directed toward effecting treatment programs that address the needs of these populations.

REFERENCES

Bograd, M. 1982. "Battered women, cultural myths and clinical interventions: A feminist analysis." in *Current Feminist Issues in Psychotherapy*, New England Association for Women in Psychology (ed.), New York: The Haworth Press.

Bowker, L. 1983. *Beating Wife-Beating* Lexington, MA: Lexington Press.

Brekke, J. in press. "Crisis intervention with victims and perpetrators of spouse abuse." in *Crisis Intervention: Theory, Techniques and Research*, Howard Parad (ed.), Milwaukee, WI: Family Service America.

Brekke, J. 1989. "The use of orientation groups to engage hard-to-reach clients." *Social Work with Groups* 12: 75-88.

Brekke, J. 1987. "Detecting wife and child abuse in clinical settings." *Social Casework* 68: 332-338.

Byles, J.A. 1978. "Violence, alcohol problems and other problems in disintegrating families." *Journal of Studies on Alcohol* 39: 551-553.

Carlson, B.E. 1984. "Causes and maintenance of domestic violence: An ecological analysis." *Social Service Review* 58: 569-587.

Cleek, M.G., and Pearson, T.A. 1985. "Perceived causes of divorce: An analysis of interrelationships." *Journal of Marriage and the Family* 47: 179-183.

Dobash, R.E., and Dobash, R. 1979. *Violence Against Wives: A Case Against the Patriarchy.* San Francisco, CA: The Free Press.

Eberle, P.A. 1982. "Alcohol abusers and non-abusers: A discriminant analysis of differences between two subgroups of batterers." *Journal of Health and Social Behavior* 23: 260-271.

Edelson, J., and Grusznski, R.J. in press. "Treating men who batter: Four years of outcome data from the domestic abuse project." *Journal of Social Service Research.*

Edelson, J. 1984. "Working with men who batter." *Social Work* 29: 237-242.

Goodman, R.A., Mercy, J.A., Loya, F., Rosenberg, M.L., Smith, J.C., Allen, N.H., Vargas, L., and Kolts, R. 1986. "Alcohol use and interpersonal violence: Alcohol detected in homicide victims." *American Journal of Public Health* 76: 144-149.

Margolin, G. 1979. Conjoint marital therapy to enhance anger management and reduce spouse abuse." *American Journal of Family Therapy* 7: 13-24.

Martin, D. 1977. *Battered Wives*. New York: Pocket Books.

McKay, J.R. 1961. "Clinical observations on adolescent problem drinkers." *Quarterly Journal of Studies on Alcohol* 22: 124-130.

Neidig, P.H., and Friedman, D.H. 1984. *Spouse Abuse: A Treatment Program for Couples*. Cambridge, MA: Research Press.

Pagelow, M. 1984. *Family Violence*. New York: Praeger.

Saunders, D. 1986. "When battered women use violence: Husband-abuse or self-defense?" *Violence and Victims* 1: 47-60.

Saunders, D. and Hanusa, D. 1986. "The cognitive-behavioral treatment of men who batter: The short-term effects of group therapy." *Journal of Family Violence* 1: 357-372.

Saunders, D. 1984. "Helping husbands who batter." *Social Casework* 65: 347-353.

Saunders, D. 1982. "Counseling the violent husband." in *Innovations in Clinical Practice, vol.1*, Peter Keller and Lawrence G. Ritt (eds.), Sarasota, FL: Professional Resources Exchange.

Sherman, L.W., and Berk, R.A. 1984. "The specific effects of arrest for domestic assault." *American Sociological Review* 49: 261-272.

Star, B. 1983. *Helping the Abuser: Intervening Effectively in Family Violence*. New York: Family Association of America.

Stewart, M.A., and DeBlois, S.C. 1981. "Wife abuse among families attending a child psychiatry clinic." *Journal of the American Academy of Child Psychiatry* 20: 845-862.

Walker, L. 1979. *The Battered Woman*. New York: Harper and Row.

Wilson, C., and Orford, J. 1978. "Children of alcoholics: Report of a preliminary study and comments on the literature." *Journal of Studies on Alcohol* 39: 121-142.

Abuse in Adult Children
of Substance Dependents:
Effects and Treatment

Patricia S. Potter-Efron, BA, CADC-III

SUMMARY. Many adults were raised in families in which members displayed both alcohol/chemical dependency and patterns of physical, verbal or sexual violence. This article summarizes the common effects of this background upon adults. Treatment guidelines are provided.

Many people have noted a connection between chemical dependency and family violence. Although it has not been shown that there is any causal relationship between the two, it is possible to claim that many children of chemically dependent families are exposed to family violence, and that this exposure occurs at a rate higher than in the population in general. Weatherly (1984) cites the 1974 Monahan study which indicated that the potential for violent behavior is increased in alcohol and opiate users, and also quotes Breiner who includes alcohol/barbiturate use in predicting severe violence. Finkelhor (1983) cites consistent statistical findings that over 50% of abuse incidents are related to the use of alcohol alone. Lewis and Williams (1986) point to the Black and Mayer study, which noted that physical abuse occurred in 25% of alcoholic families with a member in detoxification, and in 19% of opiate addicted families. The same study indicated the presence of severe neglect in 28% of alcoholic families and 32% of opiate-addicted families. Potter-Efron and Potter-Efron (1985) found 79% incidence of physical

Patricia S. Potter-Efron is a partner with Professional Growth Services, Eau Claire, WI.

or sexual abuse in 200 chemically dependent adolescents. Many parents in this sample were alcohol and/or drug abusers or dependents. Hindman (1976) states that most alcoholics have difficulty in child rearing "although not all seriously abuse or neglect their children." Pagelow (1984) also notes that children living with alcohol abusing parents are affected in many ways and states that "children in violent families are victims, whether they are the direct targets of abuse or indirectly involved by witnessing parental violence." Black, Bucky, and Wilder-Padilla (1986) note that the data from their study "indicate frequent physical and sexual abuse in the alcoholic home. Physical abuse was significantly higher at both drinking and nondrinking periods. Each family member within the alcoholic family demonstrated significantly more abusive behavior than members of the nonalcoholic family." They note as well that in their study sexual abuse was commonly twice as frequent in the alcoholic family as in the nonalcoholic environment.

Many authors also note the connections between chemical dependency and victims and perpetrators of incest. Pagelow (1984) and Coleman (1982) note that family and personal alcoholism highly correlate with perpetrators of incest. Yeary (1982) states "There are known convergent areas in the field of incest. One of these areas is the high incidence of alcohol abuse, alcoholism, or other chemical dependencies among incest cases," and Coleman notes that studies have confirmed that many chemically dependent women have histories of incest victimization. Yeary points to Weber's 1977 finding that 70% of cases of adolescents who were chemically dependent had experienced some form of family sexual abuse.

In her more recent study of adult children of alcoholics, Claudia Black (Black, Bucky & Wilder-Padilla, 1986) reviews the literature, noting that although children of alcoholics often feel guilty of provoking parental drinking, suffer deep shame about their families, and have pronounced tendencies to become alcoholic or be married to an alcoholic, the problems they have are often not obvious when they are children — these individuals may never draw attention to themselves when young, although they suffer some deficiencies as adults. Black indicates that the children of alcoholics in her study suffered more family disruptions and more physical and sexual abuse as children. She indicates also that they have more emotional and psychological problems as adults, and that they use fewer interpersonal resources than others, in their attempts to survive and to thrive in life.

Black (1982), Wegscheider (1981) and Whitfield (1986) have all written in greater depth of the effects on the child of growing up in the alcoholic family. Some of what they've suggested is echoed in the literature of grown-up abused children. For example, Gil (1983) has noted that these people have great difficulty with trusting others accompanied by difficulty in self-protection and a refusal to need, want, or expect anything from others. She also notes the loneliness and isolation of the grown-up abused person who does not believe he fits in, and the special problem this individual has in forming and maintaining intimate relationships. Leehan and Wilson (1985) point to the deeply engrained feelings of low self-worth and of helplessness which undermine the structure of the individual's life. They state also that grown-up abused children have "difficulty in identifying, acknowledging, and disclosing feelings, especially evident in the underlying, frequently debilitating, unresolved feelings of anger, guilt, and depression." Pagelow (1984) notes the tendency to low self-esteem, social isolation and emotional inexpressiveness, while underlying that tendency, grown-up victims of abuse tend to become alcohol dependent, moody, and to tolerate violence in their home of orientation. Clearly, there is substantial overlap between the concept of the adult child of a substance dependent parent and that of the grown-up abused child. In addition, children of substance abusers often have to deal with secretiveness and illegality with reference to their parents drug use, a dynamic which reinforces isolation, abusive secret keeping, and self-esteem.

EFFECTS OF ABUSE

Practices which may be termed abusive range from name-calling and verbal abuse, through mental games and physical actions, to inappropriate sexual behaviors.

In gauging the effects of abuse, it is important to not assume that verbal abuse will have less severe or long-lasting effects than physical or sexual abuse. A child or adolescent in a chemically dependent family may want to die and act on this want, as an effect of regular verbal abuse. A person may develop a crippled self-concept every bit as injurious as a bodily injury might be. Eric, age 15, is an example. Eric says he hates himself, because he makes his dad drink. He knows that other people tell him it's not his fault, but his dad finds too many things wrong with him each day to be lying. Since "my dad *couldn't* make *all* this stuff up," Eric is convinced of his own inner badness. One response Eric has to this, is to stay away from others, so that those others won't be sullied and become hurt or bad themselves by being in contact with him. Eric has become just as isolated, self-hating, and negative as a victim of physical or sexual abuse may be. He will carry these scars into his adulthood, possibly finding a compulsive behavior to ease his pain and refocus his concentration.

So generally, what are the effects of abuse? There are several characteristics common to those who have been treated abusively.

Brainwashing

Victims of abuse are often brainwashed, coming to believe that they are responsible for their own pain and the situation in which they find themselves. "Thus, abused children are told that they are bad, uncontrollable, and unloveable (Herbruck 1979). Abused wives are persuaded by their husbands that they are incompetent, hysterical, and frigid (Walker, 1979). Sexually abused children are misled to believe that their father's sexual attentions are normal and testimony of his great and genuine affection. (Armstrong, 1978; Finkelhor, 1983). Finkelhor notes that this process of brainwashing is especially "potent because families are the primary group in which most individuals construct reality." Basically, the abuser uses his power and his intimate connection with the victim to control the victim's perceptions of the situation and to manipulate the victim into staying a scapegoat and an inferior. Long-term results of such brainwashing and manipulation are severe. As with Eric, the adult child believes what he has been taught, that he is basically bad, uncontrollable and unloveable. He may feel that his own needs are monstrous, or that he is a jinx, who always brings sadness, evil, and pain to those he cares for. He feels overly responsible for others' thoughts and actions, his distorted vision making himself the puppet master of the Punch and Judy show. Ironically, of course, the real puppeteer is the abuser. But this the brainwashed victim genuinely appears to not know. He may make many sacrifices of all kinds to make up for the badness for which he feels responsible, and become a martyr, self-punishing and undeserving of anything better. Most of all, he loses connection with himself, so that he no longer knows who he is.

Loss of Trust

Abuse by a loved one violates and invades the being of the victim. Family abuse, even more than other kinds of abuse, damages the ability to trust. In the chemically dependent family, trust is already often damaged by the inconsistency of the parenting. Parenting often changes in *both* parents, when one actively drinks and the other reacts to that drinking. So the child becomes (and stays) tentative and watchful in his relationship with those close to him. Leehan and Wilson (1985) note that "Since . . . the child cannot distinguish which behaviors result in certain responses, the abused child learns not to trust him or herself," as well. The long-term effects of the loss of trust of self is a decrease in self-worth, already under siege. Over the long haul, the abused person who has lost trust in self and others, becomes cautious and demanding, testing others in relationships, and becoming oblique in the expression of his own needs. Both the fear of rejection and the need for support remain, and the abused person begins to accept others' meeting his needs as genuine, only if he has not had to ask directly for the needed commodity. The same person who cannot allow himself to express his needs directly because of his shame and fear of rejection, expects and demands others to intuit and meet his needs. Failing this, he finds a way to disown his needs, drown his wants, or blame others for their existence.

Low Self-Esteem

Low self-esteem is a common companion of distortion and other abusive practices, for both the perpetrator and the victim. While the perpetrator uses aggression and rejection of another to shore up his weak and angry identity, his behavior only confirms his worthlessness and his conception of himself as a person who lacks value. The victim often internalizes the abuse, and takes responsibility for it, as if he lacks the independent ability to define the situation in a more healthy manner. The abuser commonly gives the responsibility for an attack to the victim, and at times, the victim sees himself as more powerful than the abuser, believing that it is his own evil or inadequate character which makes the abuse happen. In the latter case, the victim's failure to distinguish between his acts and the acts of the aggressor creates a negative self-concept, a general view of the self that he is not only not worth much, but that he is even actively evil, making it necessary and right that he is treated with abuse and rejection.

A rejecting self-concept can also be created when the victim joins the abuser in being contemptuous and disgusted with himself. An example is Marta, a woman who felt flawed and dirty after being sexually assaulted by her father. Marta had been pushed away by her mother when she tried to get help, and in later years herself viewed her own being with rejection, hostility, and disgust, since she was no longer whole or perfect, but used, broken, and rejected.

Vigilance

Vigilance is another common companion of abuse. Some abusers plan actions like sneaking up on the victim, or attacking just when things seem to be going well. Some abusers are mean, sadistic and intentionally hurting. Judy, a client of mine for over a year, still had trouble trusting me. Since I am a gentle, soft-spoken person who is trustworthy in general, I was mystified about what might be happening. Judy was, too, until the day that it dawned on her that her mother had regularly prefaced abuse with soft, quiet speech. Although the physical abuse had stopped long before, even now Judy's mother would preface verbal abuse in this way; and Judy remained highly sensitive to such voice tones, knowing that softness prefaced an assault. One thing that abused children and adults learn is to evaluate carefully the tiniest scraps of information in the family environment around them. For it is these bits of information which give them an indication of the emotional atmosphere and whether or not abuse is likely in the near future. Some develop uncommonly acute hearing and reading of voices, whispering, steps, and the like. Others may develop clear but simple defensive patterns of behavior—for example, it is very common for those who have been abused to sit in a booth or against a wall in a restaurant, places where they cannot be surprised, places where they have all the environmental information available at a glance.

This vigilance is commonly carried into other marital and family environments, where the victim may be uncommonly sensitive to others' moods or where the gestural learning is inaccurate for a partner or a child—and thus where the adult child misinterprets the actions and behavior of those around them. These misinterpretations may seem threatening and may invite them, in their turn, to abuse others as a premature defense of themselves.

Helplessness

Along with vigilance, victims of family abuse live with experiences which generate emotional and behavioral helplessness. Whether the abuse occurs only when a parent is using, or at any time during the day or night, there is little that the child can do to avert it. The abuse inexorably happens. And the child living in an abusive family may learn that his behavior and the outcome of the situation are "independent occurrences." (Leehan and Wilson, 1985). His behavior—even if it is to be protective of another family member—seldom alters the existence of the abuse. Thus, his choices and actions are useless in changing the situation. Or he may learn that choices that seem to help at some times quickly become the target of abuse at another time, due to the inconsistent and unclear maintenance of family expectations. In the chaotic family, the child must decide how to behave without any guidance, and doesn't get relevant reinforcement for consistent decisions. In the rigid family the child is never given the opportunity to make decisions. "The parents take all the decision-making power and don't consider whether expectations are realistic, developmentally related or individually appropriate" (Leehan and Wilson, 1985); thus, the child is never allowed to practice making decisions as the executive of his own life. Lack of decision-making power creates people who do not know how to make appropriate decisions, or who are dependent on others to make decisions for them. It also creates people who learn, inappropriately, that decisions cross the boundaries of self and that individuals regularly are expected to make decisions for or impose decisions upon, others in the family. On the whole, it becomes impossible for him to solve the problem of abuse even if — as many victims believe — it is important to remember that many abusive parents lack security and don't know how to set appropriate limits or teach reasonable choices. Thus a parent may demand unachievable perfection, he may demand that a child master a task with no room for an error or mistake, or he may expect that a child respond to a situation with behavior he is not developmentally equipped to manage. Lyle, for example, was only two but each morning made coffee for his mother in the electric coffee pot, because she was hungover and angry with him if he did not. As the child grows, he may identify with the abuser and come to expect the same impossible performance from himself, or from his own spouse or children. Or he may be autocratic or dependent in decision-making for himself and others. Unwittingly, but surely, he perpetuates the cycle of shame, poor self-concept, and onerous helplessness.

Unresolved Events and Feelings

Unresolved events and feelings are common in the lives of those adults who were raised in chemically dependent and abusive families. There are four primary ways in which the victim of abuse demonstrates this. In the first instance, the adult who has been abused and rejected as a child sometimes demonstrates that he can have feelings, but refuses to show them, or distorts them to fit a particular mode of viewing the world. For example, the individual clings to one feeling to express all his or her needs. In the second case, the client has blocked out memories of important events and times in his life. Thirdly the client may remember events and recognize persons involved in them but be numb, blocking out or refraining from having any feelings about them. Last, the client may have split off whole parts of the self which he keeps separate and in which he acts differently from the self he primarily presents to other people. Let's take each instance singly to distinguish between them.

The adult child who refuses to express his feelings may do so because he has learned that in this way, he can have a kind of autonomy, an identity which is negative in concept but which strongly challenges his experience of helplessness. Butler (1978) quotes the statement of a person like this: "At home I kept my feelings to myself. That was the only way I could feel any sense of power over the adults in my life. If I never let them know that what they did mattered to me, then they couldn't hurt me. Nobody ever knew what I felt or thought about anything." Here is a clear case of retaining an autonomy which even abuse could not penetrate. In other cases, the adult child fails to express his feelings because as a child, he learned that catastrophe would follow a clear expression of guilt, shame, hurt, sorrow or rage. These catastrophes might consist of being ridiculed for crying, being punished for expressing anger, or being further attacked when expressing hurt. Mary is a case in point. Whenever she expressed anger, her mother would give her toys away; today she becomes frightened and sad even contemplating the expression of anger, and freezes up in therapy when talking about her mother. She rejects her own inner child and states that she wants to give this part of herself away, since she has lost so much because of it. One real problem is that Mary is so afraid of being angry with her mother she turns the anger inward on herself.

Secondly, it is common to see clients who as adults remember little or nothing of the times when they were young in the chemically dependent family. Often these blocked memories and emotions relate to sexual abuse, although this is not the only cause. Some use avoidance as a continuing defense. Sarah, for example, blocks out any time she feels uncomfortable and thus keeps herself from dealing with the abuse and alcoholism in herself and in her family, even though she has discontinued drinking. Sarah's avoidance assures her of the needed oblivion, even without the alcohol. Nina, a 17 year old, had been sexually abused by her father over 500 times, but erected a wall of denial which kept her from dating any specific occurence for prosecution. Nina had built a defensive wall which kept her from breaking down and enabled her to survive. Often alcohol and drugs are a part of this wall. Butler (1978) quotes a woman in therapy who states,

We create our own denial system. We erect a wall between us
and what has happened. There are lots of ways to build that
wall — drugs, alcohol, whatever brings immediate oblivion
will serve. If people could only find a way to look past that
wall, they might understand that many of our choices are the
only way we know how to survive.

Psychic numbing is also common in persons who have been
abused, and is seen frequently in adult children of the chemically
dependent. This process ranges from numbing feelings toward one
person to the general anesthesia of all feelings. Wayne, for example, was sexually abused by his alcoholic father when he was small.
Now he states that he cannot and does not feel anything toward his
father, even though he knows people are "supposed to" have feelings about their parents. Rick, a child of an abusive drug addict, is
different. He indicates that feelings — having any emotion at all —
are difficult for him. He entered therapy because a life situation had
made him aware that he had no pleasurable feelings and that, in
fact, he was frightened to begin to have them, feeling that happiness
would be inexorably followed by pain. What we discovered was
that he was essentially not feeling at all, that is, experience of life is
simply very shallow and superficial, and that he has learned to establish only intellectual contact with others. Therefore, he does not
have to deal with his unresolved past as the target of his addicted
father's contempt and beating — nor does he have to deal with painful feelings about himself. More than that, he never has to hope and
to be disappointed or to be close to someone who might hurt him
with their own needs or with their contempt.

Lastly, dissociation can result in a person "killing" or splitting
off an important part of the self, and remaining largely unaware of
that lost part, coping with life only with the rest of the personality.
Crisis or therapy can bring this fragmentation into clearer consciousness, and leave the adult child with the belief that he must be
crazy to have more than one self; or it may cause sudden confusing
behavior changes which add additional stress to current life circumstances. Sharon identified a highly sexual part of herself called
"Tootsie" who continually wanted to involve her in extra-marital
relationships — Tootsie dressed and behaved differently from

Sharon. In therapy, she remembered her drug-addicted grandfather had called her "Tootsie" when he was high and sexually assaulted her several times. Before remembering this, Sharon had believed she was crazy and disgustingly bad; afterwards, she could keep "Tootsie" in her place and under control.

Boundary Inadequacy

Many of the effects of abuse we have discussed here are related to a problem we shall term boundary inadequacy. Boundary inadequacy has been found to be highly correlated to alcohol and other drug abuse. "Boundary inadequacy has been defined as a pattern of ambiguous, overly rigid or invasive boundaries that is related to physical or psychological space" (Coleman and Colgan, 1986). In simpler terms, a person with boundary inadequacy does not know how to establish the boundaries of his own self and/or is unable to respect the boundaries of others. Without a clear notion of the limits and rights of the self, it becomes difficult to define a clear, individual identity for oneself. It also means that one has a distorted relationship to other people's identities, either being easily swallowed up by the identity of another (being submissive or like a chameleon), or becoming invasive and refusing to allow someone else a clear boundary. Boundary dysfunctions such as these may powerfully affect the development of a child, and his progress toward maturity. Trust is disrupted by boundary invasions, and self-trust undermined by an ambiguous sense of self-identity. Autonomy is disrupted by being "swallowed up" by another, and by getting the message that one is responsible for their actions; and when one is not sure of the parameters of identity, it is common to experience shame and guilt with or on behalf of others. These feelings simply reinforce the low self-esteem the adult child already has garnered from feeling helpless and guilty about "making" the abuser punish him. And it becomes difficult to defend against the invasions, attacks and humiliations which come from the abuser. These latter may take the form of physical beatings, sexual touch, lack of privacy, shaming interactions, excessive demands, and neglect. It is the needs of the chemically dependent person and/or the abuser which have priority, and the invaded self is sacrificed to those needs.

Rigid boundaries can be used to prevent closeness, and ambiguous ones to prevent the differentiation needed for real contact. The needed balance between self-identity and recognition and response to another's identity is put out of balance, and intimacy becomes impossible. Coleman and Colgan (1986) note that such boundary dysfunction is highly correlated to alcohol and drug abuse, and that "the children of families with boundary inadequacy will develop some form of boundary inadequacy and will interact with other individuals or their own family members in this fashion."

Thus, boundary inadequacy and invasion not only disrupts and distorts attempts at intimacy, but also actively promotes the continuance of drug dependency and of further domestic abuse and/or child abuse.

Strong needs for intimacy show up as demands and further invasions, or in the development of the role of caretaker, which posits little or no reciprocity in relationship. These boundary disturbances interfere with sharing feelings, and ability to make friends and promote the maintenance of shame and secretiveness. Strong intimacy needs may lead to a demanding stance in relationships, while strong caretaking provides a person who only feels valuable when they are meeting another's need. This kind of pairing of individuals prolongs and generationally continues patterns which encourage further shows of dependency in the family, including chemical dependency. Difficulty in communicating needs and wants clearly and equally in relationship leads to continued frustration and anger, and to feelings of rejection and helplessness.

Often patterns of relationship develop based on dysfunction within the family. Outside the family, individuals with these behavioral and emotional patterns may show an inability to make friends and to be friends to others. Social aggression and withdrawal function to cut the shamed or blaming individual off from society even further. This individual may be even more drawn to chemicals as social "lubricants" which seemingly aid the process of relationship.

Problems in Parenting

Boundary violations such as physical and sexual abuse can scar an individual significantly. An individual who has been deeply affected by abuse may experience flashbacks which interfere with his daily existence and his own parenting process. These flashbacks may deeply affect the parent and lead to abuse of a child.

> There are times when every parent has feelings toward his child which are anything but loving, but underneath the anger and aggression there flows a consciousness of what some will call love, others duty or conscience. Above all, the child continues to be seen as a child, albeit a temporarily infuriating one. To a battering parent this correct perception can disappear, the crying child perhaps being seen quite literally as the distraught parent's own mother screeching abuse . . . (Renvoise, 1978)

When something like this occurs, the child's behavior is often misperceived as an intentional act of hostility, similar to the original violation in the flashback. Whiteman, Faushel and Grundy (1987) in their review of the child abuse literature indicate that "provocations perceived as intentional arouse more hostility than those not considered personal." In the process of flashback, the child's actions may be seen as very threatening and personal.

Children's behavior which is perceived to threaten the authority or control of the parent may also be reacted to negatively by the adult child with a history of abuse. In alcoholic and abusive homes behavior may be very unpredictable or it may be rigid and very painfully predictable. In either case, the abused individual who has not been swallowed by the helplessness of despair, actively seeks to introduce elements of control into his life. Common patterns of control adopted include (1) a rigid adherence to social forms; (2) a perfectionistic criticism of the self and associated selves around him; and (3) a thorough organization of the aspects of each perceived unit of life. The reality of children is that they are "messy" and can seldom be entirely controlled within these attempts to prevent unpredictable shame. Thus, a child's actions, particularly his refusals and enthusiasms, may be seen as direct challenges to the wisdom and authority (and controlled self) of the parent. The child may once again be perceived as intentionally frustrating his parent, or as being bad and uncontrollable — an object of shame in himself, and one which calls for exacting correction.

Self-hatred

Finally, a person who has been the victim of unresolved abuse will often exhibit intense hatred of self and/or other. It is common that an individual who has been the target of regular abuse will continue this dynamic in his life even after the abuser has changed or departed (1) by finding someone else to continue to abuse him; (2) by abusing another person in the way he himself was abused; or (3) by becoming self-abusive. "What is the role of abuse in my life now?" is always a relevant question for an abused adult child. Self-destruction and self-sabotage are as common outcomes as is becoming a perpetrator of further abuse, and some abused adult children do all of the three alternatives mentioned above at once. For example, June had a history of relationships with alcoholic and abusive men. The one healthy relationship she had allowed herself to have ended in divorce, at her insistence. At the same time, she consistently behaved with verbal abuse, hair-pulling and slaps, toward the daughter who most reminded her of herself. She stated that she did not understand why her daughter behaved badly so consistently, but that she understood from her own growing experience why her daughter was so bad. June was also self-abusive, scratching herself deeply with pins at times in an effort to feel and to feel pain. Further information on self-abuse is available in the article in this volume by Wise (1988).

PRIMARY TREATMENT ISSUES

Safety First

Chemical dependency counselors are accustomed to assessing and treating substance abuse issues first. But safety is a primary and first consideration when working in the area of chemical dependency and family violence. Any person with a history as a victim of abuse needs to be evaluated for safety concerns on an immediate basis.

First, his or her personal safety is a consideration. It is not uncommon for frightened but loyal adult children to still be seeing chemically dependent parents who abuse them. For example, a client named Dione regularly visited her parents "for my mom's sake." During these visits she was always verbally abused and sometimes physically threatened and hit by her father. Even when Dione only telephoned home and talked to her mother, her mother would repeat all of her father's verbal abuse and physical threats over the telephone. Dione's sense of safety was being threatened by both parents.

Adult children of abusive substance dependents also tolerate tremendous abuse in current adult relationships, and the level of safety in each marital relationship needs to be assessed. Art, a clinical psychologist, had grown up with a violent, addicted father. A couples counselor himself, in his current marriage to a nurse he is physically beaten by her during marital fights which he has always regarded as his fault. He has never hit back, and he has never considered this a safety issue for himself, even though he has been hurt. He needs help to be aware of this problem. Suzanne, also from a violent, chemically dependent family, initially came in because she hoped to handle her husband's alcohol problem better. Initially she denied any safety problems for herself or her family, but her behavior seemed anxious and angry. When interviewed in-depth, she admitted that her husband slept with a loaded gun, and had shot up the house twice recently while drunk. Safety for herself and her children needed to be obtained immediately.

Secondly, Suzanne is an example of how adult children may fail to be oriented toward their own children's safety. She had not yet considered that her husband shooting up the house constituted a real physical danger to children she had a responsibility to protect, since she herself had been unprotected as a child. Other examples are common in working with adult children. For an incest victim to use her mother as a babysitter when her father continues to be present and addicted in the house is a tremendous safety risk for the children involved. For a young mother to raise her child in the same house with her cocaine-addicted, violent mother is a safety problem for the grandchild as well as the child. Abuse for a child from a mate must be confronted and managed responsibly, not just allowed to continue.

Thirdly, the safety of other family members with the adult child needs to be addressed. More and more, we are recognizing that those who have been abused have learned how to be abusive, and that many of them may have a capacity for being that way. Clients need to be asked directly about their own behavior during frustation and conflict, and how they handle anger and a sense of being threatened. Sometimes the adult child can easily be taught some ways to help preserve the safety of others. In other circumstances, strong intervention and/or reporting may be necessary.

Last, the safety of the client with himself needs assessment, and it's important to deal up front with these safety concerns. Dan habitually drove at breakneck speeds when he became angry with someone while June often drove her truck down railroad tracks to "feel alive." Sandra's risky, promiscuous sexual behavior was unsafe for her. These behaviors needed to be dealt with clearly and early by the therapist as part of a statement that safety first includes safety from self-abuse.

Identify Abuse

A person may have been a victim of abuse without knowing it. In fact, often the family with drug addiction is an isolated family which has developed its own rules, patterns and justifications for behavior. The way things are appears to be the right way for things to be. When we deal with chemical dependency, we have to confront denial; the same is true with family violence. In some cases, the denial is doubled. A person who cannot consider facing the shame that a parent had a drug problem also cannot face the shame of having been treated abusively, or of having had a parent who was abusive. Loyalty is very strong in dysfunctional families such as these, and the counselor will need to help the client grasp that abuse and chemical dependency have occurred without condemning the parents.

This is a difficult situation for the counselor, since it is natural to feel angry at abuse that's occurred to a client you know and care for. But it is essential to help that client recognize that abuse has occurred in order for them to see themselves in a new light, and to help them resolve the pain in their past. Some education can be done by calling attention to specific incidents related by the clients which are or may have been abusive. The individual who has grown up with a family nickname of "Turd" may not know that being called that for years is abuse. The man whose father got drunk every Friday night and ritually beat his son every Saturday for all his unnamed sins of the week before, always believed this was simply "discipline" which he imagined to be appropriate on his father's part. It is important to ask, when an adult child talks about an incident of violence, whether he knows that that incident represents abuse.

Another useful method of education for adult children is the use of Bavolek's four constructs of abuse (see Bavolek article in this publication). The constructs themselves are as follows: (1) Low empathy; (2) Inappropriate age expectations; (3) Strong belief in physical punishment; and (4) Role reversal. It has been very helpful for some clients to have the abusive environment defined by the explanation of these four concepts. As I explain each concept, I ask the adult child if he has experienced this kind of behavior on the part of his parents, and if so, to give me several examples of that behavior carried out. As he provides his own examples of ways in which he reversed roles with his parents, ways in which he was expected to do far too much or not allowed to make mistakes, ways in which he was not understood but accused or ignored, and ways in which he was physically punished, we can build a picture of what the specific painful events were that constituted his particular experience, and clearly define whether his growing up was abusive and/or neglectful. The other concept I have found applicable to many adult children is that of "severe inconsistent discipline," and this can be used in concert with Bavolek's constructs in helping to define and circumscribe the events of abuse. At the end of such a discussion the adult child can make a reasonable decision about whether he has been treated abusively; if his educated perception is that his growing up was abusive, he has some facts about what this means, and how it may have affected him. This is the beginning of the healing process.

Establish Links Between Chemical Dependency and Violence

It is important to help the adult child sort out confusion about his family and to deal with ambivalence about his situation and himself. In this process, it is important to help him determine as well as he can whether and how the family violence and the chemical dependency in the family were or are linked. Since these relationships can be so complex this is often an area of major confusion for the client. Helping to sort things out can help to clarify the adult child's attitude toward the chemically-dependent person, other family members, and himself.

The counselor can help the client to evaluate these links in several ways. The first question is whether the violence and chemical abuse are linked chronologically in any way, and whether this linkage occurs all the time, most of the time, or only occasionally. The client may need to be taught that the chemical abuse process occurs in stages, and to differentiate between the phases of intoxication, withdrawal, and procurement. It is not necessary for the counselor to show causation, and often causation is unclear. Even the understanding that a parent or mate becomes violent during withdrawal, for example, can provide cures to safety-seeking behavior and can aid the abuse victim in understanding that their behavior may not have caused the violence, but the stage of chemical use. Since most victims of violence blame themselves, this is crucial information in healing and recovery. Andrea always considered herself responsible for her mother's anger, especially since when her mom was under the influence of chemicals she seemed active and happy. It was not until Andrea understood the process of withdrawal as well as of intoxication, that she began to understand that it was not simply her behavior that created violence in her mother.

The client may also need to be educated about what drugs are most associated with violence. Since many drug-dependent people are polydrug users and abusers, a pattern of violence can be variable and hard to identify and associate. Pat was a polydrug abuser who was nonviolent when smoking marijuana or when her alcohol was moderated by marijuana use. However, when highly intoxicated on alcohol alone, she had a strong tendency to become violent. This variation was hard to identify for her husband and family, and confusing to Pat as well.

Additionally, the client may need help to identify family patterns of violence. It may occur that one parent is chemically dependent and the other violent. These may be independent variables, but can often be linked. A husband may be violent toward his wife only when she is high, or a mother abusive to her children only when her husband is building up to a binge on drugs and alcohol. One parent may be regularly sexually abusive to his daughter while her mother is so sedated she is not able to relate well to the world, or to protect her daughter. Older siblings may be violent to younger ones while their parents are too "stoned" to notice. These situations all provide examples of the links between chemical dependency and violence, where the chemical dependency is a contributing factor in the abuse. It is important to help those connected to sort out what has happened to them as understandably as possible, so that they do not blame themselves or continue to experience the world as only arbitrary and themselves as only helpless.

Assess the Damage

An essential part of the treatment and recovery from abuse is the assessment of damage. Not only the counselor needs to know the damage, but the adult child himself. One way to assess the manner of damage which allows for clear treatment planning and goal setting is to divide the areas covered into feelings, thoughts, behavior and spirituality.

In the assessment of feeling, one helps the adult child to determine which feelings he is comfortable with and can express, and which he is frightened of or denies. Identifying occasions upon which he cannot feel at all, or persons about whom he cannot feel is an important part of the therapeutic process. The third part of assessment of feeling damage is to identify negative feelings which are disproportionately strong for a healthy person—for example bitterness or vengefulness. These latter feelings will need to be appropriately directed and then lanced, so that they will not distort the person's feeling life on a continuing basis. Lastly the degree of shame and guilt needs to be examined and addressed in the feeling recovery of each adult child who has been abused.

In the assessment of thoughts, one must first examine how the individual has learned to view himself. Has the brainwashing effect of abuse convinced him that he cannot think, that he cannot learn, or that he cannot achieve? Often the result of the inconsistency combined with abuse in the chemically-dependent family is a massive confusion, which prevents the individual from engaging in reasonable decision-making processes. The client will need to be helped to recognize when he has been taught to view himself as mindless, and carefully retaught to follow a thought through from beginning to end; he will need support to take small thinking risks and act on them at first, building up to more complex thinking and more significant decisions. The adult child who has been taught he is crazy and had that reinforced by current abuse will need to discuss situations in great detail and receive on-going feedback on the appropriateness and value of his perceptions. Damage to the thinking process may be the most encompassing damage from abuse and the major barrier to new learning in life processes.

In the assessment of behaviors it is most important to focus on the impact of the abusive process on the person's present life, since past behaviors can only be accepted and not changed. The most vital question is whether a given client has the freedom to choose between behaviors or not. Many adult children who have been or are being abused experience themselves as helpless and trapped in their current behavioral patterns. For example, Joanne had grown up with an addicted mother's angry outbursts and found herself compelled to agree with whatever anyone else wanted or asked of her as a way of attempting to control her environment. On the other hand, Tom had found the only sense of identity he could gain was by rebelling constantly against a controlling father, and had continued to function that way in all his relationships with bosses and other authority figures. For both of these individuals the essential damage was that they had lost their freedom to choose behavioral responses, and it was choice that each needed to regain to live more satisfying lives in the present. Joanne was primarily affected in the area of family relations and needed to start there in regaining freedom; Tom, on the other hand, did fine with his family but had trouble maintaining a job or obtaining promotions. He had to be helped to focus on the impact of these behaviors on his work life. Any area in which a person has lost the ability to choose from a range of behaviors is one in which they have been adversely affected and where damage needs to be repaired.

In assessing damage to spirituality, the counselor should examine the questions of despair and of loss of values for these two areas have primary effects on the view a person has of their relationship to the world and/or something greater than themselves. Abuse creates despair by destroying an individual's ability to see good in himself or others or to have any hope that his situation will improve. In a sense, despair is the absence of any positive expectations, and this needs to be assessed in relation to oneself, in relation to other significant persons including the therapist, and in relationship to the environment. Long-term mistreatment causes a loss of ability to value positive actions in relation to others, and often the adoption of survival-oriented or power-oriented values such as secretiveness, dishonesty, and force. It is important to help the abused adult child look at what he values and how he acts out his values in everyday life. It is my experience that only as this damage is repaired and the adult child begins to perceive himself as a more intact and "good" person can he establish a satisfactory relationship with something greater than himself.

Not Tolerating Abuse

An important part of recovery for abused adult children of chemically-dependent families is that they be taught not to tolerate abuse in the present — not just abuse which threatens their safety, but also abuse which threatens their sense of wholeness and well-being as a person.

One element in this includes teaching them that people are victimized more often when they are drinking and using drugs, and teaching them to protect themselves in part by either abstinence or reasonable use of chemicals. For a client to alter her pattern of use because it preserves her safety, has an effect on her environment, and/or leaves her more capable of self-determined healthy action, is a powerful and healing statement for her to make both about her past and her present. It is a statement of value of herself as well.

Another element is to help her cultivate the belief that change is possible. It is not uncommon to see abused adult children in their third abusive relationship, stating to themselves and the therapist that they are fated to live with abuse. Any significant changes need to be pointed out. Often these relationships have progressed from ones in which sexual and physical abuse was common to one in which only verbal and emotional abuse occurs. The change may be from an actively drinking abuser to a recovering abuser. Although it may seem irrelevant, the person convinced that her life cannot change needs to have each of these "positive" changes noted, so that she can understand that perhaps she is and has been changing. Connie is an example. At 55, Connie has lived with drug addiction and abuse all her life. She states that her husband has a "magic spell" over her which makes it impossible for her to change herself even though she wants to. Yet in the last two years she has taken a class against her husband's wishes, attended several Alanon meetings, and begun counseling. Last week her husband told her to answer the phone while he was sitting next to it — a common occurrence. She verbally said nothing, but did not answer the telephone. While Connie is angry at herself for not standing up for herself, she needs to consistently be reminded that she is changing, and that nonverbally she did stand up for herself.

"I deserve it" attitudes often stem from a combination of brainwashing and low self-esteem, and dealing with self-esteem issues is vital in teaching the client to not tolerate current abuse. Changing self-esteem takes time, but a major aid in this effort is the focusing on strengths. Most persons who have been abused have had their weaknesses scrutinized again and again both by others and by themselves. To alter one's perspective on oneself so that strengths can be observed is a major step in changing "I deserve it" attitudes. Another is pointing out that each of us has needs (not just wants) for positive strokes and feedback, affirmation, and acceptance. It is often useful to help the adult child begin to look at relationships from the standpoint of what she needs in order to feel human.

Choosing a healthy lifestyle is a recovery issue, and defining a healthy lifestyle is part of that issue. Learning and using assertiveness and establishing connections to non-shaming peer groups are especially important steps in preventing abuse of self. Each area of life needs to be examined for its healthy and unhealthy features. Sharon, an office manager, was required to check and clean the toilet prior to its use by her boss, a woman doctor. Her relationship with her supervisor was not destroyed but enhanced the day she was assertive enough to say that this was not her job and that her supervisor would have to do this herself, as Sharon did for herself.

Dealing with Guilt

Guilt is highly significant for those who have been abused, and needs to be dealt with on several levels. Just as with the double denial system blocking out awareness of the problems of both chemical dependency and abuse, there is a double guilt system. Children of abusive chemically-dependent people may feel both guilty about the drug addiction of their parents, and blameable for the abuse.

In some cases this guilt has been formed as an alternative to a sense of helplessness. The conviction that one is responsible for the behavior of another person even if one has never been able to get them to change that behavior at least gives him a sense of importance, a sense of having had an impact. This provides a narrow grasp of identity where otherwise one would be engulfed and non-existent in the face of the abuse. Adult children with this tenuous connection to identity through guilt need help recognizing, facing, enduring and surviving the sense of being invisible and meaningless. Only confronting their engulfment by the feelings and behavior of the abuser and abusive family will enable them to develop a sense of self not based in guilt. And this, in turn, makes it possible for them to develop relationships based in health.

In other cases, this guilt stems directly from the abuse and is composed of a persistent sense of inner badness. Often a client experiencing this type of guilt finds it impossible to share and it must be identified by the therapist. Statements such as "no one should get close to me" and "people around me get hurt" need investigation. It is important to find out why the client feels that way, and if he is afraid that the therapist may get hurt from being near him. The sense of power is so strong in this experience of guilt that it borders on the delusional. An example is Jane, who was told from a young age that she made her parents drink and that she was so bad she made them punish her. When Jane's father was drunk and in a car accident, she was told that she made him so angry she was responsible for his injury. Later, when he deserted the family, Jane's barbiturate-addicted mother told Jane it was her fault because she did not keep the house clean enough. A year later, Jane lent a pair of sandals to her girlfriend for the day. That day her girlfriend was hit by a car and killed. Jane blamed herself. When I saw Jane at age 20, she was already recovering from chemical dependency but due to her conviction that she was a jinx and guilty of all the bad things that happened to family and friends, she was very isolated and allowed herself only to maintain relationships with those who were hateful and physically abusive to her. She needed to hear that I was not afraid to care for her even though she was afraid for me to do so, and she needed careful, logical, long-term unraveling of her sense of causation.

One further circumstance deserves mention here. Due to the high incidence of role reversal between children and parents in both chemically-dependent and abusive families, many adult children have developed the attitude that they must be guilty if they think about themselves. They have learned that other people's needs are far more important than theirs, and been taught that it is selfish for them to want and to need. Sometimes they even fear that they will be punished if they do what they want rather that what someone else wants — and that they naturally will deserve this punishment. These clients need education and consistent reassurance. They may also need to be taught initially that their feelings of guilt are a signal that they are taking new action — the positive action of caring for themselves — and that as they get used to this new and healthier behavior their feelings of guilt will abate.

Dealing with Shame and Self-Acceptance

Shame is a universal problem with abused adult children, even more than guilt. Shame is the feeling of inadequacy, rejection, and dirtiness that those who have been abused gain from the experience. It is increased by feeling helpless in the face of another person's power, by being humiliated in front of others and by being ridiculed and blamed on any consistent basis. Chemical dependency increases the sense of shame by its general unacceptability in the society and by the blaming of family members for other's chemical dependency. An incident which demonstrates the power of this combination is Stephen's experience. As a young boy he stayed with his polydrug-dependent father on weekends. Every Saturday evening his father had friends in to do drugs. Stephen would be sent to take a bath and then required to come out to say good night in his pajamas. Every Saturday his father would joke and play with Stephen's penis in front of the assembled company before Stephen was allowed to go to bed. Stephen felt dirty, rejected, humiliated, ridiculed — and very ashamed that his father was so stoned he would do that to him. He was not only ashamed because of the abuse but also of the way his father looked to others.

It is important to the adult child to know that the therapist has experienced and understands the feelings of shame, since it is so powerful and isolating. It is equally important for the client to understand that the goal is not to make all shame go away, but to arrive at an acceptance of the events in one's past and to accept them as part of his history. In order to do this, the therapist must help the individual move through his feelings and resolve them rather than cut them off. It's helpful to explain to clients that the only way out of a feeling is through it, and that without that feeling experience, the shame and rage are left hanging around in the background to arise and attack one's well-being on another occasion. Often it is helpful to use a metaphor, a story, or another aid to maintain the bridge between the therapist and the client in the presence of painful shame (Potter-Efron, 1987).

Giving the shame back is a useful strategy in working with adult children. The goal is to enable the client to emotionally return the

shame to the person it came from. Two examples will serve to explain this more fully. Mary was the sexually-abused daughter of an
addicted father. Though he had died several years before, she could
not seem to escape her shameful feelings, and she was so loyal to
him that she cringed at the thought of expressing her real, shame-
connected anger at the abuse. Instead, Mary was assigned to make a
bouquet for her father of things which would represent the things he
had given her. She included a rose for his love, dry highway grass
for the times he ignored her, branches with sharp thorns for the
incest, and several other objects. Then Mary took her bouquet to his
grave, and returned his gifts in an emotional but cleansing sharing
with him. She was able to accept what had happened and leave
those events in her past. Another client named Becky still had problems being shamed by her chemically-dependent mother. She had
many strong memories of shame which were reinforced by weekly
interactions with her abusive mother. Becky did not want to cut
herself off from her mother entirely but needed to find a way to
refuse to accept her shaming. So Becky went to a hardware store
and bought a shovel in order that her mother could "shovel her own
shit" from then on. She presented it to a surprised but accepting
mother. After that, Becky put her shame away, and refused to accept her mother's abuse into her own boundaries.

The single most important awareness a person consumed by
shame needs to achieve is a sense of acceptance of his own humanity, including both his strengths and defects. For some this comes
through a learned habit of self-affirmation, for others it begins with
the therapist showing pride in him and from the therapist's acceptance of his feelings. He needs to accept that he is not perfect, and
not terrible, but "perfectly human."

Assess Potential for Being Abusive

Each adult child of a chemically dependent/violent family needs
his own potential for being abusive assessed. This assessment
should include (1) an assessment of his own relationship to alcohol
and drugs; (2) a history of his responses to violent behavior of others; (3) a history of acting out behaviors he has engaged in; (4) an
assessment of his attitudes toward significant others; and (5) consid-

eration of how he responds to children, and the idea of having his own children.

Just as those who wish to preserve themselves from victimization need to be educated to the coincidence of drugs and violence, so do those who wish to protect themselves from a higher chance of becoming violent. Use of varying combinations of chemicals, times of chemical use, and similarity to learned patterns of violent chemical use should be examined. The use of a chemical to provide an "excuse" for the release of anger may need confrontation.

Whether the abused adult child has responded to past abuse by running and hiding, by fighting back directly, or by becoming violent to animals or other family members may be very important information when assessing abusive potential. Henry, for example, grew up in a family where sibling abuse was as common as parental abuse — and he was the youngest family member. He learned as a protective device to become more angry, throw a bigger fit, and hit harder to win enough power to moderate the abuse. Later in life he regularly threw fits of hysterical violence during which he would be physically extremely threatening and appear to be out of control — in order to establish his dominance if anyone disagreed with him in what he considered to be a "disrespectful" way. He counted on coworkers to hold him down to prevent his bashing in another coworker's head with a crowbar, to make sure that his would-be challenger knew he was "crazy" enough to never confront him again. Henry had made himself dangerous to himself and others in this way. In another case, Sally responded to being hit by her father by hitting her puppy and her dolls, never showing anger to anyone else. Later when she was hit by her husband, she privately hit her dog and her daughter. Publicly she appeared above reproach as a mother, and had this pattern not been located and confronted might still be behaving abusively to her children.

An adult child with a history of acting out behavior, particularly of the violent or sexual types, may be more likely to maintain behavioral patterns of abusiveness. Greg had a long history of youthful acting out as a response to a violent, addicted family life. Many years after Greg had emerged from incarceration as a juvenile and then an adult, and several years after recovery from chemical dependency himself, Greg was still engaging in a regular pattern of marital rape. An essential question is whether the individual has learned or adopted more appropriate ways of dealing with feelings, especially anger.

Attitudes toward significant others can be very important in looking at abusive potential and behavior. The adult child who cannot believe that his partner is on his side ever, is likely to become significantly more abusive to that partner than another. For example, Diane grew up in a family in which her father held all control, and all others' behavior was seen as threatening to that control. In her own marriage, Diane perceived her husband as fighting for control against her, and saw each of his small behaviors as both a direct challenge to her well-being and her very self. She was verbally, emotionally and physically abusive to him on a continuing daily basis, as she perceived her only safety to be "keeping him in line." In treating Diane, it was important for her to see how carefully she had copied her father's attitudes, in beginning to understand that she was not only potentially but actively abusive on a regular basis. Once she understood her abusive behavior, she was able to state for herself that she "reached for anger just the way my dad reached for drugs." She was able to use an addiction model to combat her daily abusiveness.

In terms of attitudes toward children, there are at least four problematic positions an adult child may hold. The adult child may fear or hate the idea of having children or of holding his children, because of the irrational fear that if he touches his children, he will damage them as he has been damaged. This attitude does not in itself indicate abusive potential, just a strong fear of it. Another more serious problem is the naive belief on the part of an abused adult child that he will never under any circumstances repeat the abusive behavior of a parent toward himself. The person who does not want to continue to perpetrate abuse in the family cycle needs to know that it is possible, and what he can do to guard against it, not just to deny it. Thirdly, the adult child may already know that something is wrong, and vaguely blame himself without making any changes in his behavior. He seems to feel that while his kids are "awful" because of him being their father, he really is powerless to help them behave better. Therefore he will focus only on stopping the "awful" behavior by yelling a lot, and hitting or spanking, but have no ideas on how to help the children learn limits or substitute new, more appropriate behaviors for the ones he classifies as "awful." This person needs to know that he has the potential for being abusive and may be abusive in some ways he can change immediately. Last, some abused adult children have been taught that children are important only so far as they meet their parents' needs. The potential for emotional abuse is profound here, and so is the likelihood that the parent who views children as serving his needs will reinforce this necessity by violent forms of control.

The primary goal here is to help the adult child assess his own abusive potential and the strengths he has to help correct any currently abusive behavior toward his children, his mate, other family members and his neighbors and coworkers.

CONCLUSION

In this paper connections between abusive practices and chemical dependency in the family have been noted through a review of the literature. Similarities between children of chemical dependents and grown-up abused children have also been noted. Nine specific effects of abuse have been described in detail, including brainwashing, loss of trust, low self-esteem, vigilance, helplessness, the results of unresolved events and feelings, problems related to boundary inadequacy, problems in parenting, and self-hatred. In addition, eight major areas for initial assessment and continuing treatment for adult children of abusive chemically dependent families have been identified and discussed. These areas include attention to current safety concerns for the adult child and other members of his family; identifying and educating the adult child in the nature and characteristics of abuse; establishing appropriate links between the chemical dependency and the violence; assessing the damage behaviorally, emotionally, cognitively and spiritually; teaching the adult child to not tolerate abuse in the present and future; dealing with guilt and responsibility; dealing with shame and self-acceptance; and assessing the potential of the adult child himself for being and becoming abusive.

BIBLIOGRAPHY

Anderson, Carole A. "The Practitioner's Initial Response to Victims of Violence," *Violent Individuals and Families: A Handbook for Practitioners.* Springfield, Ill.: Charles C. Thomas, 1984.

Bernard, M.L. and Bernard, J.L. "Violent Intimacy: The Family as a Model for Love Relationships," *Family Relations*, April 1983: 283-286.

Black, C.; Bucky, S.F.; and Wilder-Padilla, S. "Interpersonal and Emotional Consequences of Being an Adult Child of an Alcoholic," *International Journal of the Addictions*, 21(2): 213-231, 1986.

Black, Claudia. *It Will Never Happen To Me.* Denver, Co.: M.A.C. Publications, 1982.

Cermak, Timmen L., "Diagnostic Criteria for Codependency," *Journal of Psychoactive Drugs*, 18(1): 15-20, Jan-Mar 1986.

Clark, Ramsey. "A Few Modest Proposals to Reduce Individual Violence in America." *Violence and the Violent Individual.* New York: SP Medical and Scientific Books, 1981.

Coleman, Eli. "Family Intimacy and Chemical Abuse," *Journal of Psychoactive Drugs*, 14(1-2): 153-158, Jan-Feb. 1982.

Coleman, Eli and Colgan, Philip. "Boundary Inadequacy in Drug Dependent Families," *Journal of Psychoactive Drugs*, 18(1): 21-29, Jan-Mar, 1986.

Coleman, Karen H. and Weinman, Maxine. "Conjugal Violence: A Comparative Study in a Psychiatric Setting," *Violence and the Violent Individual.* New York: SP Medical and Scientific Books, 1981.

Finkelhor, David. "Sexual Abuse and Physical Abuse: Some Critical Differences." *Unhappy Families: Clinical and Research Perspectives on Family Violence.* Littleton, Mass.: PSG Publishing Co., 1985.

Finkelhor, David; Gelles, Richard J.; Hotaling, Gerald T. and Straus, Murray A. Editors. *The Dark Side of Families: Current Family Violence Research.* Beverly Hills Calif.: Sage Publications, 1983.

Flowers, Charles. "Sex Addiction: Shame and the ACOA Connection," *Changes.* Sept-Oct. 1987, Pp, 20-21, 28-29.

Forward, Susan. "Intimate Violence" *Changes.* Sept-Oct. 1987. Pp. 16-17, 36-37, 51-53.

Gelles, Richard J. "Family Violence: What We Know and Can Do." *Unhappy Families: Clinical and Research Perspectives on Family Violence.* Littleton, Mass.: PSG Publishing Co., 1985.

Gravitz, Herbert L. and Bowden, Julie D. *Recovery: A Guide for Adult Children of Alcoholics.* New York: Simon and Schuster, 1985.

Gudas, Linda. "Children's Somatic Expressions of Family Dysfunction and Family Violence." *Unhappy Families: Clinical and Research Perspectives on Family Violence.* Littleton, Mass.: PSG Publishing Co., 1985.

Hindman, Margaret H. "Child Abuse and Neglect: The Alcohol Connection." *Alcohol Health and Research World*, 1(3): 2-7.

Leehan, James and Wilson, Laura Pistone. *Grown-Up Abused Children*. Springfield, Ill.: Charles C. Thomas, 1985.

Lewis, David C. and Williams, Carol N. Editors. *Providing Care for Children of Alcoholics: Clinical and Research Perspectives*, Pompano Beach, Fla.: Health Communications, Inc., 1986.

Meacham, Andrew. "Child Abuse Comes Out of the Dark," *Changes*. Sept-Oct 1987. Pp. 20-21, 28-29.

Pagelow, Mildred Daley. *Familiy Violence*. New York: Praeger Publishers, 1984.

Potter-Efron, Patricia S. "Creative Approaches to Shame and Guilt: Helping the Adult Child of an Alcoholic," *Alcoholism Treatment Quarterly*, 4(2), 1987.

Potter-Efron, Ronald T. and Potter-Efron, Patricia S. "Family Violence as a Treatment Issue with Chemically Dependent Adolescents," *Alcoholism Treatment Quarterly*, 2(2): 1-15, Summer 1985.

Shapiro, Rodney J. "Therapy with Violent Families," *Violent Individuals and Families: A Handbook for Practitioners*. Springfield, Ill.: Charles C. Thomas, 1984.

Twentyman, Craig; Rohrbeck, Cynthia; and Amish, Patricia. "A Cognitive-Behavioral Approach to Child Abuse: Implications for Treatment," *Violent Individuals and Families: A Handbook for Practitioners*. Springfield, Ill.: Charles C. Thomas, 1984.

Van Hasselt, Vincent B.; Morrison, Randall L.; and Bellack, Alan S. "Alcohol Use in Wife Abusers and Their Spouses," *Addictive Behaviors*. 10: 127-135, 1985.

Weatherly, Dewitt L. "Methods for Assessing Potential for Violence in Clients," *Violent Individuals and Families: A Handbook for Practitioners*. Springfield, Ill.: Charles C. Thomas, 1984.

Wegscheider, Sharon. *Another Chance*. Palo Alto, Calif.: Science and Behavior Books, 1981.

Whitfield, Charles. *Healing the Child Within*. Baltimore, Md.: The Research Group, 1986.

Whiteman, Martin; Fanshel, David; and Grundy, John F. "Cognitive-Behavioral Interventions Aimed at Anger of Parents at Risk of Child Abuse," *Social Work*, 32(6): 469-474, Nov-Dec 1987.

Wise, Mary Louise. "Adult Self-Injury As A Survival Response In Victim-Survivors of Childhood Abuse." Minneapolis, Minnesota. 1988.

Wynne, Lyman C. "Developmental and Family Origins of Vengence and Violence." *Violent Individuals and Families: A Handbook for Practitioners*. Springfield, Ill.: Charles C. Thomas, 1984.

Yeary, Jody. "Incest and Chemical Dependency," *Journal of Psychoactive Drugs*, 14(1-2): 133-135, Jan-June 1982.

Alcoholism and Sex Abuse in the Family: Incest and Marital Rape

Charles P. Barnard, EdD

SUMMARY. This article focusses on two human problems frequently present among the alcoholic population that are often missed and/or avoided in the treatment process. Evidence is provided suggesting that incest and marital rape occur far more often among the alcoholic population than the nonalcohlic. Assessment and treatment guidelines are then offered for consideration.

NATURE OF THE PROBLEM

One frequently referenced study determined that alcoholics and their spouses all reported feelings of sexual inadequacy and failure (Strack & Dutton, 1971). This should come as no surprise to clinicians when considering the following: (1) Lo Piccolo and Lo Piccolo (1978, p. 435) state the three important A's in the etiology of impotence are alcohol, anxiety and anger. They go on to say that both anxiety and anger are mediated by the sympathetic nervous system, and when activated, effectively short circuit the parasympathetic nervous system which governs the relaxation response crucial to sexual functioning. Obviously, among couples where one or both are alcoholic there are typically excesses of both anxiety and anger. (2) As reported by others (Howard & Howard, 1978; Forrest, 1978), and documented by clinicians' daily experiences with alcoholic couples, a pervasive etiological factor for sexual dysfunctions between alcoholic couples is an inability to develop and main-

Charles P. Barnard is Director, Marriage and Family Therapy, University of Wisconsin-Stout, Menomonie, WI 54751.

131

tain intimate relationships. In the absence of trust and the capacity to share at an intimate level it is unrealistic to assume good sexual relations can be developed. In fact, further erosion of trust and intimacy is the more predictable phenomena, as the quarrels and difficulties in sharing increase and each spouse blames the other and distance and distrust is further escalated.

This article will focus on the existence of two particular sexual problems found among families with an alcoholic — parent incest and marital rape. As far back as 1923 (Marcuse), chronic alcoholism, or a drunken episode at the least, were correlated with the existence of incest. Recent years have resulted in much more frequent study and discussion of this early observation. Sex occurring under coercive conditions — "date or marital rape" — is a more recently identified phenomena. Studies have determined that more women had been raped by dates and boyfriends than by strangers, and that sex forced by acquaintances has more dramatic consequences than rape by strangers (Russell, 1984; McCahill, Meyer & Fischman, 1979; Resich, 1983). Finkelhor and Yllo (1985) conducted research that demonstrated 10 percent of the married women in their sample had been coerced into sex with their husbands as a result of use of physical force or the threat of same. While rape by acquaintances has focussed on dating relationships, clinicians dealing with alcoholic couples have long known of the existence of forced sex among these relationships. It appears though, that forced sex among married couples is still regarded with a "wink and an nod," rather than having the same seriousness attributed to it as occurs among dating couples. Perhaps the notion that a marriage license is a license for abuse is more widespread than we even care to acknowledge.

ALCOHOL AND INCEST

Figures vary from 15 percent to 75-80 percent of all incest perpetrators being alcoholic, or at least abusive of alcohol (Meiselman, 1978; Herman, 1983). Regardless of what the exact figure might be, both empirical data and clinical observation documents the existence of a significant correlation between alcohol and incest. Recently (Adams, 1987), the existence of a correlation between covert incest and sexual addiction was discussed, and particularly as these phenomena are observed among adult children of alcoholics. Covert incest is a term describing the existence of the feelings and dynamics of incestuous relationships, with no actual sexual contact occurring. When acknowledging the existence of covert incest, in conjunction with the disproportionate existence of actual occurrence of incest among alcoholic families, the figures can become staggering to consider. For this reason, it seems imperative for the clinician treating an alcoholic population to be familiar with the dynamics of incest.

An obvious reason for clinicians having this familiarity is to diminish recidivism potential. The recovering alcoholic who has untreated incest experiences is at increased risk for recidivism as the shame, guilt, hurt and rage continue to exist. Similarly, the incest perpetrator who has alcohol problems unacknowledged and untreated is at increased risk for recidivism as impulse control and normal inhibitory anxieties are muted while under the influence. Justice and Justice (1979), in writing about the treatment of incestuous families, have identified six problems typically in need of being addressed. These six are alcoholism, symbiosis, marital relationship, stress reduction, sexual climate, and isolation.

In this regard, alcoholism must be acknowledged as occurring in a family context, and the notion of "alcoholism as a family illness" with resultant consequences for all, accorded diagnostic and treatment importance. In the absence of this perspective, the potential for incest to go unacknowledged is increased, as the treatment effectiveness is obviously decreased.

Both incest and alcoholism have the potential for introducing homeostasis, or a state of equilibrium into a family, albeit pathological in nature. The couple who experiences difficulty with intimacy and sexuality can have episodes of intoxication as a regulator of distance to insure against the existence of prolonged periods of closeness and maintain a pathological equilibrium in this respect. Similarly, the presence of a parent-child incestuous relationship can maintain equilibrium of the alcoholic's sense of sexual virility and maintain the delicate balance of the tenuous marriage. Obviously the emotional and physical costs of maintaining equilibrium in these fashions is exorbitant. Effective treatment must address family-related issues in order to eliminate the potential and need for the family's equilibrium being preserved in these fashions.

While each family has its idiosyncratic uniquenesses, we know that as families become more dysfunctional their creative potential is diminished and they blur into sameness. Uniqueness and creative, growth enhancing differences are directly proportional to the degree of health present. Table I lists the most frequently observed similarities in family dynamics that are in need of being addressed with the alcoholic and incestuous family. Typically, the elements of Table I constitute issues that are in need of treatment among recovering families.

Blurred generational boundaries. As the marriage of the alcoholic and spouse deteriorates, potential for a child being elevated to the position of surrogate spouse is proportionately increased. Either the alcoholic, or spouse, become more likely to enlist a child as their confidant and person to share with that which normally occurs between spouses. In the process, the marital schism is intensified and the child is denied the opportunity to engage in age-appropriate and developmentally important tasks of childhood. Significant family therapy pioneers (Haley, 1976; Minuchin, 1974) have described

Table I

Characteristics of the Alcoholic/Incestuous Family

1. Blurred generational boundaries
2. Dysfunctional marital dyad with fragmented parental dyad
3. Deterioration of marital sexual relationship
4. Short circuiting of normal inhibitory anxieties
5. Muffled and distorted family affect
6. Family roles calcified and narrowly circumscribed rules
7. Family is isolated emotionally and physically
8. Excesses of belongingness or separateness and rigid homeostasis
9. Sibling relationships pathologically disturbed
10. Intimacy and trust problems
11. Dependency issues

this phenomena of blurring generational boundaries in the family hierarchy as being inevitably linked to immediate and long-range behavioral problems. Those who have described difficulties among children of alcoholics (COAs) have described this occurrence as a primary factor of disturbance (Lewis & Williams, 1986; Gravitz & Bowden, 1985; Ackerman, 1983; Black, 1981). Obviously this phenomena can directly relate to the development of incest, or at least covert incest (Adams, 1987).

Dysfunctional marital dyad, with fragmented to nonexistent parental dyad. This phenomena is a direct corrollary to the preceding concern. Lewis and colleagues (1976), as well as Satir (1972), have described the parents as the "architects of the family." If the architects are dysfunctional it is reasonable to assume the structural integrity of the family structure will not provide an environment that fosters growth and health. Consequently treatment must address the dysfunctions extant in the marital and parental dyad.

Deterioration of the marital sexual relationship. As identified in the introduction to this article, marital sexual dysfunction among couples with one or both being alcoholic should be expected until demonstrated otherwise. Inhibited options for expressing one's sexuality in the marital subsystem is one ingredient that can serve to fuel an incestuous relationship. The multifaceted factors contributing to the erosion of sexual expression and satisfaction must be treated to reduce potential for recidivism of both the alcoholism and incest.

Short circuiting of normal inhibitory anxieties. Alcohol acts on the brain in such a way that inhibitory anxieties are short circuited, just as the activation of the defense mechanisms of repression and suppression observed in incestuous relationships does the same. Consequently the alcoholism and incest become ingredients in a vicious cycle that escalates. The more drinking, the greater the likelihood of incestuous behavior, the more incestuous acts, the more shame and guilt to be denied/escaped, the more drinking, and so on.

Muffled and distorted family affect. There is poor modeling of appropriate expression of emotions such as affection and anger, so learning is diminished. Self-esteem is also diminished and this serves to impede productive expression of affect. Subsequently a very limited component of the human emotional keyboard is accessible to these families, and that which is available is typically expressed inappropriately.

Family roles are pathologically assigned and calcified with narrowly circumscribed rules. Roles in these families are rigid in their assignment and not considerate of individual differences and a variety of situations (Black, 1981; Wegscheider, 1981). For instance, one child is ascribed the role of being the "cute one" who others cuddle regardless of age or circumstances, such as the circumstance of another child being hurt and in need of "cuddling." Or, one parent is the tyrant and the other always appearing submissive and dependent. The roles in these families are typically calcified and do not leave room for negotiation of the roles or discussion of the rules. Instead, the lethal sameness of the family organization and operation prevails.

The family is isolated, emotionally and physically. Denial and the perceived need to keep secrets fuel the isolation of the family. Shame, guilt and distrust are underlying ingredients of this process. Justice and Justice (1979) describe the insecurity and possessiveness that evolve, resulting in the children being prevented from having normal social contacts as the whole family becomes increasingly isolated. The family needs to learn how to make it's boundaries more permeable, allowing family members contact with those outside of the family, and those on the outside access to family members.

An excess of belongingness or separateness to the detriment of the other, and rigid homeostasis, or "stuckness." Minuchin (1974) has discussed how individuals need to experience a sense of "belonging to," and then develop a sense and capacity for being "separate from" in order to develop a productive sense of identity and self-esteem. The family under discussion will most typically provide one or the other of these experiences to the detriment of the other, resulting in people who feel fragmented or partial. Belongingness to the point of feeling suffocated and squelched, or separateness to the point of feeling alienated and lonely prevail. Self-doubts and esteem issues predominate among those from this type of environment and prevent them from acting in ways that would promote a change. Consequently, the destructive family structure is maintained.

Sibling relationships come to be pathologically disturbed. Those children "elevated" to the position of surrogate spouse develop grandiosely inflated senses of self-esteem, combined with anger over belng denied a "normal childhood," and those ignored develop self-esteem problems that provide an essential ingredient for being abused as adults. The resultant hurt, jealousy, frustration, and self-esteem issues culminate in pathological sibling relationships in the form of avoidance and/or a desperate clinging to one another for stability absent in the parent-child relationships.

Intimacy and trust problems. As intimacy and trust problems may have fostered the marital quarreling and schism that exists, the quarreling itself serves to further intensify the intimacy and trust struggles. The children observe the deteriorating marital relationship and find it difficult to trust or rely upon either parent. For children it is a short step from being unable to be intimate and trust the two most important people in their life to generalizing this perception to people in general. The result is a family of people who do not trust, and experience difficulties in attempting to be intimate.

Dependency issues. Bowen (1974) has described the difficulties alcoholics experience in relating interdependently. Dependence, or symbiosis, is more characteristic of their relationship style. Functional autonomy, in combination with a desire and capacity for intimacy is practically non-existent in their behavioral repertoire and relationships they are a part of. The dependency on alcohol is just one manifestation of the dependent nature that is so pervasive in their lives. The behavior that is so reflective of dependency, or characteristic of the antithesis of dependency generated by their fear of closeness, is easily observed among the family members where one or more is alcoholic and incest is occurring.

ALCOHOL AND FORCED SEX OR RAPE

As with incest, alcohol and marital rape are frequently identified together. One-third to two-thirds of rapists, and many rape victims, are found to be intoxicated (Amir, 1971; Meyer, 1984; Rabkin, 1979; Russell, 1984). More recently, forms of sexual aggression have been discussed under the rubric of "date rape," inferring a relationship other than marriage. As domestic abuse has become more visible, sexual aggression is also coming to be identified as a significant component. In fact, contrary to the inference of "date rape," studies have clearly identified that rape and other forms of sexual aggression are significantly correlated to length of the relationship.

Some have suggested the very fact of intoxication among alcoholics may diminish the rate of acknowledging the occurrence of rape in a marital relationship. Both spouse and others may be prone to "excuse" the behaviors because of the presence of alcohol and intoxication. Richardson and Campbell's study (1982) clearly demonstrates that individuals perceive an intoxicated male perpetrator as less culpable, and appear to assume "the alcohol made him do it." Conversely, female victims who were intoxicated were perceived as being more responsible for the sexual aggression and generally immoral and more aggressive. Certainly this study suggests the existence of sexist stereotyping that promulgates potential for further under-reporting of marital sexual aggression among the alcoholic and general populations.

Another study (Richardson, 1981) demonstrated that alcohol intake enhances the likelihood and intensity of male aggression toward females. The likelihood of marital rape in the alcoholic relationship becomes even more realistic when acknowledging other considerations as well. For instance, Gelles (1972), in writing about domestic violence, has suggested that marital arguments between spouses typically focus on one another's weaknesses. Acknowledging that a common struggle among male alcoholics is low self-esteem, it is easy to realize that when a male feels threatened by a female while he is intoxicated, she may find herself at considerable risk for being aggressed upon, including sexual aggression.

Considering the likelihood that rape and other forms of sexual aggression are occurring far more frequently in alcoholics than is generally acknowledged, what may account for this under-reporting? The following constitute some possible reasons.

1. Clinicians not being sensitive to this dynamic among couples as a result of reasons such as: diminishing the male's personal responsibility/culpability because of the intoxication; and, acceptance of rape myths such as, "she probably provoked him," "she probably liked it," or, "he didn't have any other choice."

2. Timothy Cermak, a psychiatrist who was the first to initiate treatment of children of alcoholics as co-dependents, writes that co-dependents minimize the amount of violence in their relationships (1986). He reports believing that they do not view themselves as victims of physical or sexual abuse except in the most extreme cases, and even then they frequently take the blame. Many co-dependents seem to believe they "caused" the abuse, or "deserve" to be treated in that fashion. Consequently the co-dependent spouse stays in the relationship in spite of repeated episodes of abuse and fails to identify and report the physical and sexual abuse. In fact, Cermak has offered the following as he endeavors to establish co-dependence as a more widely accepted and understood human problem: "One of the most reliable symptoms of co-dependence is the inability to leave a chronically abusive relationship behind, whether that relationship is ongoing or past" (Cermak, 1986, p. 33).

3. Clinicians, and society, continue to accept traditional sex-role stereotypes and assume the female should be passive and accept her "lot in life." Various studies have demonstrated that this "traditional perception" results in agreement with notions such as women never admit they want sex and the role of men is to overcome their resistance, and that leading a man on justifies force (Check & Malamuth, 1983).

4. Roman Law gave men absolute control over their spouses and children, including the capacity to sell or condemn them to death. This notion was transmitted into the English Law with little change until the 14th century. Although obvious changes have occurred in recent years, there are still those that believe the male prerogative regarding his wife is tantamount to a sacred notion. Unfortunately, many wives who were physically and sexually abused by their fathers may even espouse this notion.

5. The couple becomes dependent upon the sexual aggression as a mechanism for experiencing closeness. Lenore Walker (1979), writing about the cycle of violence, has described how couples report a "honeymoon period" of closeness following aggressive episodes. Similarly, Hanks and her colleagues (1977) found among battered women of alcohol-abusing men that they reported feeling closest after aggressive episodes. In this respect, the couples become dependent upon the aggression as a means of regulating dis-

tance in their relationship. Obviously, treatment must address the development of more productive ways of negotiating and regulating the issue of emotional distance.

SUGGESTIONS FOR THERAPISTS

Obviously, the exposition of a treatment strategy with accompanying techniques is beyond the scope of this article. In the absence of a more encompassing presentation, the following are offered as general considerations for the therapist who works with this population.

1. When working with a family with an alcoholic adult male, assume sexual abuse (incest and/or marital rape) has occurred until proven otherwise. Other factors present that may intensify concern are: a passive, dependent mother, and/or mother who is debilitated by illness or other disorders; a weak, to non-existent mother/daughter relationship; a history that suggests use of harsh physical discipline, recognizing sexual abuse and physical abuse are highly correlated; a father who is extremely jealous and controlling of "his females;" and, a daughter who is a frequent runaway and acts out in other ways as well. While not suggesting any, or all of the above being present should result in a definitive diagnosis of sex abuse, we do know the above behaviors are highly correlated with the presence of sexual abuse (Barnard, 1984).

2. To find out if sex abuse is occurring, one must ask. To do so, the therapist may need to confront their own uneasiness with exploring this area with clients, because often times it is this very uneasiness which prevents the sex abuse from being disclosed. In fact, it is not unreasonable to assume some families do not disclose to therapists because they sense the therapist's discomfort. The therapist can be helpful by approaching the area of human sexuality in a direct and matter-of-fact fashion. By doing so, permission is communicated to the family to feel more at ease in discussing this area.

3. In treating these families, the therapist should directly address how affection and anger can be expressed, received and resolved in this family. As suggested earlier, often the management of affection and anger constitute the core of sexual abuse issues. Consequently,

treatment should be focussed on more adaptive means of expressing anger and affection in the family, while also enhancing the family's conflict resolution skills. Until these areas are addressed, and new skills developed by the family, they will continue to be at risk for reoccurrance of the sex abuse, as well as the alcoholic being more vulnerable to slip back into abuse of drugs.

4. In treating these cases it is easy to become caught up in focussing on the individuals involved. For instance, the perpetrator gets referred to a perpetrators group, the victim is referred to a "survivors group," and the other family members are referred elsewhere, or just forgotten. While treatment for the individuals is an important element of the recovery process, one must not forget to treat the family. Steinglass (1987), and his colleagues, have written about the "dry alcoholic family." They use this concept to convey the notion that individuals in families may be treated, but without addressing how the individuals have pathologically fit together, the family may not achieve significant change. Steinglass and associates discuss how their research demonstrates that families must be helped to address issues such as presented in Table I of this article, if there is to be increased hope for significant change in their recovery. Without this effort, the family will be like the alcoholic who stops drinking, but continues on a dry drunk. To facilitate this effort, an inventory such as the Family Inventory of Recovery Elements (Barnard, in press) can be employed with families.

Treaters must be cautious about yielding to the temptation of doing what they are most comfortable with, and just treating the individuals. By not addressing the "invisible patient"—the family—the individuals will not be helped as much as otherwise might be the case. Helpers must be ever cognizant of the fact that people do not present with just intrapersonal dynamics, but also interpersonal dynamics. To treat at only the intrapersonal level, seems similar to the process of a mechanic who gives a 6-cylinder car a tune-up by changing only 4 of the spark plugs.

5. At a larger level, we must continue to work to change the attitudes of friends, family members, professionals, and society in general regarding issues of sexual abuse. The ignorance and insensitivity that prevails regarding incest and marital rape continues to

serve as a catalyst to keep victims prisoners of their guilt and shame.

CONCLUSION

Alcoholism has come to be accepted as a multi-faceted disease that requires effective diagnostic work to determine how and what to treat. This must then be followed by a comprehensive treatment effort. This article has described the correlation that exists between the presence of alcoholism and sexual problems; specifically, incest and marital rape.

The sensitive clinician will attend to determining whether or not sexual problems are evident among the recovering people encountered. Studies were discussed in this article that suggest the wise clinician will assume sexual problems exist until proven otherwise. Assuming sexual problems such as marital rape and/or incest are discovered, they must be treated to promote the recovery of all involved. Some general treatment guidelines were also discussed. Incomplete, partial treatment is likely to vastly increase the potential for relapse of many pathological behaviors, including the drinking, among the recovering population. Those who ignore assessment and treatment of the sexual domain among alcoholic individuals and families are guilty of gross professional tunnel-vision.

REFERENCES

Ackerman, R.J. (1983). *Children of alcoholics: 2nd edition*. Holmes Beach, FL: Learning Publications, Inc.

Adams, K.M. (1987). Sexual addiction and covert incest. *Focus on Chemically Dependent Families*, 10, 3, 10-11 & 46.

Amir, M. (1971). *Patterns in forcible rape*. Chicago: University of Chicago Press.

Barnard, C.P. *Alcoholic families: The invisible patient*. In press.

Barnard, C.P. (1984). Alcoholism & incest: Issues in treatment. *Focus on Family & Chemical Dependency*, 7, 2, 29-32.

Black, C. (1981). *It will never happen to me!* Denver: M.A.C.

Bowen, M. (1974). Alcoholism as viewed through family systems theory & family psychotherapy. *Annals of the New York Academy of Science*, 233, 115-122.

Cermak, T.L. (1986). *Diagnosing & treating co-dependence*. Minneapolis: Johnson Institute Books.

Check, J.V.P., & Malamuth, N.M. (1983). Sex role stereotyping and reactions to depictions of stranger versus acquaintance rape. *Journal of Personality & Social Psychology*, 45, 344-356.

Finkelhor, D., & Yllo, K. (1985). *License to rape: Sexual abuse of wives*. New York: Holt, Rinehart & Winston.

Forrest, G.G. (1978). *The diagnosis & treatment of alcoholism*. Springfield, IL: Charles C. Thomas.

Gelles, R. (1972). *The violent home*. Beverly Hills: Sage Publications.

Gravitz, H.L., & Bowden, J.D. (1985). *Guide to recovery*. Holmes Beach, FL: Learning Publications Inc.

Haley, J. (1976). *Problem solving therapy*. San Francisco: Jossey-Bass Publishers.

Hanks, S.E., & Rosenbaum, C.P. (1977). Battered women: A study of women who live with violent alcohol-abusing men. *American Journal of Orthopsychiatry*, 47, 2, 291-306.

Herman, J. (1983). Recognition & treatment of incestuous families. *International Journal of Family Therapy*, 5, 2, 81-91.

Howard, D., & Howard, N. (1978). Treatment of the significant other. In S. Zimberg et al. (Eds.), *Practical Approaches to Alcoholism Psychotherapy*. New York: Plenum Press.

Justice, B., & Justice, R. (1979). *The broken taboo*. New York: Human Sciences Press.

Lewis, J.M., et al. (1976). *No single thread: Psychological health in family systems*. New York: Brunner/Mazel.

Lewis, D.C., & Williams, C.N. (1986). *Providing care for children of alcoholics*. Pompano Beach, FL: Health Communications, Inc.

LoPiccolo, J., & LoPiccolo, L. (1978). *Handbook of sex therapy*. New York: Plenum Press.

McCahill, T.W., Meyer, L.C., & Fischman, A.M. (1979). *The aftermath of rape*. Lexington, MA: Lexington Books.

Marcuse, M. (1923). Incest. *American Journal of Urology & Sexology*, 16, 273-281.

Meiselman, K.C. (1978). *Incest*. San Francisco: Jossey-Bass Publishers.

Meyer, T.J. (1984). Date rape: A serious campus problem that few talk about. *Chronicle of Higher Education*, 29, 1, 12.

Minuchin, S. (1974). *Families & family therapy*. Cambridge, MA: Harvard University Press.

Rabkin, J.G. (1979). The epidemiology of forcible rape. *American Journal of Orthopsychiatry*, 49, 634-647.

Resick, P.A. (1983). The rape reaction: Research findings & implications for intervention. *Behavior Therapist*, 6, 129-132.

Richardson, D. (1981). The effect of alcohol on male aggression toward female targets. *Motivation & Emotion*, 5, 333-344.

Richardson, D., & Campbell, J.L. (1982). The effect of alcohol on attributions of blame for rape. *Personality & Social Psychology Bulletin*, 8, 468-476.

Russell, D.E.H. (1984). *Sexual exploitation: Rape, child sexual abuse, & workplace harrassment*. Beverly Hills: Sage Publications.
Satir, V. (1972). *Peoplemaking*. Palo Alto: Science & Behavior Books.
Steinglass, P. (1987). *The alcoholic family*. New York: Basic Books, Inc.
Strack, J.H., & Dutton, L.A. (1971). A new approach in the treatment of the married alcoholic. *Selected Papers, Twenty Second Annual Meeting: Alcohol & Drug Problems Associations of North America*. Hartford, CT.
Walker, L.E. (1979). *The battered woman*. New York: Harper & Row.
Wegscheider, S. (1981). *Another chance*. Palo Alto: Science & Behavior Books.

Children at Multiple Risk:
Treatment and Prevention

Rodney J. Johnson, MSW
Mary Montgomery, MSW

SUMMARY. Children who are exposed to disruptive family situations frequently endure multiple stress factors. Three such closely linked factors are chemical dependency, family violence, and family disruption. The authors discuss the nature of the risks to these children and a framework to provide both treatment and preventative counseling. A specific program designed for children from violent homes is described.

INTRODUCTION

Much has been written recently about the many difficulties faced by children growing up in our fast-paced society. For children who experience the problems of family violence, chemically-dependent parents, and family disintegration, the journey to adulthood can be very dangerous and can have serious lifelong consequences.

After several years of counseling hundreds of battered women and court-referred perpetrators of domestic violence, the staff of the Wilder Community Assistance Program attempted to address one of these problems by developing a program for children living in violent homes. The initial rationale for this programming was to provide preventative services to a high-risk population in an attempt to influence the intergenerational transmission of family violence. After three years of working with these children, a far more complex view of risk has emerged.

Rodney J. Johnson is Director of Community Social Services, Amherst H. Wilder Foundation, St. Paul, MN. Mary Montgomery is a counselor in the Community Assistance Program, Amherst H. Wilder Foundation, St. Paul, MN.

These children are not only at risk of transmitting family violence in the next generation, but they are also at serious risk of displaying mental health and adjustment problems during childhood. In addition, the interplay between witnessing family violence, suffering child abuse, observing chemical dependency in a parent or parents and experiencing parental separation, increases the likelihood that developmental problems will occur. Unfortunately, these problems occur simultaneously in families with considerable frequency.

This article will develop a rationale for how these children are at risk, describe a program for children from violent homes, summarize the results of an evaluation of the short-term effects of the programming, discuss the issues of chemical abuse, family disruption, and child abuse in the families served, and finally point to the possible integration of philosophy and programming efforts to reach more children similarly at risk.

AN INITIAL VIEW OF CHILDREN AT RISK

The consequences associated with family violence include the obvious suffering of the abused, but that is only the beginning. The effect on families and the community escalates as the emotional and physical damage is passed from one generation to the next (Walker 1979).

In reviewing domestic violence research in 1980, Gelles reported that one of the consistent conclusions ". . . is that individuals who experienced violent and abusive childhoods are more likely to grow up and become child and spouse abusers than individuals who have experienced little or no violence in their childhood years." Our clinical experience has shown that the majority of men and women entering our adult domestic abuse counseling program have previously been victims or witnesses of violence themselves. Despite the fact that all family violence is not explained by this theory, the increased risk of future violence from the current victims of family violence is too strong to ignore.

More evidence for the strong association between spouse abuse, child abuse, and even sibling violence is provided by recent studies. According to Walker's study, 53% of men who assaulted their partners also physically abused their children. She reports that 28% of mothers who are abused are abusing their children. The risk of a mother abusing her child during the times that she is being battered is 8 times higher than when she is not being battered (Walker, 1984). In addition, violence between siblings has been found to be directly proportional to the level of parental violence directed toward the children (Finkelhor, Gelles, Hotaling and Straus, 1983). Gelles, Walker and Finkelhor all agree that there is a strong link between victimization and violent behavior and that the role of the family in the perpetration of violence is critical.

THE EFFECT OF MULTIPLE RISK FACTORS

Professionals working with children in specialized counseling settings need to be aware that the problems of family violence, chemical abuse, and family disintegration are frequently linked. Screening for all these factors should become standard practice in any setting working with any one of the problem areas. In addition, it is important to understand how children are affected and what type of integrated intervention approaches would be helpful.

Rutter (1979) has reported results of a study in which children who experienced multiple chronic risk factors were found to have elevated rates of psychiatric disorders. While children experiencing a single risk factor were no more likely to have psychiatric problems than children with no risk factors, as soon as the second factor occurred, the risk of childhood psychiatric problems increased four times. The risk of psychiatric disorders continued to climb as further concurrent stresses occurred. The type of family risk factors examined by Rutter included severe marital discord, low social status, large family size, paternal criminality, maternal psychiatric disorder and psychiatric hospitalizations. Although these factors do not exactly match the risk factors discussed in this article, the concept of chronic stresses that potentiate each other may well apply.

In another study, stressful family conditions including chemical abuse, family violence and family instability were found to be related to the actual use of, and the perceived need for, mental health services for exposed children (Mueller, 1987). Again, as the number of stressful conditions increased, the parents increasingly felt their child needed mental health counseling and actual use of such services increased. These results are consistent with Rutter's findings and the risk factors discussed are similar to those found among the children from violent homes.

The obvious conclusion is that reducing the number of stressors for children will minimize the risk of childhood mental health problems, even if all the stressors cannot be eliminated. Preventative work with parents in each of the problem areas must continue to be a focus for the future. Realistically, however, we know that many children will continue to be exposed to multiple stressors in their families. It is essential that we begin to examine the most effective ways of helping these children.

Recent literature (Rutter 1979, Garmezy 1985) has begun to examine protective factors that help children raised in the worst circumstances to survive and lead reasonably productive lives. Although far too extensive to review here, a few factors they discovered seem to relate directly to this discussion. These include self-esteem, scope of opportunities, positive relationships, and adequate coping skills. In general, the factors of mastery and adaptability seem to exert a protective influence. As the investigation of protective factors continues, the ability to assist children in surviving disadvantage should improve. We need to know how children beat the odds more than we need to know how they succumb to them.

These early explorations of protective factors seem to suggest that the acquisition of coping skills could be useful in helping children survive difficult circumstances. As Rutter (1983) points out, stressful experiences can either increase the risk of poor outcomes when subsequent stressors occur, or they can have a "steeling effect," allowing for more adaptive responses to further stressors.

BUILDING A GENERIC COUNSELING APPROACH FOR CHILDREN EXPERIENCING MULTIPLE STRESSORS

Regardless of how specialized a counseling setting may be, it seems reasonable to believe that a generic set of coping skills could be taught that would be useful to the children in combating multiple stressors. We offer three basic building blocks which should be systematically taught.

1. *Children are not responsible for the problems of their parents or any other adults.* They did not cause violence, chemical dependency, divorce, or any other problem.
2. *Children can't change the behavior of their parents or any other adults.* They can't cure violence, chemical dependency, divorce, or any other problem.
3. *Children can control their own behavior and cope with the difficulties they face.* They can develop and follow protection plans. They can find supportive adults to help them grow and mature. They can learn problem solving skills that are not physically abusive and that do not involve the abuse of chemicals. They can learn to succeed in future relationships. They do not need to be alone. They can help others. They can be remarkably successful.

Any setting working with the problems of parents, including adults who are violent, chemically dependent or experience difficult divorces and separation, must also consider the needs of the children. Helping a parent will often improve the situation for the children, but it won't necessarily help the children overcome their reduced ability to handle future stress, or reduce the effects of modeling their parents' behavior. Children need to work through their own issues in order for healthy growth to continue.

A PROGRAM FOR CHILDREN
FROM VIOLENT HOMES

The Domestic Abuse Children's Program was instituted in February, 1985. This program is one component of an array of counseling services offered by the Community Assistance Program under the auspices of the Amherst H. Wilder Foundation, Division of Services to Children and Families.

The program serves children of parents who have received domestic abuse services from the Community Assistance Program. All of the children have lived in violent homes. The main emphasis of the program is to provide preventative counseling and education to children in an effort to break the intergenerational patterns of abuse.

A group format is utilized in an attempt to reduce the child's sense of isolation and shame. Age appropriate groups are conducted for children 3 to 12 years of age. Services are also provided for adolescents, however, these will not be discussed in this article. Group sessions are held once each week for 1-1/2 hours, over a 12-week period. Each group has 5 to 6 participants and is facilitated by 2 counselors. Because 4 groups are usually conducted at the same time, siblings can be accommodated in separate groups. Counselors keep in touch with parents through personal contacts and letters. The final session allows all parents, children, and counselors from the different groups to gather together in parting celebration.

The groups combine education and supportive counseling to address specific issues related to abuse and other family problems. Some of the topics include: abuse and who is responsible; personal protection plans and support networks; the effects of violence; feelings; self-esteem; alcohol and drug abuse; grief and loss; separation and divorce; personal power; choices; and non-violent problem solving.

The Domestic Abuse Services for adults, offered by the Community Assistance Program, serve as a guide for the Children's Program. By utilizing similar formats, we ensure that parents and children are receiving consistent information. For example, adult groups begin with a discussion of the types of abuse (verbal, emotional, physical, and sexual) and the cycle of violence with its three phases of tension building, blow-up and honeymoon or calming-down phase. In the children's program the types of abuse are presented as talking and touching for younger children and as physical, verbal and sexual for older children. The cycle of violence becomes the anger volcano and children learn about the rumbling, explosion, and cooling lava phases.

Also in the adult program, clients learn to observe cues in the tension-building phase so that they can act on their control or protection plan before a violent incident occurs. The children learn to take action when they hear or feel the rumbling phase of the anger volcano. Children learn to protect themselves when they are afraid that they may be hurt, or someone they love will be hurt, through personal "safety plans." These very specific plans include what they can do and who they can talk to.

The counseling approach is as important as the concepts that are taught. Much of that approach is designed to offset the learning that takes place in violent and chemically-abusive homes. Children raised in such environments learn that one person often has absolute control over another; that play, involving noise and healthy movement, is disruptive and may contribute to a violent incident; that conflict is dangerous; and that assertive expression of feelings is undesirable.

The counseling is designed to empower children through information and support. Each child's experience is considered unique. For some children the violence they have witnessed or experienced may be the primary stressor, for others it may be a parent's chemical abuse and for still others it may be the parents' separation.

The program is structured to serve children of all ages, interest levels and special needs in a non-authoritarian group process. Even the most active or acting-out child is accepted into the program and counselors adapt to individual needs. The group content is rich in interesting activities which allow children to learn while having fun. Counselors provide clear definitions and much repetition of critical themes such as: "That's abuse;" "That's not my fault;" "I have a choice;" and "I have a right to feel safe." At the same time, the children are allowed to tell their stories at their own pace and in their own way.

Children are allowed to move freely around the meeting room even during group discussions. The rooms are stripped of potential dangers and are small enough so that the child who does decide to separate from the group will still be able to hear the discussion. Children are also allowed to make noise and are sometimes encouraged to do so as when they are asked to shout in unison, "It's not my fault" or "I'm special."

Whenever possible, male and female counselors work together in a group. They talk with each other, sometimes disagree and have fun together. The counselors attempt to get in touch with the child in themselves, as they laugh and play in the children's world.

This child-centered approach presents counselors with their biggest challenge. Some of the children's behaviors are disruptive and destructive. Counselors must attempt to modify these behaviors utilizing a series of creative techniques including distraction, gentle touch, verbal reinforcement and concrete rewards including stickers, badges and balloons. Conflict between the children is allowed. In fact, the groups are loosely structured enough so that it occurs naturally. The children are encouraged to work through the conflict with the support of the counselors who, when needed, may suggest problem-solving strategies and suggest feelings words.

Healthy expression of feelings is a theme that runs through all the group sessions. In addition to special activities designed to teach a feelings vocabulary, the children learn throughout the program that their feelings are okay, that there are words to match feelings, that feelings change over time and that people may experience more than one feeling at the same time.

Teaching this information about feelings sets the tone for children to express feelings about family members and to change those feelings from week to week. Sometimes children talk about love for a parent who they also fear or feel anger toward. They may say one week that they love their father or mother and the next week that they hate them. These statements are confusing and frightening to parents and children may be told that they don't really feel that way. Counselors let the children know that they believe them. Children will also tell counselors how they feel about them. They may say that they like one better than the other. As counselors model acceptance of these preferences, they teach the children that adults can handle their feelings.

A group for children three and four years of age is unique to this program. Because this is the critical age for imitation and for socialization of ways to express anger, as well as the age when children are developing self-concepts, the work with these children is essential in breaking the intergenerational cycle of abuse. Topics are similar to those taught in the other groups. Methods used include art, music, dance, and story-telling. Coloring books, which address topic areas in a form that is understandable and interesting to the children, have been designed for this age group.

The following examples serve to illustrate the importance of the groups for the children:

> When Brian, age 5, told his mother that he had been sexually abused by his stepfather, he also told her that he knew that it

was not his fault because he had learned that in his group. This was the first time he had discussed the abuse with anyone.

Melissa, age 11, knew that the worst violent incidents against her mother would occur when her father had been drinking. She talked of waiting up for her dad to come home from the bar long after her mother had gone to bed so that she could "take care of him." Once he was asleep and the house was quiet, she would allow herself to relax. Through the group, Melissa learned that she was not responsible for her father's actions and that she couldn't change his behavior.

Relieved of the responsibility for her parents, Melissa has begun to be a child again and will find fun and worthwhile activities to do for herself. Melissa and her mother both have developed safety plans to use should the potential for a violent incident occur.

Jason, age 6, would run to stand between his mother and father whenever he thought that his mother was in danger. He would tell his dad to stop, but usually the violence continued. Counselors attempted to relieve Jason of all responsibility for stopping the violence. In cooperation with his mother, the staff helped him develop a personal protection plan that allowed him to be in a safe place when violence might occur.

Kelly, age 9, had become increasingly isolated and fearful due to the violence in the home. Her mother was alarmed by her lack of interest in friends and activities. She spent most of her time in her room and was afraid to have her mother leave the house. Kelly talked openly in group of her sadness, fears, and loneliness. She was very much influenced by other children's stories that were so similar to her own. Group members began to encourage her to call them and to become involved in after school activities. Kelly made progress and her mother also learned new ways of helping her. Kelly said she liked the group because she didn't feel different any more.

John, age 3, told his group that he felt sad because his father was going to die. Further exploration revealed that John's father had recently entered a chemical-dependency program. John had been told by his mother that his father drank too much, was sick, and had gone to the hospital. Since John had also been told that his grandfather died "because he drank too much," he assumed that his father would also die. John's problem provided counselors with an opportunity to discuss drug abuse in simple terms with the group and to alleviate John's fears.

Parent conferences are conducted at the conclusion of each group. At that time, the counselors make individual recommendations based on the needs of each child. Children in need of outpatient mental health services are referred to the Wilder Child Guidance Clinic for further counseling. Where chemical dependency is an issue in the family, the children are frequently referred to the Children Are People support groups.

COUNSELING TECHNIQUES IN PRACTICE

The educational and supportive counseling offered in each group meeting regardless of the topic, is designed to reinforce the three generic building blocks of preventative counseling with children.

- Children are not responsible for the problems of adults.
- Children can't change the behavior of adults.
- Children can only control their own behavior and cope with the difficulties they face.

To illustrate how these themes are integrated into the counseling process, two group sessions will be described in some detail.

Abuse Session

Opening Discussion: The session begins with a clear definition of abuse that provides a framework for further work. Permission is then given for children to talk openly about any abuse they have experienced and they are relieved of all responsibility for that abuse.

Ask the children if they know what abuse is. As the children offer examples, group them into three categories of abuse: (1) physical, (2) verbal, and (3) sexual. Write these categories on the board and ask for more examples of each. Some children may want to know if it is okay to use swear words as examples. Explain that it is okay at this time. Discuss the issue further by asking some of the following questions. "Have you seen or heard someone being abused? What did you do? How did you feel? Have you ever been abused? How did you feel? What did you do? Was it your fault? Whose fault was it?"

Abuse Drawings: Ask group members to draw something they have seen or heard that was abusive. Have each child share the story behind their drawing with the group and then hang it on the wall.

The drawings allow for further exploration of abuse in the children's lives. Children can often draw what they cannot say. Using this method, they sometimes come up with new forms of abuse not yet included in the definition. For instance, one boy drew a man and woman having intercourse, called it "visual abuse" and said that he had been forced to watch pornography.

Self-Esteem Exercise: Because talking about violence may bring out feelings of sadness, anger, and helplessness in the children, it is important to introduce a self-esteem exercise that emphasizes the children's personal power over their own lives. Have the group members imagine that they have the power to change anything they want. What would they change: in their school; in their home; in the world? Ask them to write these down and discuss, "How would it feel to have that kind of power? How does it feel when you think you don't have power? We have power over some things, but not others. We do have power over what we do and how we act."

Wrapping Up: The wrap up is designed to bring information and experience together with essential points that the children should remember. Counselors acknowledge their feelings, take a stand that abuse is not okay and that they have a right to feel safe, and again relieve them of responsibility.

Ask older groups of children to take notes while you write important points on the board. Write, comment, and invite discussion on each of the following:

1. Abuse hurts
2. Abuse is not okay
3. Abuse can be (a) physical, (b) verbal, (c) sexual
4. I am not responsible for someone else's abuse
5. I have a right to feel safe

Ask the children to keep these notes in their folder and to go over them once in awhile.

Feeling Good: Because this is a difficult and emotional session, ending on a positive note is very important. Tell the children that, "Abuse makes us feel bad." Then ask, "What are some things that make us feel good?" Ask them to write down five things. Let them share and discuss their list. Tell them, "It is important to know what makes you feel good. It is okay to feel good." Explain that sometimes people who are feeling bad about themselves will put down others for feeling good. Ask, "What can children do when that happens?"

Closing: Give a reward to each child for "feeling good." The children are also given a homework handout. The exercise reads, "When I see or hear abuse going on, I feel . . ." There are five clouds in the middle and a list of feelings words to choose from at the bottom. The children are asked to choose five feelings and write them in the clouds.

The children are then given a letter to bring home to their parents stating: "We discussed abuse today in group. We talked about three different kinds of abuse—physical, verbal, and sexual; some feelings we have about abuse; and how it is not our fault if we are abused or someone we love is abused. Your children are bringing home some homework on this topic. You can share with them how you feel when abuse is going on. If you have any questions or concerns, please feel free to call us."

Drug Abuse Session

The Opening Discussion: The session begins with a definition of drug abuse that is developed through a combination of the children's comments and the counselor's input. Children are asked, "What are drugs?; What are examples of different kinds of drugs? How do drugs affect the way people feel, think, and act?" The children may also provide examples from their personal experience.

Feeling Exercise: In previous sessions, the children have discussed how feelings can be a basis for actions. Now they are asked to give examples of what people do when they feel sad, lonely, confused, bored, angry, etc. The counselors use the examples to develop the idea that in response to difficult feelings, some things people do help them feel better and others make them feel worse. The counselors then help the children relate this concept to drug use by explaining that people who abuse drugs feel better for awhile, but then end up feeling worse. The concepts of loss of control, addiction, illness and treatment are discussed.

Self-Esteem Exercise – Group Story Telling: This exercise provides some relief from a difficult topic and reinforces the concept that the children have a right to feel good about themselves. It is possible during the exercise to point out that people who feel good about themselves are not as likely to take or abuse drugs.

Start a story with the statement, "I feel fantastic about myself when . . ." Ask each child to contribute a sentence to the story. Older groups of children can take turns writing. The result is a creative flow of thoughts that serves as a release for the children and a rich source of information for the counselors.

Family Exercise: Ask the group members to stand up and hold hands. Then ask one child to pretend to fall down. Discuss the experience with the group. Ask, "What does this do to the circle? What does it feel like to be the one falling down? What does it feel like to be the one trying to hold up the person who is falling?" Discuss how this role play is similar to how drug abuse affects the family. Everyone tries to compensate for the break in the circle. Ask the group, "Has this happened in your family? What have you done? Have you seen it happen in other families?" Point out that they cannot control the drug abuse of a parent. They can only reach out for support and talk about it to people they trust. They did not make it happen and it is not their fault.

Family Feelings: Do an exercise on family feelings by asking the group to complete sentences like, "When my mom is sad, she . . ." When my sister is happy, she . . . " "When my dad is angry, he . . ." Use positive and negative feelings for each member of the family. Ask, "What do you do when your mom, dad, sister does that? How do you feel? Do you ever want to make it better? Are you responsible for how others feel or act?"

Closing: Counselors give awards to the children for talking about drug abuse and hand out a letter to be taken home to their parents. The letter could read: "We talked about drug use today, how people act when they are using drugs and how it affects the family. The children learned that when a family member is addicted to drugs, it is not the child's fault and they cannot control it. Please talk this week about drug use in your home. What is acceptable to you and what is not, and how drug use may have affected your family. The children did very good work today on this difficult subject."

PROGRAM EVALUATION RESULTS

A formal evaluation of the Children's Program was conducted by the Wilder Foundation's Research Center for the 49 children attending groups during 1986. Children ranging in age from 3 to 12-years-old were served in 9 groups divided according to age. The Program's long-term objective, as stated earlier, was to prevent these children from repeating their parents' violence in relationships when they become adults. Obviously, it is too soon to tell if this objective will be accomplished. However, four short-term objectives were measured.

It was anticipated that children would gain information about domestic abuse, develop a protection plan, learn non-violent problem solving, and view their group experience in a positive light. Information on these objectives was obtained through parent and child (age 9 and older) questionnaires completed at intake and upon completion of the program.

Not only did the results indicate that the objectives were met for most children, but the parents indicated ". . . that the program often had a positive effect on the whole family, including the parents' behavior toward their children" (Mueller 1987). Parents reported better communication with their children and more use of non-abusive discipline. "Furthermore, about half the parents indicated that their children were settling arguments more often without hitting or name-calling since being in the group" (Mueller 1987).

Overall, the results indicated attitude and behavior changes in both the children and their parents which were greater than anticipated. Long-term follow up would be needed to see if these changes can stand the test of time and result in less family violence in the next generation.

The authors were able to establish the degree to which these children experience multiple problems by utilizing information provided through this evaluation and by reviewing the clinical records of all family members. Because program participation was limited to children who had at least one parent in a family violence program, it is not surprising that most of the children had witnessed violence in their homes. The following discussion will address the possible effects of this stressor as well as other significant stressors on the children.

Witnessing Violence

Forty-six of the 49 children in our study (94%) had witnessed violence in the family. Most of the violence was in the form of a physical assault on their mother by their father. The assaults ranged in severity from pushing and restraining to choking and stabbing. The children often talk about these experiences in their groups.

A 9-year-old indicated he jumped on his father's back in an attempt to save his mother from being stabbed with a knife. A 4-year-old child said he fantasized having a gun that he could use to shoot his father down to "peanut size" when the father was assaulting the mother. A 6-year-old talked about the time his father tried to drown his mother and how afraid he was that the sharks would eat her. A 3-year-old said that she saw her mother fall into the "anger volcano" and that she tried to pull her out, but couldn't.

Eth and Pynoos (1985) in their book, *Post-Traumatic Stress Disorder in Children*, include a discussion of children as witnesses of personal violence. They observe that "children who witness extreme acts of violence represent a population at significant risk of developing anxiety, depressive, phobic conduct and post-traumatic stress disorders, and are in need of both clinical and research attention." The focus of their discussion is on children who have witnessed the murder of a parent, rape of a mother or the suicidal act of a parent. Although the acts of violence that most of the children in this study have witnessed are not usually as severe, they are, nevertheless, personal acts of violence that may affect the children in some of the ways described.

Some of the children in the Program had witnessed extremely brutal acts of violence, including attempted murder. The fact that these acts were committed by a family member would seem to increase its impact on the child. This is an issue that needs further investigation.

Chemical Abuse

Although a causal relationship doesn't appear to exist between abuse of a partner and abuse of alcohol and drugs, research does demonstrate that men who abuse their partners also frequently abuse alcohol and drugs. Walker (1984), utilizing results from her own study and a review of the literature, reported chemical abuse rates for men who batter ranging from 61% to 85%. These figures suggest that many children who are experiencing family violence are exposed to chemical abuse as well.

Since the program evaluation was not originally designed to research chemical abuse in the children's families, this information was only available on 20 of the 36 families included in the study. These families accounted for 29 of the original 49 children. Interviews with mothers of the children at the time of their intake into the Women's Domestic Abuse Program revealed that: in 14 of the 20 (70%) families, the father abused alcohol and drugs; in 6 of the 20 families (30%), both the father and mother abused alcohol or drugs; 7 of the 14 fathers and 3 of the 6 mothers with chemical problems had been through chemical-dependency treatment; and in 8 of the 14 families experiencing chemical abuse problems, a parent had been involved in either AA or Alanon. Although the numbers are small, the 70% rate of chemical abuse in families where battering has occurred is consistent with other studies.

Chemical abuse by parents appears to be a major stressor in the lives of many of the children in this study. These children experience a chronic type of stress associated with a parent or parents who are at least intermittently out of control. Children who are raised in chemically-abusive families have been reported to have difficulty in trusting their environment and in establishing healthy boundaries (Children Are People, Inc., Support Group Training Manual, 1985). They may also avoid emotions, feel overly responsible for others, and be at risk of developing mental health problems.

Child Abuse

Child abuse is also prevalent in this population. At the time of intake, 29% of the children were identified as victims of abuse and 22% of the families were involved with a county child protection agency. During the time of this study, 7 reports of suspected child abuse were made to Child Protection based on children's statements to counselors in group. Three of the reports involved suspected physical abuse, while four involved suspected sexual abuse.

Research indicates that abused children have disproportionately high rates of mental health and behavior problems (Browne and Finkelhor, 1986; Lamphear, 1985; Mueller, 1987). Mueller notes that abused children also experience a greater number of stressful events in their lives, beyond abuse, than children who are not abused. The higher rates of mental health problems found in this population may be influenced by these other stressors as well.

Family Disruption/Separation/ Divorce Issues

Thirty of the 49 children (61%) involved in the evaluation were living in single parent homes at the time they entered the program. Observations of the children during the process of group indicated that many experienced multiple separations from their fathers as mothers separated, reunited and separated again in their own efforts to free their lives of violence. Counselors frequently heard from children one week that they were happy because daddy was back, and the next week that they were sad because he was gone again. When children were asked to draw pictures of their families, they usually excluded the father from the drawing, as if to tell us that they have not only lost the parent from their home, but from their lives. The stress of many separations is sometimes intensified by the presence of police in the home at the moment of separation. One child said that he thought the police were going to shoot his dad, another talked of seeing his dad "tied-up" by the police, and still another said that her daddy didn't live at home, he lived in jail.

Wallerstein (1980) reported that the central event for children in the separation/divorce process is the separation, not the divorce. Children experience a variety of feelings at this time including . . .

"anxiety, sorrow, anger, guilt and an overall heightened sense of their own vulnerability." It is evident, then, that still another significant stressor is affecting this population of children. The Wallerstein study (1980, 1984) which has longitudinally documented the differential effects of divorce and separation on children, is an excellent source of information on this topic.

CONCLUSION

The problems of family violence, chemical dependency, and family disruption place children at considerable risk when they occur in isolation. When they occur in combination, the risks appear to increase exponentially. Unfortunately, children are often affected simultaneously by these three chronic problems. The consequence for them may be a wide range of mental health problems in the short run, and maladaptive behavior in the long run as problems are transmitted into the next generation.

Programming for these children with a focus on the acquisition of coping skills seems critical. This programming can profit from the growing information available on protective factors that help children to survive in adverse environments. The hope for the future should not be based entirely on trying to protect children from less-than-ideal family situations. Professionals must also concentrate their efforts on building stress-resistant children, if we are to turn the tide for the next generation.

BIBLIOGRAPHY

Browne, A. and Finkelhor, D; 1986. "Impact of Child Sexual Abuse: A Review of Research." *Psychological Bulletin* 99: 66-77.
Children Are People, Inc. Support Group Training Manual, 1985. 493 Selby Avenue, St. Paul, MN 55102.
Eth, S. and Pynoos, R.; 1985. "Children Traumatized by Witnessing Acts of Personal Violence: Homicide, Rape or Suicide Behavior." In S. Eth and R. Pynoos (Eds.), *Post-Traumatic Stress Disorder in Children* (pp. 19-43) Washington, DC: American Psychiatric Press.
Finkelhor, D.; Gelles, R.; Hotaling, G.; Straus, M.; 1983. *The Dark Side Of Families*. (pp. 219-231) Beverly Hills: Sage Publications.
Garmezy, Norman; 1985. "Stress-resistant Children: The Search For Protective Factors." In J.E. Stevenson (Ed.), *Recent Research in Developmental Psycho-*

pathology. Journal of Child Psychology and Psychiatry Book Supplement, No. 4. (pp. 213-233) Oxford: Pergamon Press.

Gelles, Richard J.; 1980. Violence in the Family: A Review of Research in the Seventies. *Journal of Marriage and the Family* 42: 873-885.

Lamphear, V.; 1985. "The Impact of Maltreatment on Children's Psychosocial Adjustment: A Review of the Research." *Child Abuse and Neglect* 9: 251-263.

Mueller, Daniel; 1987. "Health and Well-Being of Children." A Report from the Needs Assessment of Children in Ramsey County, Minnesota. Wilder Foundation Research Center.

Mueller, Daniel; 1987. "Evaluation of a Program for Children In Abusive Families; 1986 Report." Wilder Foundation Research Center.

Rutter, Michael; 1979. "Protective Factors in Children's Responses to Stress and Disadvantage." In M.W. Kent and J.E. Rolf (Eds.), *Primary Prevention of Psychopathology, Vol. 3, Promoting Social Competence and Coping in Children* (pp.49-74). Hanover, NH: Univ. Press of New England.

Rutter, Michael; 1983. "Stress, Coping and Development: Some Issues and Some Questions." In N. Garmezy and M. Rutter (Eds.), *Stress, Coping and Development In Children* (pp.1-41). New York: McGraw-Hill.

Walker, L.; 1979. *The Battered Woman.* Ch. 7, p.3. New York: Harper Colophone.

Walker, L.; 1984. *The Battered Woman Syndrome.* New York: Springer Publishing.

Wallerstein, Judith S.; 1980. "Children and Divorce." *Pediatrics In Review* 1(7): 211-217.

Wallerstein, Judith S.; 1984. "Children Of Divorce." *American Journal of Orthopsychiatry* 54(3): 444-458.

Child Maltreatment
and Alcohol Abuse:
Comparisons and Perspectives
for Treatment

Stephen J. Bavolek, PhD
Hester L. Henderson, PhD

SUMMARY. There is growing empirical and clinical evidence that shows an association between alcohol abuse and child maltreatment. Professionals treating families for alcohol abuse need to become aware of the possibility of child maltreatment. The purpose of this chapter is to identify indicators of child abuse and neglect, to discuss commonalities among child abusers and alcohol abusers, and to discuss perspectives for treatment.

The use of alcohol and the use of force within a family is well documented in the literature on family violence. Numerous clinical and empirical studies have identified a relationship between alcohol abuse and interpersonal violence in the family, particularly child abuse and spouse abuse (Coleman & Strauss, 1983; Spielier, 1983). While the relationship between alcohol abuse and family violence is

---

Stephen J. Bavolek is Research Associate Professor in the College of Health, University of Utah. Dr. Bavolek is nationally recognized for his work in child abuse and neglect prevention and treatment and parent education. He is principal author of the Nurturing Programs for Parents and Children, Parents and Adolescents, and Teenage Parents; and the Adult-Adolescent Parenting Inventory (AAPI). Hester L. Henderson is Assistant Professor in the Department of Exercise and Sport Science, University of Utah. Dr. Henderson is the director of the Special Physical Education teacher training program at the University of Utah, has written two books on behavior management, and has coauthored the Nurturing Program for Parents with Developmental Disabilities and their Children.

165

explored in greater detail in other studies in this volume, the purpose of this paper is to alert the professional who treats alcohol abuse to the possibility that child maltreatment may also exist within the family. Specifically, the focus will be threefold: (1) to recognize the physical, emotional and behavioral characteristics of abused children; (2) to explore the similarities between alcohol abuse and and child maltreatment; and (3) to identify sound principles of treatment for families experiencing both alcohol abuse and child maltreatment. Professionals treating families for alcohol abuse must be able to recognize indicators of child abuse and neglect for several reasons:

1. As a professional working with families and children, you are mandated to report your suspicions of child maltreatment to the local department of social services, police, or county sheriff.

2. In addition to the treatment of chemical dependency, your responsibility extends to increasing the overall functioning of the family. The maltreatment experienced by family members needs intervention designed to replace old, learned abusive parenting patterns with new nurturing patterns.

3. The treatment and prevention of alcohol abuse and child abuse and neglect go hand in hand. The strategies and programs created to treat both maladies are interdependent. Coordination of both services to the families is imperative.

To increase your skills in identifying children who are suspected victims of abuse and neglect, it is necessary to understand several important issues about child maltreatment.

CHILD MALTREATMENT IS A PROCESS AND A PRODUCT

Like alcohol abuse, child abuse and neglect is a way of life for many families. Abuse and neglect are the ways a caregiver inappropriately interacts with a child usually with some end goal in mind. The goal may be to make the child comply with the caregiver's demand (sit up straight; eat all your food; no running in the house; stop your crying; etc.); to punish the child (hitting the child on the buttocks, face, etc.); or to show dislike for the child (name calling; use as an object for sexual gratification; ignoring the child's needs, etc.). In this sense, child maltreatment is an ongoing process. All parenting processes, whether they be healthy or unhealthy, always lead to a product. Some of the products of child abuse and neglect are usually seen in bruises, welts, unmet developmental needs, low self-esteem, and/or the exhibition of aggressive behaviors in the child. These products are generally referred to as "manifestations" or "indicators." Suspicions of child abuse and neglect are based on these indicators because generally the abusive parenting processes go unobserved. Although indicators give us information to base our suspicions on, the absence of "overt" indicators does not necessarily mean a child is not being abused or neglected. Some families are more capable of hiding the physical and psychological indicators of abuse and neglect than others.

Children are abused in many different ways and to differing degrees. Some are abused daily, some five times daily, some only once every two months. Some children are severely whipped causing major trauma to the body, others are burned with cigarettes, still others are hit with a belt on the buttocks or slapped in the face with a hand. Although the frequency and severity of the inappropriate caregiver-child interaction differs with each example, the process remains the same. That is, whether the child was abused with a hand, belt, or whip once a day, five times a day or once every two months does not change the process. The process which is the inappropriate interaction between caregiver and child, differs only on the continuum of frequency and severity.

CHILD ABUSE AND NEGLECT DEFINED

Child abuse is generally defined as an act of aggression that has been committed to the child which may require medical attention or create concern for the child's well-being. The abuse may be physical, sexual or emotional. Abuse to children is often defined in terms of an act of commission — a course of action which leads to the occurrence and/or repetitions of the offense. Common acts of commission are situations in which a parent is the actual perpetrator of the offense or situations where one parent perpetrates the offense and the other parent condones the act; thus, setting the stage and providing opportunity for a repetitive pattern.

Child neglect is often viewed as the failure of the parents to provide their children with the minimum care and supervision expected by a society and, in effect, are accused of failing to fulfill their parental responsibility. The failure to carry out their parental responsibility is referred to as acts of omission and generally results from neglect of duty or from inadequate and ineffective functioning. The line separating these two criteria is not always sharply defined. Neglect to children can relate to the child's physical appearance; home living conditions; and/or lack of parental supervision.

IDENTIFYING PHYSICAL ABUSE IN CHILDREN

Identifying families who are experiencing physically abusive interactions can be achieved by being aware of physical indicators. Physical indicators are the most obvious to spot and often provide the professional with the "hard information" many seek in order to substantiate their suspicions of physical abuse. Keeping in mind that child maltreatment exists on a continuum and that physical as well as behavioral indicators will vary in frequency and severity, no series of indicators, however slight or inconsequential they may appear to be, should be dismissed. The following physical indicators serve as guidelines to assist professionals in recognizing physical abuse in children.

Physical abuse should be suspected when any of the following conditions exist:

1. The child shows evidence of repeated injuries. There are signs of new injuries before old injuries have healed (skin abrasions, fractures, etc.).

2. The history is not consistent with injuries. The way the child states receiving the injuries is not consistent with the type of injury (falling on the playground and bruises or welts on the legs or arms, or buttocks).

3. The child complains of abdominal pain. Internal injuries have developed which are the result of punching, kicking, or hitting the child in the midsection.

4. The child has unexplained injuries. The child refuses to state

how the injury occurred or offers several contradictory explanations as to the origin of the injury.

5. The injuries are bilateral and appear clustered on the child's body. The injuries of physically abused children usually appear on both sides of the body (both sides of the back or buttocks, both legs or arms, etc.) and are clustered around a particular bodily area. A child who is repeatedly spanked on the buttocks will show evidence of bruises on both sides without evidence of trauma to other bodily areas. Explanations of the injury which suggest the child fell down would be inconsistent with the type of injury.

6. The child shows evidence of the following injuries:

    a. Bruises, welts, scars on the face, lips, or mouth or on the large areas of the torso, back, buttocks, or thighs. Injuries will usually appear on both sides of the body, in unusual or clustered patterns, or may be reflective of an instrument used to inflict the injury (rope, paddle, coat hanger, stick, etc.)

    b. Burns from cigars or cigarettes usually inflicted on the palms of the hands, the soles of the feet, the arms, or the scalp. Dunking burns indicative of immersion in hot liquid. Such burns usually have a clear line of immersion which differentiates abuse from accidental injuries. Areas commonly traumatized are the hands up to the wrist (glove-like appearance), the feet just above the ankles (sock-like in appearance), or the buttocks and genital areas.

    c. Ocular injuries manifested in dislocated lens, retinal and subretinal hemorrhage usually caused by grabbing the child and shaking the child violently. Bruises or "black eyes" caused by trauma to the ocular region are also common.

    d. Restraint injuries occur as a result of the child being tied with a rope or cord. The injuries commonly appear around the mouth (being gagged), the wrists and/or ankles (being tied), or the neck or torso (being hung).

    e. Head trauma appears as bald patches on scalp resulting from hair pulling.

IDENTIFYING PHYSICAL ABUSE
IN ADOLESCENTS

The physical abuse of adolescents is displayed in four specific patterns: the first pattern is abuse that begins when the child becomes a teenager over issues peculiar to adolescence such as dependency, autonomy, adolescent privileges and rights. The adolescent seeks to make more decisions relating to self, wants to spend more time with his/her friends, and generally seeks to be treated with more respect. Such perceived "rebellion" by the parents is often the basis for the abuse.

The second pattern is abuse that is a continuation of abuse from childhood where maltreatment is not new to the family. In this pattern, abuse is not particular to the victim's age or developmental state. It is suggested that roughly half of abused adolescents are graduates of abuse as children.

The third pattern is abuse that evolves from mild or moderate corporal punishment and crosses the line to become abuse. It is often difficult to distinguish this pattern from the first pattern. Slapping/Spanking the child escalates into beatings in adolescence. Parents find themselves losing control as the child's strength, size, confidence, and independence increase. The parents then feel more force is necessary to punish and control.

The fourth pattern is abuse as a result of differences over expectations, dependency, autonomy, and social control. The family returns to behaviors which characterize the parent-child relations when the teenager was a toddler. Many parents who had difficulty with children during "terrible two's" may also have difficulty during adolescence.

Physical abuse of adolescents includes any non-accidental injury caused by the youth's caretaker, such as beating, branding, or punching. By definition, the injury is not an accident, but neither is it necessarily the intent of the youth's caretaker to injure the youth. Physical abuse may result from strict discipline or from punishment which is inappropriate to the adolescent's age or condition. The nature of the physical abuse may vary: (a) it may be a "one-time" beating or punch; (b) it may be episodic abuse, or long-term, chronic abuse; (c) it may include physical restraint, confinement, or torture.

It is important to remember that some of the physical indicators common in young children, such as serious or multiple fractures, burns, and serious internal injuries, are rare in adolescent abuse cases. The following physical indicators of physical abuse may be present in adolescents.

1. Unexplained bruises and welts on the face, lips, mouth, or eyes; and in various stages of healing. Such injuries may include bruises of different colors, old and new scars close together; injuries in clusters forming regular patterns, or reflective of the article used to inflict them (electrical cord, belt buckle); or injuries on several different surface areas (indicating that the youth has been hit from different directions.

2. Unexplained fractures to the nose, facial structure or extremities and/or swollen or tender limbs.

3. Unexplained lacerations and abrasions to the mouth, lips, gums or eyes, or on the arms, legs, or torso.

IDENTIFYING EMOTIONAL ABUSE

The National Center on Child Abuse and Neglect defines emotional abuse as child abuse which results in the impaired psychological growth and development of the child. It frequently occurs as verbal abuse or excessive demands on a child's performance and results in a negative self-image and disturbed or disordered behaviors. Emotional abuse may occur with or without physical abuse.

Four forms of emotional abuse appear to be the most common.

1. *Rejection.* An explicit refusal to accept the child is rejection. Researchers have characterized rejection as a psychologically malignant force in human development and have found that rejection increases when parents are given unrealistic total responsibility for children in the absence of support, encouragement, and feedback from the outside. Children thrive on acceptance and are consumed by rejection.

2. *Coldness.* Children need a rich and varied emotional experience with their parents if they are to form a valid and reliable picture of the world and to place themselves appropriately within that

picture. When the parent-child relationship is cold, the child is deprived of a necessary element of social experience. Without this experience to work with, the child develops gaps in his/her social skills and emotional development. The child who is exposed systematically to coldness from the parents is seriously impaired in future relationships.

3. *Inappropriate control.* Parents who either dictatorially overcontrol their children or who abdicate responsibility for controlling them by placing their children at risk for impaired development, particularly if they couple this inappropriate control with rejection and coldness. In one sense, of course, a parent who refuses to act responsibly in the area of control is rejecting the child, either by not tolerating autonomy or by not accepting responsibility.

4. *Extreme inconsistency.* Children can learn to adapt to, and indeed can survive and thrive on, a wide variety of realities. The existence of very different cultures is testimony to the flexibility of human nature. Firsthand observation and systematic research demonstrate that children can develop "normally" in a variety of value systems, social arrangements, and cultures. However, when there is no consistent presentation of reality or when there is little clear definition of what is real, what the standards are, what is expected, and how social relationships (including the family) work, the child's development is in jeopardy. Extreme inconsistency in which the child is not given a firm foundation of reality is, therefore, a common form of emotional maltreatment.

IDENTIFYING SEXUAL ABUSE

Sexual abuse of children and adolescents is defined as exploitation for any sexual gratification. Sexual abuse, like physical abuse and emotional abuse, exists on a continuum of severity and frequency. The sexual abuse of children and adolescents includes rape, incest, fondling of the genitals, exhibitionism, voyeurism, and pornography. The assessment of physical indicators of suspected sexual abuse is always determined by a medical examination by a physician. There are, however, other physical and behavioral indicators that can, when seen in concert, alert the alcohol abuse counselor to possible sexual abuse. These include:

1. *Apparent pain in sitting or walking.* Be alert for evasive or illogical explanations. Encourage the child to have a physical exam.

2. *Pregnancy.* Although teen pregnancy may not be the direct result of incest, factors leading to overt or promiscuous sexual activity by the teenager may have earlier roots in incestuous family activities.

3. *Direct reports from the children.* Children very seldom lie about such a serious matter; concealment is much more the rule. Not all children are able to tell their parent(s) directly that they have been or are being molested. As a counselor, you may be the child's only confidant. Do not simply disregard the child's story as nonsense. Follow the proper channels and report the case.

4. *Distorted body image.* Children may depict themselves as being ugly or being disfigured. Many sexually abused children express low self-esteem, shameful, self-depreciating, and self-punitive feelings.

5. *Sex play.* Occcassionally sexual abuse is indicated by subsequent sex play between peers or when the child acts out the sexual incident with dolls.

6. *Drug use/abuse.* Use of alcohol and/or drugs may be the child's avenue for handling guilt and anxiety about having been sexually abused or perpetrating sexual abuse upon younger children.

7. *Indirect allusion.* Sometimes sexually abused children will confide in teachers with whom they have a good rapport and feel may be helpful. The confidences may be veiled and vague but allude to a home situation by indicating, "I'm going to find a foster home to live in," "I'd like to live with you," or, "I'm afraid to go home tonight."

8. *Seductive behaviors.* If children identify sexual contact as a positive reinforcer for attention, they may adopt seductive behaviors with both peers and adults.

EMOTIONAL/BEHAVIORAL INDICATORS OF ABUSE

It is often said that the most severe trauma a child suffers as a result of abuse is not physical but emotional. The physical wounds often heal—but the emotional scars which have resulted from the acts of violence often never heal. These emotional scars may manifest themselves in the following behaviors:

1. *Extreme fright*. Some children manifest extreme fright upon any and all contact. They often whimper and attempt to hide under the sheets.

2. *Apathy*. Some children exhibit profound apathy to the point of apparent stupor, although they do not withdraw from tactile stimulation.

3. *Emotional blunting*. Children may resemble cases of "shell shock" in adults. They display a profound blunting of all external manifestations of inner life. They may sit or lie motionless, be devoid of facial expression, or be unresponsive to all attempts at evoking recognition of the external world.

4. *Aggression*. The effects of harsh physical punishment upon a child often leads to the development of serious violent and delinquent behaviors.

5. *Emotional problems*. Serious emotional illnesses may develop as a result of severe and persistent physical abuse. Self-destructive behavior, suicidal attempts, and self-mutilations are found to be significantly higher in abused children than in non-abused children.

6. *Pseudomaturity*. Children develop extremely precocious skills in initiating social contact with adults as a means of guarding and protecting themselves.

7. *Hypervigilance*. Some abused children become hypervigilant. These children become watchers for any sudden adult movements. Some develop a remarkable ability for perceiving the mood of adults, while others "test the waters" by verbally notifying the caretaker in advance of what the child is going to do (I'm gonna go to the bathroom now; Can I color on this piece of paper?).

8. *Personality shifts*. Abused children may develop a "chameleon nature." That is, their behavior shifts and changes in accordance to the inconsistent environment of their parents.

9. *Ego restrictions*. Abused children may suffer restriction of various ego functions. The child may not attempt new tasks and avoids antagonizing adults.

10. *Declarations of failure from child*. The child openly states

that he/she can never do anything right after making an error or mistake.

11. *Feelings of worthlessness.* The child perceives him/herself as being worthless, a failure, and unacceptable and disappointing to adults.

12. *Defeat/Rebellion.* Children may quit school and become truant. Some may leave home and become runaways, while others quit the family (psychologically) and become incorrigible.

13. *Defiance.* Children may defy parental and adult authority. Some may continue to go to school, but refuse to perform; some may stay at home but refuse to do their chores; and some may stay out late with a group of friends of which their parents disapprove.

14. *Delinquency.* Children's reactions to inappropriate parental expectations may lead to more seriously delinquent behaviors like pregnancy, stealing, vandalism, and/or alcohol/drug involvement.

IDENTIFYING PHYSICAL NEGLECT

Child neglect may be defined as an act or acts of omission on the part of the caregiver(s) responsible for the well-being of the child. Recognition must be given to the fact that neglect, like abuse, may exist in many gradations, ranging from incipient stages to truly gross proportions. Neglect may be classified into two main categories: physical and emotional. Although recognizing neglect is not always easy, you should suspect neglect when the following conditions exist:

1. The child's physical appearance and health is markedly different from members of his/her peer group or culture.

2. The type of neglect presents a serious hazard to the child's overall well-being and development.

3. The neglecting condition is consistently present.

Indicators of Physical Neglect — The Child

Physical neglect of the child relates to the direct care of children birth to 18 years in terms of their bodily needs and appearance. The

following characteristics indicate a child is being physically neglected:

1. Filth and dirt on the child's body or clothing.
2. Vermin in the child's hair or on his/her clothing.
3. Insufficient clothing. The child may lack essential parts of
clothing like shoes, jacket, etc. The child wears the same clothes
each day or has clothes badly in need of repair (shoes with holes, or
lacking soles/heels; unfashionable torn jeans, jacket, etc.).
4. Insufficient medical care. The lack of medical treatment for a
health problem or condition which, if untreated, presents a problem
or danger to the child. Such medical needs can include psychiatric/
psychological treatment, dental needs, orthopedic needs, ocular
needs, and medical needs.
5. Inappropriate clothing for weather. The child may be dressed
in a light-weight jacket in sub-zero weather, or wear no socks or
gloves in winter, etc.
6. Undernourishment or malnourishment. The child may appear
underweight as a result of not eating or overweight as a result of not
being fed a balanced diet. Many physically neglected children resort to begging or stealing food from others.
7. Body odors. Offensive body odors which are the result of not
bathing regularly.

Indicators of Physical Neglect —
The Environment

Physical neglect of the environment relates to the overt conditions of the physical appearance and condition of the home. The
following characteristics indicate a child is living in a neglecting
environment.

1. Filth and dirt in the overall appearance of the home.
2. Lack of (indoor or outdoor) sanitation facilities.
3. Overcrowded living or sleeping conditions.
4. Vermin or rodent infestation.
5. Inadequate or defective heating, plumbing, or electricity.
6. Broken plaster in walls and ceiling, or defective flooring.
7. Dirty dishes stockpiled in the sink, leftover food and garbage
   scattered about the house.

8. Inadequate protection from the elements (broken windows, leaky roof, etc.).

Indicators of Physical Neglect —
Lack of Parental Supervision

Physical neglect may also relate to situations where children and adolescents are left alone without adult supervision for substantial periods of time. The following conditions indicate a child is being neglected.

1. Working parents make no arrangements to care for their children.

2. Leaving children unattended at night while parents are out of the home for whatever reason.

3. Leaving children and adolescents unattended for a substantial period of time.

IDENTIFYING EMOTIONAL NEGLECT

Emotional neglect is an intangible which is difficult to measure. It may be defined as the failure to provide psychological nurturance necessary for a child's psychological growth and development. Professionals very seldom witness parents emotionally neglecting their child(ren). Instead, behavioral manifestations are often viewed.

Indicators of Emotional Neglect

1. *Lack of support.* There is failure on the part of the parents to provide the emotional support necessary for the development of a healthy personality. Parents fail to provide the child with consistent age-appropriate guidelines, or may overprotect the child and inhibit appropriate social and emotional growth of the child.

2. *Lack of empathy.* Many parents demonstrate an inability to be empathically aware of their child(ren)'s needs. Parents feel they will "spoil" the child by providing "too much" love. For many, a high premium is placed on the child being good, behaving appropriately, and learning to be obedient.

3. *Child used for need gratification.* By direct actions, or through less obvious (but equally meaningful) implications, the child is used

as an object for need gratification of the adult. The child is expected
to perform in the role of a surrogate husband, wife, mother or father
in a family where one parent is absent or incapacitated.

Behavioral and Emotional Indicators
of Child Neglect

Children who are being neglected may exhibit a range of extreme
behaviors. The following serve as behavioral and emotional indicators:

1. *Poor parent-child interactions.* Some neglected children
"take over" and begin to care for their parents sensing the parent's
own intense neediness. Neglected children may distrust adults entirely and not make any demands or they may cling and demand
attention of any adult with whom they come in contact.

2. *Personality adjustment problems.* Neglect is most clearly
manifested in a child's poor personality adjustment. Many appear
listless and withdrawn, harbor feelings of being unwanted and
abandoned, and exhibit low self-esteem.

3. *Peer interaction problems.* Many neglected children fail to
develop social relationships and are most often considered loners.
Due to the nature of neglect, children will display extreme possessiveness of toys and games, may be resentful of other children or
adults and become destructive, or may steal articles of clothing or
food from others.

4. *Academic retardation.* Neglected children often demonstrate
an "academic retardation" that is not a true indication of their abilities. Speech and language developmental delays are common.

PARENTS WHO ABUSE AND NEGLECT
THEIR CHILDREN

In recognizing families who are experiencing abuse and neglect,
three common characteristics of the parents become apparent. From
an assessment of personality, although abusive and neglecting parents have often been referred to as mentally ill, the fact is, less than
15% of the parents who abuse their children have been identified as
emotionally disturbed. Clinical data have generally identified abu-

sive parents as exhibiting narcissism, neediness, immaturity, low self-concept, poor self-esteem, demand to be nurtured, and poor ego control. Bavolek and Comstock (1983) found that parents tended to score high in anxiety, aggressiveness, and independence while indicating a low integration of social roles which is manifested by a tendency to "follow one's own urges." These traits exemplify characteristics of adults who exhibit narcissistic personality disorders.

Abusive parents often feel intense ambivalence and inconsistency. They seek attachment to family members but are unable to establish healthy relationships. Abusive parents often express a lack trust in self and others and fear dependence or independence due to unmet dependency needs. Many are unable to play with children and expect perfection in self and family. They lack self-control and seek to control others through feelings of insecurity.

Polansky (1979) found that neglecting parents are cognitively knowledgeable of socially acceptable parenting practices but do not consistently exhibit them. Many neglecting parents exhibit a tendency to infantilize their children by restraining the development of normal independence and autonomy, again, feeding their own dependency needs. Their impulsiveness and general feelings of detachment only serve to reinforce fears of abandonment and separation in their children. Additionally, Polansky indicates that neglecting parents are understandable humans with whom one could empathize and sympathize. Their adjustment problems are pervasive and are not limited to child abuse and usually exhibit long standing feelings of inadequacy.

The inability to handle stress is often cited as another causal factor in the maltreatment of children. Parents often feel overtaxed and are unable to handle the condition or situation. Stress can result from situational crises, the environment, socio-economic status, family or personal sickness, or marital problems. Behaviors of the infant are perceived as being deliberately annoying, such as prolonged crying, or failure of the infant to meet the demands or needs of the parent. Self-confidence, ingenuity, and useful knowledge of how to seek help are necessary to cope with stress and crises. Because abusive and neglecting parents seldom display these qualities, crises and stress have a greater impact on them.

The third common characteristic among abusive and neglecting parents is the fact that the vast majority were abused or neglected as children by their parents. In essence, child abuse and neglect are patterns of learned behavior and are replicated in subsequent generations.

Bavolek, Kline, and McLaughlin (1979) have identified four parenting patterns which often lead to abuse and neglect. Although parenting behaviors are not practiced outside the dimension of an individual's personality, understanding and identifying specific inappropriate parenting behaviors can lead to goal directed instruction.

Pattern A: Inappropriate Parental Expectations of the Child

Beginning very early in the infant's life, abusing parents inaccurately perceive the skills and abilities of their child. The infant is expected to perform in a manner incongruent to what may reasonably be expected for his/her developmental stage. The basis for this problem stems from the abusing parents' lack of a knowledge base relative to the capabilities and needs of a child at each developmental stage. Treated as if the child was older than he/she really is, the child is often left to care for him/herself. Inappropriate expectations frequently surround such activities as eating, bathing, toileting, etc.

Pattern B: Inability of the Parent to be Empathically Aware of the Child's Needs

Empathic awareness of a child's needs entails the ability of a parent to understand the condition or state of mind of the child without actually experiencing the feelings of the child. Abusing parents often demonstrate an inability of being empathically aware of their infant's/child's basic needs. Based on a fear of "spoiling" their child, abusing parents often ignore their child which results in the child's basic needs being left unattended. The child is seldom loved or nurtured. A high premium is placed on the child being good, acting appropriately, and learning to be obedient. However, what constitutes "good" behavior is seldom clarified.

Pattern C: Strong Parental Belief in the Value of Punishment

Physical attacks by the abusing parent are not usually a haphazard, uncontrolled, impulsive discharge of aggression by the parent onto the infant/child. On the contrary, studies appear to indicate that abusing parents utilize physical attacks as a unit of behavior designed to punish and correct specific bad conduct or inadequacy on the part of the child. Abusing parents not only consider physical punishment a proper disciplinary measure but strongly defend their right to use physical force.

Pattern D: Role Reversal

Abusing parents often look to the child for satisfaction of their own emotional needs. Usually described as a "role reversal" the child is expected to be the source of comfort and care; to be sensitive to and responsible for much of the happiness of his/her parents. The child is further expected to make life more pleasurable for the parents by providing love, assurance, and a feeling that the parent is a needed, worthwhile individual.

COMMONALITIES BETWEEN ALCOHOL ABUSE AND CHILD MALTREATMENT

The commonalities between alcohol abuse and child maltreatment have important implications in providing treatment to either or both types of dysfunction. Stor (1980) found characteristics of physical abusers generic to alcohol abusers. One of the commonalities was control—the right to control others which is often reflected in extreme jealousy. In alcoholism literature, the alcoholic is often described as exhibiting jealousy as a result of sexual dysfunctioning and mental changes. McClelland (1972) refers to the alcoholic's need for power—the need to control others and/or the environment.

Another shared characteristic among child abusers and alcohol abusers is blame—projecting blame and anger onto others. Alcoholics blame others for their drinking; child abusers blame their children for not complying, being obedient, or meeting their needs.

A third characteristic is the confusion of the abuser's own role and a disturbed perception of his/her action (Bavolek & Comstock, 1983; Stor, 1980). Alcohol abusers and child abusers confuse their own roles and responsibilities with those of their family. Alcohol abusers tend to be grandiose with friends in bars and neglectful of their family's needs. When confronted at home with their behavior, they often become outraged and frequently resort to abuse (Speilier, 1983).

Violent family background is yet another common characteristic of child abusers and alcohol abusers. The alcohol literature has noted the disruptiveness in alcoholic families and has discussed in great length the neglect and physical violence common to many alcoholic families (Jackson, 1954).

Finally, poor impulse control also seems to be common to many alcohol abusers and child abusers. In an early study, Delamater (1968) found that individuals who lack adequate impulse control, yet are socialized into societal norms, use alcohol to deviate from their controlled behavior. This provides an explanation for the abuse of alcohol and subsequent violent behavior.

TREATMENT CONSIDERATIONS

The research presented in this paper and throughout this volume substantiated that alcohol abuse and child abuse and neglect tend to co-exist. Treatment, it would appear, should be available to treat both disorders conjointly, rather than independent of each other. Research this author has been conducting over the past five years has focused on developing a comprehensive treatment program for families experiencing child abuse and neglect (Bavolek & Comstock, 1983; Bavolek & Bavolek, 1985; Bavolek, 1988). The Nurturing Program is a family-based program designed to reparent members of dysfunctional families by replacing old, unwanted, abusive patterns of parenting with new, more nurturing patterns. The philosophy of the Nurturing Program to treat child abuse and neglect has important principals for treating families in which there is abuse of alcohol and children. *The single most important aspect of effective treatment is to include all family members in the program.* Family-based treatment approaches treat the family as a system. Since all members play a role in keeping the dysfunction going, all members need to be involved in learning new behaviors. Results of research conducted with abusing and neglecting families during a three-year period in the early 1980s found 80% of the abusive families who agreed to participate in a 2 1/2-hour weekly program completed all 15 sessions. Only 20% of the nearly 120 families who began the program dropped out. Among the families who completed the program, significant, positive pre and post-test changes were found in parenting attitudes, family interaction patterns, knowledge of nurturing parenting techniques, and desirable personality traits, i.e., positive self-esteem and self-concept, reduction in anxiety, increase in self-discipline, etc. (Bavolek & Comstock, 1983).

Reparenting the entire family seems to be a second important factor in treating alcohol abuse and child abuse. Reparenting is a therapeutic procedure of creating new, positive experiences for parents and children which will replace old, negative experiences. Since learning requires both a blend of new thoughts with new feelings, instructional activities have to engage family members at the cognitive (knowledge) and affective (feelings) levels. Since family dysfunction is expressed through feelings, treatment programs which engage clients strictly in a cognitive level have a slim chance of success.

Finally, treatment must focus on self and on role. A healthy human being will do a better job in any family role (father, mother, daughter, son, etc.) than an individual who views him/herself as inadequate, incapable, and incompetent. The research is clear; unless individuals develop a more positive regard for self, a more positive regard for others is just a dream.

CONCLUSION

The purpose of this paper is to provide information about child abuse and neglect to professionals who work with families in which at least one parent is abusing alcohol. Since the existence of child abuse and neglect and alcohol abuse go hand in hand, to more effectively treat the family, professionals must be able to recognize suspected cases, understand the family dynamics, and be able to implement treatment programs which will increase the overall functioning of the family by addressing the alcohol dependency as well as the abuse and neglect. It is certain that neither the violence, the neglect, or the alcohol abuse can be effectively treated in isolation. Recognizing the extent of a family's dysfunction is the first step in its effective treatment.

REFERENCES

Bavolek, S.J. (1988). *The Nurturing Program for Parents and Adolescents*. Eau Claire, WI: Family Development Resources, Inc.

Bavolek, S.J. and Bavolek, J.D. (1986). Validating the home-based nurturing program for parents and children birth to 5 years. Final report, University of Utah.

Bavolek, S.J. and Comstock, C. (1983). Nurturing program for parents and children. Eau Claire, WI: Family Development Resources, Inc.

Bavolek, S.J., Kline, D.F., & McLaughlin, J.A. (1979). Primary prevention of child abuse: Identification of high risk adolescents. *Child Abuse and Neglect*, 3, 1071-1080.

Coleman, D.H. and Strauss, M.A. (1983). Alcohol abuse and family violence. In E. Gottheil (Ed.), *Alcohol, Drug Abuse and Agression* (pp. 104-124). Springfield, IL: Charles C. Thomas.

Delamater, J. (1968). On the nature of deviance. *Social Forces*, 46, 445-455.

Jackson, J.K. (1954). The adjustment of the family to the crisis of alcoholism. *Quarterly Journal Study on Alcohol*, 562-568.

McClelland, D.C. (1972). *The drinking man*. New York: Free Press.

Polansky, N.A. (1979). Help for the help-less. *Smith College Studies in Social Work*, 49, 169-91.

Speilier, G. (1983). What is the linkage between alcohol abuse and violence? In E. Gottheil (Ed.), *Alcohol, Drug Abuse and Agression* (pp. 125-126). Springfield, IL: Charles C. Thomas.

Stor, B. (1980). Patterns in family violence. *Social Casework Reprint Series*, 5-12.

Adult Self-Injury as a Survival Response in Victim-Survivors of Childhood Abuse

Mary Louise Wise, PhD

SUMMARY. The presence of adult self-injury is often listed as a descriptive indicator for a history of childhood sexual or physical abuse. The overlap between families in which both chemical dependency and sexual abuse occur is now accepted knowledge. A predominant dynamic for both problems is the shame, bound family system. The author presents a therapeutic perspective of adult self-injury as a coded survival response to childhood abuse in which shame, denial, and self-injury are intricately interwoven. Specific messages in self-injury and therapeutic responses to self-injury are discussed.

"Self-Injurious Behavior," "Self-Destructive Behavior," "Deliberate Self-Harm," "Self-Mutilation," and "Self-Abuse" are clinical labels used to describe actions by a person toward her/himself that result in physical harm to the body. Self-injury ranges in degree of immediate and long-range severity from mild or superficial effects, to permanent physical damage, to life-threatening dangers. Examples of self-injury include cutting, burning, picking sores, hair removal, ingestion of harmful substances. Very recently, researchers (Summit, 1981; de Young, 1982) have presented data indicating that self-injury is a subsequent behavioral manifestation of children who have been physically abused. Clinicians and researchers (Brown, 1985; Charmoli, 1986; Gelinas, 1983; Miller, 1984; Simpson, 1981) have recognized adult self-injury as one of the indications of childhood sexual abuse in the adult client's life.

Mary Louise Wise is a licensed consulting psychologist in Minneapolis, MN.

SELF-INJURY AS SURVIVAL

Until the long-lasting effects of childhood sexual abuse became better understood, attitudes of professionals toward self-injury often included fear, judgment, disgust, and/or fascination with the details of abusive trauma in people's lives. Statements are often made by professionals that self-injury by clients challenges the skill of clinicians, or that it is a difficult therapeutic problem to confront. Adults who self-injure have been viewed as too difficult to work with, as manipulative, or as having behavior problems to be modified. These reactions and views seem to reflect the response of others to people who self-injure, rather than a perspective on the nature or meaning of self-injury in people's lives. Today, therapists informed by contemporary literature (Fossum & Mason, 1986; Gelinas, 1983; Horowitz, 1976; Simpson, 1981), are hearing and seeing the coping strategies that victim-survivors have developed in a family system of abuse, shame, and denial.

The author uses the phrase victim-survivor in reference to someone who experienced childhood abuse and in whom the internalized effects of victimization are ongoing. Equally, the phrase victim-survivor refers to the person's physical and emotional survival of the childhood abuse, and the defensive abilities developed for ongoing survival. Often, an individual victim-survivor is more aware of one dimension of this paradox; either (1) aware of the feelings and effects of victimization, perhaps feeling immobilized in life because of them, and less aware of the strength used in survival; or (2) aware of an adamant commitment to survival, protection and strength, without being in touch with feelings of vulnerability. The first person may feel inadequate in life and in fact, life may be a maze of difficulties and crises. The second may have what appears to be a confident, competent, highly successful life, yet may carry ever-present, devastating feelings of emptiness and shame, which, along with an inability to be vulnerable, damage self esteem and limit interpersonal relationships. These examples highlight the extremes, whereas individuals are likely to show tendencies in one direction or the other. The paradox is that the victim-survivor is simultaneously *both* victim and survivor. Owning both dimensions brings out the potential wholeness in being able to know one's vulnerability and need for protection, while also knowing one's strengths and abilities to survive. Both dimensions were present at the times of childhood abuse, and have been active in the life patterns the person developed as she/he continued to live in relation to the effects of abuse. Kaufman (1980) describes an array of defensive strategies a child may develop in response to shame and abuse, and the subsequent process of internalization and adult life patterns.

Self-injury is one of the crossroads in the paradoxical nature of being a victim-survivor. Self-injury itself is a further violation to one's own being, and simultaneously a survival response pattern to internalized victimization.

SHAME-BOUND FAMILY SYSTEMS

Hidden within a shame-bound family system, abusive events are kept secret from outside the family, and are often denied within the family as well. Self-injury can be an outward, visible signal from the self-injuring person to her/himself, and/or to others, about the internalized pain of the victimization. Lindberg and Distad (1986) have identified self-destructive behaviors (substance abuse, perfectionism, isolation, and depression) as logical responses of adolescent incest victims in their attempts to alleviate stress or assert some control over the helplessness experienced in the incest.

The shame-bound cycle described by Fossum and Mason (1986, p.107) offers a model for the oscillation between compulsive control and abusive release so prevalent in shame-bound families and in individual family members. In the control aspects, shame is often expressed covertly through attitudes of being overly critical, self-righteous, rigid, blaming, pleasing and placating. The excesses in the control phase involve efforts to control self and others; these move into a "breakout" release phase to escape the pressures of control and shame. Fossum and Mason list abuse of alcohol, drugs, food, sex, money, physical abuse, sexual abuse, verbal abuse, and self-mutilation as routes of escape from excessive levels of abusive control.

Children in a shame-bound, abusive family system are taught a self-abusive pattern of surviving stress, pain, injury and betrayal. Fossum and Mason state that "Children growing up in a family with an alcoholic or otherwise compulsive/abusive parent, integrate this cycle (control-release) as part of their own system with shame at the center" (1986, p.103). Without intervention and recovery from the underlying shame process, the multigenerational patterns of abuse continue, perhaps in different forms in each successive generation. For example, a person who was raised in an alcoholic family may maintain adamant control over active drinking in her/his current family, and yet continue the shame-based attitudes, values, and behaviors in response to which, her/his children may develop escape/release patterns such as becoming alcoholic, self-abusive, or injurious to others.

In her article on self-injurious behavior in incest victims, de Young (1982) reports that over 57% of the 45 women in her study injured themselves as children, between ages 9-12, beginning soon after the initial incest event. de Young also reports that self-injuries were often kept secret, since disclosure of the incest or the self-injury might disrupt the delicate balance of the family. This suggests the beginning of a process of repressing the fact of abuse, for the sake of survival. The consequences of abuse, however, are not eliminated by repressing direct knowledge of the experience: "The inability to remember the trauma, to articulate it, creates the need to articulate it in 'the repetition compulsion'" (Miller, 1984, p.162). Miller adds that self-destructive enactments take on the function of concealment (p.315) and organize the present suffering (self-injury) in accordance with the pattern of the past (the victimizing event). "As a result, the child or adolescent has no choice but to remain silent until the symptoms she later developed as an adult provided her with a substitute language in which she was able, and compelled, to tell the truth" (Miller, 1984, p.321-22).

DEVELOPING A THERAPEUTIC PERSPECTIVE

The author's professional experience with adults who self-injure began within an agency with a specialized, intensive therapy program for adult women who were victim-survivors of childhood incest and family abuse. This program is described by Hildebrand (1982), Myers (1980), and Wise (1985). The women in this program either already identified themselves as having been sexually abused in childhood, or identified themselves as having problems/

symptoms known to be related to childhood abuse. The program included educational components on shame and on self-destructive behaviors. Clients were asked to identify the messages of their self-destructive patterns, asking questions about how these self-injuries began, and how they might relate to the pain, secrecy, betrayal, or helplessness they experienced when abused. In this agency, therapists worked with commitment to go beyond the identification of self-injury as a symptom of childhood abuse, to hearing and believing the painful and shame-filled experiences of abuse that underly the self-injury. Most clients responded positively to receiving respect from therapists for their efforts to survive, rather than additional shaming for behaviors they already knew created more violation and shame. In this context, clients could begin to unravel and understand the sources and meaning of their patterns of self-injury which had long been a confounding source of shame in their lives. Clients were offered therapeutic opportunities in which they could learn new and non-shame-based survival skills.

As the author's understanding from hearing the life-stories of clients continued, and as their patterns of self-injury began to change toward non-shame-based abilities to claim their own truths about their lives and to develop healthy patterns regarding control and release, the author's perspective about the dynamic survival functions of self-injury broadened to include other psychiatrically-labeled symptoms as survival patterns. These symptoms are seen as the outer signals of the victim's inner, often unconscious determination to survive and to preserve her/his true experiences in the face of denial. Table 1 presents some of the patterns identified through the author's work with clients who self-injure, and the dynamic functional aspects of these survival-directed behaviors.

The relationships shown in Table 1 between injurious behaviors and patterns of functional survival responses are not intended to be either all-inclusive or mutually-exclusive categories. The author's experience indicates that in each person's life, the ways that self-injury becomes a survival response to abusive life situations is individually unique. The following list describes some of the factors in the development of survival response messages. These ideas have come directly from clients' life-stories and their unfolding therapeutic work. Note that the patterns are posed as possible paths of development, not as definitive ones, based on the author's support of the

TABLE 1. Functional Aspects of Survival-Directed Behaviors

Defensive or Injurious Behaviors	Survival Responses or Strategies
Behaviors that protect from pain and/or express pain	Function or meaning in the survival process
Minimizing; denial; numbness; separation from body.	Mental or sensory blocking of awareness of the pain, betrayal, or neglect of needs.
Chemical use/abuse; eating disorders.	Discovery of ways to alter feelings physiologically that mask or disguise pain.
Hospitalizations; incorrigibility; illegal activity; accidents; running away.	Desperate attempts to speak out about hidden pain, fear. Also actions that provide a means of being removed from an abusive situation.
Bodily injuries such as cutting, burning, bruising.	a) Validation of emotional (invisible) pain; b) Release from feeling crazy or bad (related to intense family denial system); c) A visible action that keeps alive a bodily memory path to the original abuse.
Promiscuity; prostitution.	Continuation of patterns learned through abusive sexualization by others.
Caretaking; role-reversals; isolation/clinging; helplessness.	Continuation of patterns through which interpersonal contact was possible in the family.
Self-blame.	A belief that is an attempt to have a degree of power or control. Maintains a base for ego development.

client's right to discover and name her/his own survival patterns for her/himself. These individual messages are the links to the truth of her/his experiences of abuse (see also Table 2).

1. When internal experiences of pain seem unreal and afterward incomprehensible, self-injury may give more reality to the subjective pain.
2. Self-injury may be a way of reenacting (actually or symbolically) against herself what was done abusively to her. (The most powerful statement of this pattern is in Miller's work regarding repetition compulsion [1984].)

3. Accumulative denial (by family, or subsequent internalized denial by the survivor) may intensify the subjective feeling of craziness or unreality. Self-injury may restore a sense of realness to the person—a way to make oneself more real in a world that gets progressively distorted from reality. (This is similar to de Young's [1982] description of ego-reintegration as one of the functions of self-injury.)
4. Bodily and/or emotional numbing may periodically culminate in self-injury that restores a direct sensory experience of one's ability to feel, to know one's aliveness.
5. The victim-survivor often believes she is bad. Self-punishment based on this belief about her badness, may be expressed in self-injury whenever particular needs, feelings or thoughts are experienced.
6. Self-injury may be an attempt to alleviate or diffuse immediate emotional pain and to keep painful memories suppressed. This pattern may continue until a time in her life that offers enough safety and support for her to be able to remember the past more directly. Sometimes patterns of this sort, such as chemical dependency, may need to be specifically treated before the client will regain access to the underlying pain/abuse.
7. Self-injury can originate or become a memory link to childhood abusive experiences, either to the experience as a whole, or to specific injuries during the abuse.
8. Self-injury may be an act of establishing a sense of control over the pain she feels. This may relate to feelings of helplessness she experienced during the victimization.
9. Self-injury may be a way to physically get away or be removed from a currently dangerous or crazy situation when no other form of protection seems available.

SUMMARY OF PERSPECTIVE

For the victim-survivor of childhood abuse, defensive or self-injurious behaviors originated as those individuals' patterns of response to real, environmental and family dangers. Children (or adults) do not just suddenly become self-injurious. They have already tried other ways of getting help: Ways to have their needs acknowledged and met safely; Ways to protect themselves from

TABLE 2

Additional Examples Description of self-injury	Person's understanding of its survival function
1. Cutting upper thighs, where Dad masturbated against her when she was 5 years old.	Cutting kept it real--a scar-- it really happened. I was hurt here.
2. Hitting knee with hammer to make bruises and swelling.	It made my pain visible, something to then soothe and care for. No one saw my pain about being abused.
3. Periodic drinking in large amounts during high school and college.	I would drink when I was out socially. I had to drink a lot to keep from feeling so much shame, or I wouldn't be able to be around anyone. Other kids drank too, so I wasn't so different. I dreaded that they might find out that my father had been sexual with me.
4. Hitting head with a rock.	It released the "awfulness" feeling. The inner shame gets too overwhelming from time to time. Afterward I can cry and feel my emotional pain.
5. Repeated cutting of legs and arms.	Sometimes for relief, sometimes because I deserve to be hurt or punished for being bad. Something inside feels like too much for me to know about.
6. Daily drinking of alcohol during high school, continuing pattern until age 30.	Although I only drank a little each day, it helped me not to be so aware of the tension in my family. I'd feel better, even though the abuse and the tension around it continued. Both my parents knew I was drinking and acted like it was okay. They drank too.
7. Repeated scratching of head sores.	I just thought it was a bad habit. But when my memories came back about being abused at age 6, I remembered saying inside, "I'll do this so that I can remember that this really happened."
8. Smoking marijuana	Until I quit using drugs, I didn't remember being sexually abused. Looking back, I know that anytime I felt this one feeling, sort of restless and scared, I would smoke dope. When I stopped, it was that same feeling that led to my memories. I needed a lot of support when those feelings would come.
9. Injury to genitals during masturbation.	When the chaos and family tension would build up, my father would force me to have intercourse. It

TABLE 2 (continued)

Additional Examples Description of self-injury	Person's understanding of its survival function
	was painful, but it seemed to relieve the family tension. Things would settle down then. Pain to my genitals still helps me feel relief from confusion and stress.
10. Bursts of rage, physically pounding walls, bruising arms and hands.	Anytime feelings of neediness come into awareness, I feel rage and self-hate. I hated myself for needing my father's care. If I hadn't needed his attention and care, he couldn't have abused me.
11. Biting inside of cheeks.	I believed if I told about being abused, I would be kicked out of the family. I remember now that anytime I wanted to tell, I would bite the inside of my cheeks. I just thought it was a nervous habit until I was able to tell about the abuse; then it became a signal that I wanted to speak out about my life.

violation of body and self; Ways to find validation for feelings, thoughts, experiences, rather than denial. As Kaufman states in his book, *Shame: The Power of Caring* (1980), "If self-injurious behaviors weren't needed for survival, no one would develop them." A child in an abusive family develops protective "symptomatology" to protect her/his emotional integrity and personal reality in the face of abuse, family denial of abuse, the shame-bound cycles in the family. The shame cycle and the messages from the abuse become internalized in the victim-survivor. Self-injury, although destructive, is actually a signal of inner health and survival, a signal of "sane" reactions to incomprehensible abuse, a signal that the person is insisting on the reality of the pain/betrayal/loss that she/he has experienced.

Self-injury may continue from childhood into adulthood, or may reappear in an adult's life when memories of the abuse are triggered. Self-injury patterns continue to carry the coded truth of buried pain, fear, betrayal and loss, and keep alive the reality of their abusive experiences. Although self-injury is in varying degrees harmful to survivors of abuse, these patterns will likely continue, and at times intensify, until the realness of the childhood abuse and of their feelings about the abuse are known, expressed, heard, and believed.

SUGGESTIONS FOR THERAPY

The practical therapeutic first step to take with clients who self-injure is to bring self-injury out into the open. This may mean verbally acknowledging that you see the physical scars and are willing to hear about the experiences of self-injury and the experiences of abuse to which the self-injury may be related. This opening can be structured naturally and intentionally into individual or group therapy settings. Bringing self-injury out where it can be talked about offers clients the opportunities (1) to own their experiences of self-injury; (2) in group settings, to hear others own their self-injuries; (3) to loosen the shame around self-injury; (4) to receive understanding and support; (5) to lessen isolation. Critical in this process is the client's need and right to be heard and respected, not labeled or explained.

In working with clients who self-injure, the author believes that clients feel most respected by a therapist when they themselves are encouraged to identify how their self-injury might be related to the pain of being hurt in the past. It becomes the therapist's responsibility then, to be sensitively aware of issues about self-injury and to introduce the idea of self-injury as survival. In facilitating a client's exploration of self-injury patterns (individually or in group), the therapist might ask about any memories of self-injury during childhood. Because memories of abuse are often buried, questions about first remembered self-injuries, when they happened, what was happening in the family at the time, etc., may help the client begin to unravel the personal truth that the self-injury represents. Sometimes questions about the feelings/thoughts that come before and after self-injury can help the client discover the survival pattern of the injuring, even without a specific abuse memory connected to it. Questions about what others' responses to self-injury can be helpful in hearing the client's pain around not having been seen and heard. Introducing the question, "How did/does your self-injury help you survive, emotionally or physically?" not only opens a non-shaming path for growth, but also furthers the client's process of uncovering and speaking out about abuse/betrayal and shame, to which the self-injury has been linked. This provides a foundation for recovery and healing.

THERAPEUTIC RESPONSES TO SELF-INJURY

The remainder of this article will focus on some of the interactional messages that occur between client and therapist, including helpful and unhelpful attitudes and actions from therapists in response to clients' self-injury.

Three UNHELPFUL ways to respond to self-injury are:

1. If the therapist responds with disgust or with judgment to present or past self-injury, the client often receives the message that the therapist cannot handle hearing about the shame, the horror, and the pain of the self-injury experiences or the original abusive experiences. The message may also be a reconfirmation of family messages that she/he is disgusting and unworthy of attention or care.

2. If the therapist views self-injury as a manipulation by the client for attention, the therapist may reenact the family's response to the client's pain, the family adults' refusal to see the reality of her/his pain. Viewing self-injury as manipulation focuses on the effects of the client's behavior on the therapist, rather than focusing on the core significance/meaning of this behavior for the client. The other person's reality is more important, at the expense of the client's buried pain being unheard.

3. Helping a client "manage" or "reduce" self-injury may be necessary, but as the prime strategy for healing, it may bury the voice that carries the truth of her/his pain. What a client needs at times of self-injury are presence, understanding, care and respect. Incidents of self-injury are not best met by discipline, primarily because self-injury is not about being bad or difficult. Even life-endangering self-injury involves aspects of self-preservation, taken in desperate attempts to manage deeper personal pain.

Ten HELPFUL ways to respond to self-injury are:

1. The single most important message is "I believe that *your pain is real.*" Affirm the presence of the pain behind the self-injury.

2. Convey your respect. "I respect your efforts to survive, even though self-injury is involved. Self-injury carries some strategy you

have created to help you survive. It may be time, now, to begin developing new ways to live through your pain without hurting yourself, but I am glad you survived. You did it the best way available to you at the time.'' It is crucial that the client's survival strategy thus far be affirmed and valued.

3. Acknowledge that because self-injury has had physical and/or emotional survival value, the client may hold onto it tightly, and may feel terrified of living without this pattern.

4. When self-injury begins in adulthood or resurfaces in adulthood, this may indicate that memories are rising to awareness, or that the client is closer to experiencing feelings about past abuse. Asking about times she/he may have self-injured as a child may open a door for memories.

5. When memories of and feelings about abusive experiences arise and are brought out of silence, the client may experience an increase in self-injury, or an increased urgency to self-injure. Your belief that this is not a sign of worsening condition, but rather an indication that the client is ready to move closer to feelings and memories, may help the client experience these without devastating degrees of shame, and may decrease the likelihood of self-injury.

6. However frightening, upsetting, painful, annoying the therapist finds a particular self-injury to be, it is most important to affirm the belief that the client's pain is real and that you see it and can be with her/him to help. Remember not to let your own reactions to the self-injury take precedence over what the self-injury means for the client.

7. Helping the client move toward pain and remembered abuse involves communicating confidence that the client has already survived the original traumas, and that you are willing to join in her/his journey to reapproach those experiences. New patterns for survival will need to begin developing before the client can let go of the self-injury pattern.

8. Therapy will likely include times when anxiety, fear, pain and shame intensify. These may be times when urgency to self-injure increases. If the client self-injures, remember to respond with concern for the injury per se, *and* more importantly, with care about what the client is experiencing (pain, fear, shame, etc.).

9. When relationships (with therapist, with group members) have

developed, the client may be ready to move toward a time-limited decision to not act on her/his pain with self-injury, and to attempt new options personally and interpersonally for support and care around feelings and experiences.

10. As self-injury patterns begin to change for the client, she/he will experience and recognize feelings and needs that were denied, betrayed or neglected in childhood. The client may have had little or no appropriate learning in how to live with these feelings and needs. The client may literally not know what it is that she/he is feeling or wanting, and will need opportunities to learn. This is a genuine need for developmental discovery and learning through modeling, instruction, experimentation, identification, practice, rebellion, etc. The most likely places for this learning to occur will be along people the client trusts, i.e., the therapist, supportive group members or friends, and in programs that offer experiential and didactic learning.

LIFESTORY EXAMPLES

The first lifestory example offers a view of how self-injury and its paradoxical survival functions unfold during the remembering and healing process for one person who is a victim-survivor of childhood sexual abuse and neglect. Following the lifestory, the author presents additional brief examples of self-injury and the survival functions that various individuals have identified. It is important to remember that the survival messages and functions that become coded into patterns of self-injury are very individual in nature. Self-injuries that are similar in outward appearance, even in a single person's life, may have different functional paths. As a person is heard and believed about being abused, and as she/he is not shamed for the very behaviors that furthered survival, her/his story will unfold with its own unique messages.

A Lifestory

When Martha (age 23) began therapy in an incest therapy program, she had been sober for two years, and was active in AA and Alanon groups.[1] She had begun drinking and using other drugs at the age of 14, and remembered being sexual with boyfriends in order to stay away from home where her oldest brother (age 26, when she was 14) would force her to be sexual with him. This pattern of escape continued until she left home (age 18) to live with her boyfriend. Martha entered a chemical dependency treatment program (age 20), married, and has maintained her sobriety since she became pregnant (age 21). She entered the incest program because she had begun to fear that her husband or brother would sexually abuse her two year old daughter. She had never talked about the abuse she had experienced, and had seen a television program that advised that help was available.

It was extremely hard for Martha to verbalize what her brother had done to her and made her do with him. She said she felt horribly dirty and ashamed. She believed that if she told, no one would like her or be friends with her. She was amazed that the women in her therapy group believed her, and did not believe the abuse was her fault. Martha began to regain earlier childhood memories: running away from home at age 11 and being brought back by her brother. She began to recognize how absent her parents were and how often she was left "in her brother's care." After sharing childhood pictures with the group, she began to recognize her vulnerability as a child. She learned that shame (the feeling of "being inherently bad") results from how one is treated as a child ("If I weren't bad, why would they hurt me?"). She was increasingly able to verbalize the specifics of the abuse.

After six months in the therapy program, Martha began to have nightmares. When she woke from them, she did not remember the content, but she reported feeling about seven years old, and that the soles of her feet hurt. She then told her therapist that sometimes when she felt the shame (which she could now identify as a feeling, not as a fact of her badness) building up inside, she would cut the soles of her feet with a razor or broken glass. Usually small cuts, but deep enough to hurt when she walked. Martha said that she felt relief after the cutting, but that she also felt considerable shame about doing it. The therapist reminded her of the possible connection between self-injury and hidden pain, and asked if there might be some way that cutting her feet had helped her survive abusive situations either now or in the past. At this point, Martha remembered a picture of herself at age seven in which both her feet were bandaged. She remembered running on very sharp rocks in a vacant lot until her feet bled, and being carried home by her brother.

Martha's time of remembering continued for several weeks, as layer by layer, she recovered her lifestory. She remembered being sexually touched by her brother as early as age five, and remembered running away from home at age seven after the first time this brother penetrated her. She remembered her mother telling her that if she tried to run away again, she would let her go so far that her feet would hurt too much to be able to walk back home. It was shortly after this warning that Martha recalls running on the rocks and injuring her feet. She remembered thinking that she had to do this to keep herself from running away again, because she had nowhere to go and she would not be able to get back. By the time she was 11-14 and could get away with boyfriends and drinking, she had forgotten cutting her feet on the rocks. She began to connect her current foot-cutting and the feeling of wanting to cut, with current times when she felt shamed and unwanted, and with wanting to get away from anything she felt trapped in. She was gradually able to stop cutting, and to use the feeling of wanting to cut, or the feeling of pain in her feet, as signals[2] about her feelings and needs. She began taking non-injurious actions in response to her feelings and needs.

Martha was in the therapy program for 14 months. During this time of uncovering memories, learning about shame, unraveling the survival patterns of her self-injury, Martha's life began to show marked changes. Her outlook on life became more open and positive. She began to be hopeful for her own life, and for her daughter's life. She made numerous relationship changes, bringing people into her life who were both caring and respectful.

In closing, the author acknowledges placing a primary emphasis on the therapist's willingness to openly learn from the client's behavior and life, and on the importance of the therapist's perspectives and attitudes toward clients who self-injure. Through attitudes, therapists can offer a non-shaming relationship and environment in which the client can feel safe enough and respected enough to begin claiming her/his own truth. How the therapist accompanies the client in her/his journey, begins in attitude and spirit, and then develops in form and technique.

NOTES

1. For acceptance into this incest therapy program, chemically dependent clients were required to be stable in their sobriety, and to maintain their participation in supportive groups. The therapeutic focus on recovering memories and validating feelings is central to the healing process, and precludes any use of substances that would take clients further away from feelings. Although sobriety followed by incest therapy is a preferred order of treatment, there are many times that validation of a person's pain and grief about having been abused is a crucial component that anchors her/his chemical dependency recovery program.

2. This awareness is a subjective dimension of the paradoxical crossroads between being victim and survivor. Shame seems to be the carrier: if you get lost in the feelings of being bad, worthless, dirty, awful, then wanting to self-injure just adds to your shame. Unraveling how you internalized shame, recognizing that shame is a result of how you were treated and what you were taught to believe, you can then begin to learn new messages about yourself, such as "I am worth protecting, even though I was not protected from abuse, and even though I have tried to protect myself in the past using ways that hurt me." You can then learn new ways to protect yourself, to connect to new people who are supportive and respectful, and to learn new ways to treat yourself that are respect/care-based rather than shame-based.

REFERENCES

Bernard, C. (1983). Alcoholism and incest; improving diagnostic comprehensiveness. *International Journal of Family Therapy*, 5, 2, 136-143.

Brown, A. (1986). Child Sexual Abuse and Incest: Definition and Behavioral Indicators. Workshop materials-International Conference on Multiple Personality/Dissociative States.

Charmoli, M. (1986). *Incest in relation to sexual problems, abusive relationships and sexual orientation*. Unpublished dissertation, University of Minnesota.

de Young, M. (1982). Self-injurious behavior in incest victims: A research note. *Child Welfare, 61*, 577-584.

Fossum, M.A. & Mason, M.J. (1986). *Facing shame. Families in recovery*. New York: W.W. Norton & Co.

Gelinas, D.J. (1983). The persisting negative effects of incest. *Psychiatry, 46*, 312-322.

Hildegrand, E. (1982). Treatment of adult incest survivors. Available from author: Marstrandsgade 7, 2100 Copenhagen o, Denmark.

Horowitz, M.J. (1976). *Stress response syndromes*. Jason Aronson.

Kaufman, G. (1980). *Shame: The power of caring.* Cambridge, MA: Shenkman Publishing Company, Inc.

Lindberg, F.H., & Distad, L.J. (1985). Survival responses to incest: Adolescents in crisis. *Child Abuse and Neglect, 9,* 521-526.

Miller, A. (1983). *For your own good. Hidden cruelty in child rearing and the roots of violence.* NY: Farrar, Straus, Giroux.

Miller, A. (1984). *Thou shalt not be aware: Society's betrayal of the child.* NY: Farrar, Straus, Giroux.

Myers, B. (1980). Incest. If you think the word is ugly, take a look at its effects. In K. MacFarlane, B. Jones, & L. Jenstrom (Eds.), *Sexual abuse of children: Selected readings.* Washington, DC: National Center on Child Abuse & Neglect, Office of Human Development Services, U.S. Dept. of Health and Human Services.

Simpson, C.A. (1981). *An exploratory study of self-mutilation.* Unpublished dissertation, University of Kansas.

Summit, R. (1984). The child sexual abuse accommodation syndrome. *Journal of Child Abuse and Neglect.*

Wise, M.L. (1985). Incest victim-survivor paradox: therapeutic strategies and issues. Program #124, Annual Convention, American Assoc. for Counseling and Development. (Audio cassette, AVW AudioVisual, 2254 Valdina St., Suite 100, Dallas, TX 79207.)

Victims as Victimizers:
Therapeutic and Professional
Boundary Issues

Lindsay A. Nielsen, MSW, CCDP

SUMMARY. This paper is devoted to the intricate issues that confront the Substance Abuse Therapist working with the victim/victimizer. What will hopefully become clear is that what once used to be polarized into two distinct diagnostic categories, victim and perpetrator, is now being recognized as an ongoing intra-personal interplay. When a person is victimized over the course of time, that person learns and internalizes the entire process of victimization, much as the person who grows up in an alcoholic home learns the entire process of addiction. This intra-personal dynamic has behavioral, cognitive and affective components that manifest inter-personally, or relationally. In effect, this means that clients will "act-out" their boundary issues within their relationships, including the relationship with the therapist in overt and covert ways. Boundaries evolve interpersonally and are healed interpersonally. The role of the therapist is to provide the milieu for that healing. This can only occur if the therapist him/herself has ethical boundaries. Some of the issues explored in the paper are: dual role of the therapist, resolution of victim/victimizer issues, myths, accountability in treatment, transference/countertransference, group issues and professional self-care.

INTRODUCTION

Just as a thermostat regulates heat, so do boundaries regulate closeness and distance in a relationship. Boundaries regulate physical touch, sexual touch, emotional connectedness, the kind and

Lindsey A. Nielsen is in private practice in Minneapolis, MN.

amount of information that is shared, and all other behaviors that occur between people. Thus, victimization of any type can be described as a process of boundary violation (Evans, 1987).

Individual and family boundary patterns are altered by chemical abuse and addiction (Coleman, Colgan, 1986). Growing up in a family system that has the combination of abuse and addiction will hinder the natural development of a healthy boundary structure. Boundaries, like everything else in a family such as this, are inconsistant and often illogical. A child will not learn appropriate boundary functioning. S/he will mimic what s/he experiences. This renders a child unable to distinguish appropriate relationships. Thus, as clients from either alcoholic or abusive family systems know little about what constitutes boundary-appropriate behavior, especially in an asymetrical relationship, they are particularly vulnerable to boundary-violating behavior, and thus to the harmful effects of *professional boundary violations* (Nielsen, Peterson, Shapiro, Thompson, 1986; Colman, Colgan, 1986).

Maintaining appropriate professional boundaries is obviously a fundamental requirement of any counseling or therapy. Appropriate boundaries are significant as an entity however, when related to the healing of victimization, as the process of victimization is characterized by layer upon layer of boundary violation. The violations usually occur first and most significantly in the parent/child relationship which, like the therapeutic relationship, is asymetrical in power. Constant and critical attention to therapeutic boundaries is thus mandated, in order to allow for a corrective experience.

Boundary restructuring is a key component in the healing process from both addiction and abuse. It is mandatory for the clinician treating victims/victimizers to behave in as ethical and boundary-appropriate a manner as possible. For the therapeutic relationship to be healing, a clear commitment to ethical behavior is required by the therapist.

There are specific ethical concerns in relation to treating those engaged in, or emerging from an abusive system. The population is especially vulnerable, the transference and countertransference issues are particularly powerful, and the therapist is by necessity working with the dual role of assisting with the healing of the victim while also working to prevent the continuation of the cycle of abuse.

Some of these ethical issues prescribe a clear course of therapeutic response, as society has already set limits on certain kinds of behavior. For example, if a client is assaulting his/her children, and the therapist knows of this behavior, there is little question as to at least one of the necessary courses of action, since therapists are bound by law to report the abuse immediately. The professional boundary issues left to consideration are then related to the necessary dual role of being the therapist and in some respects also being the enforcement officer.

Other professional boundary dilemmas are less clear in terms of a prescribed course of treatment. Therapists are often faced with the knowledge that there are no laws which will guide their therapeutic response when the abuse is less overt. Child protection requires certain criteria to be met in order to become involved. The abuse which is present in a family system will often not fall within these guidelines, but can be as therapeutically harmful as more overt abuse. An example of this is a father screaming at his seventeen-year-old daughter that she is a whore and a slut, slaps her, but doesn't leave any bruises. The effects to the seventeen-year-old may be just as destructive as if he had left bruises, but the father will not become involved with the legal system and is in the position to be able to decline treatment for himself and for his daughter.

Another boundary dilemma for clinicians in relation to abuse includes the dual focus which is necessary for effective treatment of clients. Helping clients work with both their victim and their victimizer issues arising from an abusive upbringing can be difficult.

When victimization was a new area of study, ethical issues appeared to be less complex. There were the victims (who "we" were working with) and there was a separate group who were the victimizers. It is now understood that these two groups are often one and the same. While it was clear that most victimizers had been victimized, it was not as clear that the victims we were working with, also had, and were continuing, to victimize others. This victimization wasn't always extreme or overt. Often the clients were verbally attacking those closest to them, even if they weren't physically hurting them. The harmful effects to the client's relationships were still significant.

Another myth active at one time in both the fields of victimology and the field of Substance Abuse was that all victimizers were male. Women were the victims, men were the perpetrators, except in cases of physical or verbal abuse of children. While it was recognized that women victimized their children physically, it was not recognized that they also victimized them sexually. Over time it has become clear that both men and women can be victimizers, but that they simply act-out their victimization differently.

Many types of abuse are theorized to be "about" rage, and the power to act on that rage. As women do not have the same power as do men, in terms of physical strength, resources, and systemic support (Kenworthy, Koufacos, & Sherman, 1976), they tend to act-out against those with less power, such as their children or in the case of self-perpetration, themselves. When living in an abusive system, whether this be familial or societal, everyone in the system learns to cope abusively. The abuse may be subtle or may be overt. All people in an abusive system carry on the rules, roles and myths which enable victimization. Abuse dynamics, whether acted-out overtly or covertly get passed onto the next generation.

One aspect then of professional boundaries and ethics that is important to consider is the effect of the clinician's own myths and beliefs about abuse, and about the process of abuse on their work with clients. Myths present in society about victimization include: "Victims are to blame," "Victims wouldn't have been victimized if they had been sober" (thus sobriety will keep someone safe), "Women want to be raped," "If you put yourself in a dangerous situation, you deserve what you get," "Men are never victims," "Women are never perpetrators," "Violent people can't stop themselves from being violent," "If the person has insight or remorse about the abuse, they will stop being abusive," "The abuse will stop when the abuser gets sober," "It's o.k. to hit children as long as you don't leave any marks or cause any 'permanent' damage."

We have all been socialized with these myths, to one degree or another. An exersize that is helpful for both therapists and clients to do is to write down all of the myths they can think of and then discuss any parts or aspects of them that are still believed, either intellectually or emotionally.

Myths and stereotypes affect the therapist's work if the therapist is not aware of them. For example, if the clinician is afraid to address perpetration issues, or is blind to them, with either men or women, s/he will be unable to effectively treat abuse.

There are special issues for professionals when working with the combination of chemical dependency and abuse. While the correlation between abuse and chemical use has been widely recognized, litle research has been done regarding effective treatment strategies. Myths widely held in the field of Chemical Dependency expound the idea that once a violent person maintains sobriety, the person will discontinue violent behavior. Clinicians have not found this to be true. Additionally, some people are able to control overt violent behaviors, but their thinking pattern (beliefs) remains unchanged. Another area of misunderstanding includes blaming a person's victimization on their chemical use. Describing a woman's rape as a consequence of her chemical use is blaming her for another person's criminal behavior. This is ethically wrong and will cause further trauma.

When it was recognized that although often combined, abuse and chemical dependency each were problems that required different attention, clients were often treated in separate programs. There is currently a push to attempt a combined-treatment approach, which is different than attempting to deal with abuse as a by-product of addiction.

BOUNDARIES AND BOUNDARY VIOLATIONS

Boundary setting is both an individual and a relational process. Each individual has a boundary structure, as does each relationship. Individual boundaries develop from both individual and relational processes. Boundaries are both taught and maintained through the rules or norms of a relationship. The rules of relational boundaries are formed with the understanding of the nature of the relationship. In other words, the jobs performed by a relationship define it's boundaries.

Abuse is the violation of both personal and relational boundaries and is best viewed on a continuum (Schaefer, Evans, 1986; Nielsen, 1984). These violations can be overt, and include inappropriate sexual or physical connections such as incest and violence, or can be covert and include emotional and developmental neglect. These actions can also be active or passive. Failing to care for a child by nurturing them is for example, a passive action, but one that affects the child as much as does active abuse.

Thus if the therapeutic relationship is to be reparative, it must allow for appropriate dependence and independence, as is needed by the client. Keeping the relational boundaries open enough, in order to model to the client that the world holds safety outside the therapeutic relationship, is crucial to allow for the clients successful exit from therapy. Referring a client to workshops, or groups run by other therapists, to self-help groups, or having a consulting therapist come into a session when the therapist feels "stuck" are all ways to "open up" the therapeutic boundaries. Clients often feel "lucky" to have found one person they feel they can trust. For many clients, the therapist is the first person they have ever felt this kind of trust with. For true healing to occur, the client needs to become clear about who in their life has not been trustworthy rather than to continue projecting onto the entire population. It is part of the therapist's job to not remain perfect and idealized, and to assure the client verbally and behaviorally that there are many more trustworthy people "out there."

CONSEQUENCES OF VICTIMIZATION

Boundary violations always prompt an emotional response. People tend to respond with varying levels of grief, shame, anger and guilt. A break in the relational bond occurs. Even one incident of significant violation can cause a major shift in the child's boundary functioning. The world can move from a safe place to a dangerous one within minutes.

Case Example

As a young child, Mary remembers feeling happy and secure. When, at age seven, Mary was asked by her father, who had come home drunk, to set the table, she refused. Mary's father took her outside, and whipped her. During the whipping, Mary screamed for him to stop and for her mother to help her. She remembers seeing her mother and her older siblings all huddled together nearby, but no one came to help her. Mary describes that her relationship with her father from that day forward turned distant, and that she never again trusted her mother or siblings to take care of her. The relational bonds were never reconnected, and to Mary the world became a frightening place. Mary later made the statement, "Never again did I feel safe, or trust that someone close to me was predictable."

It is common for people to try to make sense of boundary violations by applying information until the pieces "fit" as a way to explain the emotional stress they are experiencing. In an abuse system, the information that one supplies is skewed to fit an abusive system. For example, Johnny makes sense of his mom hitting him by saying to himself that which echos what he has learned, that indeed the abuse was his fault, and that it is an appropriate response to him, or to his behavior. Therefore Johnny learns to cope with those same types of behaviors in others by being abusive.

When a person is violated there are two processes taking place. The first process involves the immediate consequences of the violation, and the second process is related to the learning of abusive dynamics and strategies within the system.

The immediate consequences may be physical, as well as emotional. The physical consequences can be permanent, depending on the type of abuse experienced. Early sexual abuse, battering, or rape are all forms of victimization which often leave permanent physical scars. The immediate emotional consequences are present regardless of the type of abuse. Shame, anger, betrayal, grief, and dissociation are all comonly experienced with boundary violations (Peterson, 1986). These are also typical emotional responses clients have when abused by a therapist or counselor (Schoener, 1984; Nielsen et al., 1986; Coleman & Schaefer, 1986).

The secondary process that is occuring is a learning process. This process often has a more permanent effect than do those immediate consequences of the actual overt abuse. These consequences include the developmental effects to the individual's personality and relational structures, an important component of which is the learning of inadequate boundaries.

The violated child learns to view boundary violations as the norm. S/he then incorporates this system into her/his psyche, and into their relational rules, values, and world view: How people can and should be treated, what behavior is acceptable, rules around privacy or lack therof, and of who is in charge of one's own and other's boundary decisions. If your physical boundaries are not respected, you will not learn to respect others', and furthermore, you will not internalize respect as a value. Respect in this context will be like a foreign word. You can hear it, and possibly understand it intellectually, but you won't be able to really understand its meaning, or apply it to your own behavior.

Following is a partial set of rules individuals from abusive family systems have brought with them into the clinical setting.

- If I feel bad, it's someone else's fault.
- If someone is abusive to me, it's my fault.
- If I can control other people well enough, they won't hurt me.
- If I understand, I shouldn't have feelings.
- Touch is not safe.
- If I have feelings, I will go crazy or even die.
- If I tell the family secrets people will go away, or I will lose my family, or I will die.
- If someone shows me care, they must have an ulterior motive.
- Authority figures can't be trusted, so I must control them, charm them, caretake them or intimidate them into giving me what I need.
- Being used is the same as being loved.
- Not being abused is the same as being loved.
- In order to receive attention or be loved, I need to be special, especially good or especially bad.
- It's o.k. to touch someone physically or sexually even if they don't say it's o.k., or want me to.
- When the conflict inside gets to be too painful or anxiety provoking, it's o.k. to strike out and attack.
- When someone makes you feel bad (i.e., shameful) it's acceptable to attack that person out of a feeling of rage.
- A person is either good or bad.

The function of the abusive family rules is to maintain the status quo and to legitimize abuse, invasion, and neglect. It takes the constant attention of the therapist to address the abusive rules when they are in operation. Additionally, it is required that the therapist conducts him/herself professionally in a way that is a continual contradiction to the rules.

In an abuse system one learns and incorporates all the different aspects of victimization, including perpetration. The learning process is believed to be responsible for the creation of future perpetrators and is a process learned by all members. The roles learned may be gender and age specific, but the process of abuse, if not treated, will persist. The ways in which individuals act-out the system varies, but there are usually some consistant components.

Perpetration against self and others, boundary inadequacy, a distorted sense of power and powerlessness, and a shame/rage-based identity structure are usual consequences of an abusive system. Each one of these constructs dictate a special attention paid to professional boundaries when working with victims and perpetrators.

Setting limits with the client, using words to describe a client's behavior such as abusive, offending, or mean, when these words fit, maintaining clear boundaries, reframing a client's sense of powerlessness into fear of action, or fear of consequences, and identifying shame and a model of coping with it, are all ways to routinely attend to these dynamics.

TRANSFERENCE ISSUES

Transference is a process which is inherent to therapy. The client experiences an ego-regressed state that allows the therapist to increase in power and energy and the client to decrease. In other words, the therapist gets "big" and the client gets "little" (Ellis, 1987).

Transference is defined by the psychiatric glossary of the Psychiatric Association (1975) as "the unconscious assignment to others of feelings and attitudes that were originally associated with important figures, parents, siblings, etc. The transference relationship follows patterns of its prototype."

Theoretically, in the context of the therapeutic relationship, the client behaves by the rules and norms familiar to them. As the therapist responds, the client, partially due to the special power of transference, incorporates a healing and corrective experience. This experience can only be corrective if the therapeutic response is an appropriate one. It is the client's job to reflect openly the rules and norms of an abusive upbringing. It is the therapist's job to place these behaviors and underlying beliefs in the framework of abuse and respond in a non-abusive, or non-neglectful fashion.

Failing to set limits with a client cannot be corrective because the therapist is then reinforcing the earlier experience of neglect.

COUNTERTRANSFERENCE

The issues of countertransference are particularly challenging when working with clients from an abusive system. These problems become even more difficult if the therapist also grew up in an abusive situation, as the client's work will periodically trigger the therapist's own family of origin issues.

One of the most difficult aspects of working with abused and abusive clients is that the client's abuse issues get acted-out with the therapist. The ways in which this occurs affects the therapist's countertransference struggles. For example, if a client who has required a great deal of energy and care implies or directly states that the therapist is not trustworthy, competent or ethical, the therapist is hard pressed to not get his/her feelings hurt. S/he may also feel angry and resentful with the client. Empathizing with the client about how the situation feels, but then also asking the client to distinguish between their trust issues and the trustworthiness of the therapist by asking if the therapist has lied to them, if the therapist has not fulfilled expectations, or if the therapist has failed to be accountable, are all ways to clarify that trust is about behavior, and is not about "magical," intangible principles. Addressing the manner in which the client chose to "deal with" their fear (by accusing the therapist of not being trustworthy) as a breach in the therapeutic relationship, while teaching the client a different way to talk about their lack of trust, is often effective. It is imperative that clients get feedback about the impact of their behavior on their relationships. Punishing the client by withdrawing from that client only serves to reinforce the abusive and neglectful dynamics that are already being acted-out. Assuredly, clients who have been abused or have been abusive will lack trust and, given the rules of the family system, will interpret that lack of trust as totally about them or totally about others. Therapeutically using this situation as a way to teach clients how to assess their feelings is an ethically responsible and respectful way to process trust issues in a significant relationship.

Working with victims/victimizers is often a very difficult process. It is not uncommon for the therapist to experience a deep sense of distress in relation to what one's clients have had done to them, and at what their clients have done to others. At times the therapeutic process feels hopeless and the therapist feels inadequate. Given the individual and relational dynamics present for the client, the therapist will be constantly monitoring and therapeutically responding to victim or victimizer behavior. Often, clients will attempt to "victimize" the therapist. Periodically the therapist will respond personally, rather than professionally. It is important for the therapist to curtail this, as the therapist is then more vulnerable to victimizing the client overtly, or covertly. The therapist will then become untrustworthy, and support and reinforce the abusive system.

Given the inherent vulnerability of the therapeutic relationship, supervision and case consultation is a necessary tool for on-going professional boundary maintenance.

STRUCTURAL ASPECTS AND THE PROCESS OF POLARIZATION

Given the characteristics of the client population, structural issues within the therapy are of great therapeutic value. The parameters of the therapeutic setting can allow, or fail to allow for a healing and corrective experience. Clients from abusive systems are usually ignorant of the appropriate roles and rules of an asymetrical relationship, have not experienced respectful treatment, expect neglect, expect dishonesty and betrayal, and often don't understand the concept of accountability.

Clients with boundary inadequacy will exhibit the issues in various ways. Asking the therapist personal questions, attempting to caretake the therapist, attempting to close the boundaries of the therapeutic relationship, or demanding special treatment can all be examples of role dysfunction. Clients disallowing any connection, or dependence on, the therapist is also a sign of role dysfunction. Consider the following scenario:

> A client, at the end of group, asked the therapist if the therapist had really felt what she said she felt in response to another client's work. The client whispered the question in a conspiratorial manner.

A number of significant things occured in this interaction. The client was attempting to make her relationship with the therapist special and secret, and she was attempting to triangulate with the therapist against the other client. She was also expressing her own lack of emotional response to the group member, and expressing her lack of trust in the therapist, by assuming the therapist would in the first place lie to the other client and then share that secret with her. The characteristics of the client's abusive upbringing were clearly operating. Addressing the issues, in group, from that framework was an effective change strategy.

The therapist has a responsibility to be accountable to the client just as the client has a responsibility to be accountable to the therapist. The therapist and the client, however, don't have the same job to do, so this process of accountability will appear differently. It is not in the best interest of the client to be allowed to behave irresponsibly or disrespectfully in the therapeutic relationship, regardless of the reasons for the behavior. Nor is it good for a client to be allowed to be disrespectful, neglectful or abusive to group members, whether this is manifested overtly or covertly. A client failing to show up for appointments, consistantly being late, not keeping the therapeutic financial contract, and not attending to homework or other commitments are all ways clients exhibit a lack of accountability.

Anytime a person's identity has been developed within the structure of an abusive system, it is probable that the person will develop an identity in accordance with the roles of both victim and victimizer. Many people become "stuck" in these roles, even when not confined to an abusive system. This life stance is one of powerlessness, bitterness, co-dependence, and blaming.

Present is the belief that the world has been unfair and will continue to be unfair. While this is a true statement, the belief is used to justify an inappropriate self-or-otherwise destructive response. Addiction, perpetration, depression, and rage are viewed from a framework of powerlessness. Using one's history as a justification for continuing to be self-or-other destructive is as much about the inherent powerlessness of the victim stance as it is about the powerlessness of addiction.

One of the problems with this stance is that a polarization occurs. In clients who are in denial of the abuse or the ramifications of the abuse, the parents often are idealized. As they progress through therapy, come to understand the abuse, and reclaim feelings, parents are then polarized negatively. Both polarizations serve to keep the individual developmentally "stuck."

A paradoxical aspect of this, however, is that most victims feel totally to blame and are hesitant to (overtly) blame anyone else. The process renders the client unable to see both parts of themselves and others. To see only the part of their parents' behavior that was abusive or "bad" then allows them the right to hold their parents responsible. In an abusive system, the norms disallowing confrontation of the abuse are so powerful that to break them requires a polarization. The person believes that if s/he breaks the non-confrontational law, s/he will lose the family, and any hope of future connection anyway. Making the family totally bad is a defensive strategy to reduce the grief. The client is fighting to stop feeling like they are bad and responsible for the abuse and neglect they have experienced. The internal dissonance that abuse creates is extreme. "How can the same Dad who reads to me, and helps me fly a kite, also beat me, or sexually abuse me?" To resolve the dissonance, the child dissociates inside, and then also splits the parent into two, a good Dad, and a bad Dad. One minute Dad is idealized, and the child is bad, and the next minute Dad is bad and the child is good. Often when people are in therapy working with the abuse, they will have contact with their family, at which time the family behaves well. The client then feels "crazy." "I must have made all this up" is commonly heard after the holidays. When polarized, there is no room for both abusive and non-abusive reality.

This same process of polarization will occur with the therapist. At any given time, the therapist will be viewed as good or as bad.

The therapist must interrupt this process during both phases, using a non-shame-based philosophical framework. If the client continues to remain in a shame-based philosophical system, where one is either totally bad or one is completely good, they are destined to flip from one role to the other. It is thus the job of the therapist to present family of origin accountability from a non-polarized position and help the client express their feelings about both parts of the family. In this way the therapist is saying: "Yes, your parents did hurt you, they did make serious mistakes, and it's o.k. to remember the other times as well."

Accountability is a foreign concept in most abusive families. There is blame and there is irresponsibility but there is rarely a true system of accountability in place. Expecting accountability from a client may in fact trigger shame as the client will hear the feedback as blame, and as a statement that you think they are bad. As time and trust progress clients will begin to understand that you, the therapist, respect them and yourself enough to expect and offer accountability. Accountability in action would include times the therapist apologizes for being late, or says to the client, "I'm sorry I can't really pay enough attention to what you are saying when you speak so quietly." In these two examples the therapist has shown both emotional and behavioral accountability.

Giving clients a copy of a "Clients Bill of Rights," informing them of legal and ethical commitments, reporting any abuse that is necessary to report, being clear in financial and other business matters, and maintaining clear and consistent professional boundaries with the client are all ways to structure in accountability and offer reinforcement for the therapeutic work.

PERPETRATION ISSUES

As with all abuse dynamics, perpetration issues show up on a continuum with both overt and covert forms of perpetration present. These dynamics are seen both individually and relationally. Relationally, a client who verbally attacks a therapist for being late, or for disappointing them in some other way is exhibiting these perpetration issues overtly. A client who asks very personal questions or watches the therapist in a way that "feels" invasive is exhibiting perpetration in a more covert manner.

Perpetrator mentality includes all of the dynamics cited earlier, but there is a different process of rationalization that occurs. All information is distorted or skewed to legitimize perpetrator behaviors.

- The world has been unfair to me so therefore I have the right to retaliate in whatever ways I can.
- No one's ever given me anything so why should I give anyone else anything?
- Everyone else does it, so why shouldn't I?
- It feels good when someone else hurts for a change.
- It wouldn't bother me, so why should it bother you?
- I get to do what I want.
- It's not my fault.
- I don't have any feelings, so I can't empathize with yours.
- I have a right to take whatever I want.
- I like to "get over" on people.
- Revenge feels good.
- Everybody does it, so I'd be a fool not to.
- People are "screwed up" anyway, so hurting them is o.k.

This framework is obviously a dangerous one. Therapists must not assume that their clients think as they do or have the same feelings or values. It is essential to determine how a client justifies his/her behavior.

Clients also perpetrate against themselves with self-mutilation, starvation, binging and purging, chemical abuse, performing painful masturbation, verbally shaming themselves and with continued involvement in abusive relationships. While all of these behaviors can become addictive and thus become primary problems, they must also be viewed as a part of the larger issue of self-victimization.

Sometimes the way abuse is acted out can be more covert. Taking excessively hot showers or continually placing oneself in dangerous situations are examples of less overt self-destructive behaviors. The individual is continuing and reinforcing the abusive

dynamics learned in his/her family of origin. These behaviors conflict with the process of healing, similar to the effects of chemical
abuse.

It is often very difficult for therapists to conceptualize a dual
victim/perpetrator mentality in one person. The psychoanalytic concept of dissociation helps to clarify this concept. Dissociation is
best viewed on a continuum from healthy adult functioning to a full
blown Multiple Personality Disorder, the latter comprising fully
split off autonomous personalities embodying specific, rigid, behavioral, cognitive, and affective states with no knowledge of each
other.

As was mentioned earlier in this paper, when existing in an abusive system one internalizes the system, its rules, beliefs and emotional states. In an unintegrated personality, which characterizes
most of these clients, there is a lack of acceptance regarding fanta-
sies, impulses, needs, desires and thoughts. When repressed and
dissociated, they are given enormous power and will find expression, directly or indirectly. When these different states are expressed, by harming someone else or the person him/herself, the
individual may not seem to be themself. In reality, the person is
acting out a part of themself, one which isn't expressed in legiti-
mate ways. In treatment of victimization it is imperative to explore
the thinking patterns and gain understanding as to how two different
patterns, victim/perpetrator, can exist in one person.

It is the therapist's responsibility to directly address these issues,
as a therapeutically corrective experience is contingent upon the
therapist behaving in a non-neglectful, non-abusive manner. Talking about the issues without limit-setting is of little therapeutic
value. It is akin to the situation in which a client has insight about
abuse but continues to have abusive contact with a parent, without
setting limits.

Setting limits regarding self-destructive behavior doesn't mean
that the therapist expects nor demands perfection, or an overnight
change. It means that the therapist expects commitment from the
client, and continual improvement with these issues. It is thus essential to openly, and continually explore how the abusive dynamics are being acted-out.

It is therapeutic to place the issues in a wholistic abuse framework with the client. It is often easier for clients to view themselves in a victim role rather than in one of perpetration. By ignoring the ways the client perpetrates against themselves and against others, therapists fall into enabling and solidifying a client's victim/victimizer identity which is clearly not in the client's best interest. Issues of perpetration are almost always present. Learning to view the system as a whole, with themselves playing all the roles, will be the most effective in terms of interrupting the generational cycle.

Learning to view one's parents in perspective, and understanding the origins of the abuse that are separate from them can be a freeing experience. It helps the client really understand that the abuse wasn't their fault, but in fact was the abuser's responsibility, and was about the abuser's history. This understanding, however, without accountability, can be dangerous. While understanding the origins of the abuse, it is still necessary for them to learn to hold their parents accountable for their behavior. This accountability has to extend to the client's behavior as well, to really make an experience corrective.

GROUP DYNAMICS WITH VICTIMS/VICTIMIZERS

Therapy groups are a powerfully corrective medium for many people who have been raised in an abusive family system. A group can also be destructive if it is allowed to take on the characteristics of an abusive system. In this case, individuals repeat, without interruption, their roles as victim, by getting everyone angry at them, of victimizer, by attacking other group members, and of neglect, by not giving to one another.

In this situation, the group facilitators have an immense job to do. The facilitators become like the surrogate parents of the group. If they in any way sanction verbal or emotional abuse they are, in effect, reinforcing the members abusive upbringing. It is then more likely that the patterns will go on unchecked or even get worse. They must also model appropriate nurturing, support, and confrontation, in order to teach the members these skills.

Co-facilitating is usually a better system than solo facilitating a group of this kind. It will help the therapists most effectively to use the opportunities for healing which present themselves. Co-facilitation also offers support for the therapists. When co-facilitating, it is less likely that any form of role-reversal will occur with the clients. It is simply easier to maintain boundaries when there are two clinicians involved.

When intaking clients to the group it is essential to talk with the referring therapist if the person is not already working with one of the facilitators. During the process of the group experience, therapeutic consultation should remain consistent. An individual will often present much differently in group than in individual therapy. This consultation also reduces the likelihood that a client's attempts to triangulate or polarize will be successful.

A therapy group will reflect all the dynamics of the members' family of origin. Co-dependence, trust issues, accountability, victim and offender behavior, intimacy struggles, dishonesty, "bullying," shame and rage, despair, powerlessness and neglect issues all become apparent as the group develops. The rules and boundaries which are part of an abusive family system will also be in operation in the group. The following rules are commonly grappled with:

- A person is either totally good or is totally bad.
- When the going gets tough, the tough either attack or withdraw.
- You can't expect anything from people anyway.
- People are only out for what they can get.
- If people are nice to you, it's because they want something from you.
- Authority is incompetant so you need to take over for them.
- There is only so much to go around so everyone needs to fight and compete for what little there is.

The boundary issues one would expect to see in group include both of the extreme ends of the continuum of interaction. Group members will be attempting to merge or disengage at any given point in time. Members will attempt to give advice, say what the others are feeling, invade boundaries, and exhibit the tendency toward dual-role functioning. At other times members will talk about extremely painful issues and receive nothing from other members, because the group members have dissociated, or are self-focused.

When this occurs it is crucial to call attention to the neglectful dynamics which are in operation. Members often report that they didn't know how to respond so "went away or got shameful," or that they were thinking about their own issues. Using this situation to teach about neglect can be helpful to the clients. If the group facilitators take over and fill in the silence without noting the neglect, the group loses a learning opportunity. It is still the therapist's job to make interpretation of behavior, appropriately nurture the clients, role-model and set limits.

Controlling behavior also becomes a central theme in the group. Most of the members have equated control with increased safety, safety from abuse, and safety from the feelings associated with abuse. The controlling behavior may be passive or active in its expression. Active controlling is characterized by members who bully in the group, or manage the group, and passive control is reflected in the use of silence and powerful non-verbal communication. Using those opportunities to teach about the negative consequences of this type of controlling and to help the clients go underneath the behaviors to the feelings which are present can be effective. This technique is also helpful when hearing a client talk about abusive behaviors. Often the client can trace back to feeling shame or rage or other types of anxiety or stress before being abusive.

Modeling ethical decisions, apologizing for mistakes, directly confronting abusive behavior in a firm and caring manner and ongoing group processing are all strategies to make the group safe for the members, and to provide a corrective experience. If these don't occur, a vital piece of the therapy doesn't take place. There are many people who have been treated for victimization or perpetration problems who never address the systemic aspects of the abuse, and so are in a position to continue the system, even if the overt types of abuse aren't occurring. Consider the following example.

A thirty year old female client, whose issues include a "chronic victim stance" begins her time in group talking about how she has come to understand that it was her parents job to stop her from being mean and vicious to her younger brother. Her husband has helped her to realize that this is one of the consequences of the neglect by her parents. Given this, she now believes she can stop feeling responsible for having hurt her brother and how she later hurt one of her friends. The group supports the client's new insight. The therapist, who is also supportive of the clients new understanding, reminds her that she is still accountable for her abusive behavior and that she still needs to make amends to her brother and to the friend. The group becomes angry at the therapist. The therapist explains that not holding yourself accountable for your own actions, even when they are learned and supported in an abusive system, is a way of staying "stuck" in, and perpetuating that system.

In this situation, the group is joining with the abusive system. All of the members want the client to feel comfortable, non-shameful, and exonerated of any wrongdoing. They have been able to see for some time, the effects of the neglectful family dynamics on their group member. They are also trying desperately to not feel responsible for what was done to them and for what they have done to others. They all have their own secrets about siblings. If the therapist joins with the group in polarizing, and playing good vs. evil, the clients will have to struggle with their own guilt and their own secrets privately. If, on the other hand, the situation is addressed in an open and non-shaming manner, there is an invitation to other members to courageously look at their own behavior and to give the same kind of feedback to group members. It also teaches them to not accept abuse even when they can understand and feel compassion for the person who is acting abusively.

Therapists and group members can inadvertantly reinforce victim/victimizer behavior. Behaving toward the person as if they are helpless and powerless, joining in seeing others in the client's life as "bad," and the client as "good," not holding the client accountable in group, failing to confront perpetrator behaviors, and not distinguishing between childhood powerlessness and adulthood powerlessness all serve as reinforcers for the roles.

PROFESSIONAL SELF-CARE ISSUES

When working with victims/victimizers for any length of time, professional self-care issues are of primary concern. The rate of burnout for professionals is high (White, 1986). The earlier stages of burnout include an internalization by the therapist of the hopelessness and cynicism experienced by most of these clients. A type of spiritual despair and depression can develop for clinicians.

Most people live with an enormous amount of denial, which allows for a shelter from the realities of lives not their own. While this denial isn't always positive in terms of the effects on the world at large or on their own life situation, it does allow for a certain degree of emotional protection. When listening to details of victimization, one is not allowed this particular type of shelter.

Violence and addiction affects all of us on a daily basis. It is a part of the world we live in. We can't not be affected by abuse. When working with abuse victims and perpetrators day in and day out, the therapist has to develop strategies to cope with their own response to the devastation they are seeing. For this process to be one which doesn't render the clinician ineffective, it has to include a rather spiritual and philosophical component. "What does my role as a therapist include when dealing with a global issue like abuse?" "What can I do and what can't I do, and where do I channel the knowledge and concern I have for humanity?" These questions are grappled with on an ongoing basis. It is difficult, but proper, to keep one's own despair and anger about abuse out of the therapeutic relationship, except when it is therapeutic to express it. To hear someone talk specifically about perpetrating against themself or someone else with either no remorse or with a sense of "glee" can be a horrifying experience, and one that will evoke an emotional response.

When working with an abuse population, there is little the clinician doesn't hear about in detail. A depression can develop related to the sense of helplessness and hopelessness one experiences when one consistantly hears and sees such violence and trauma. Even if the clinician hasn't experienced much direct abuse him or herself, it becomes clear how violent the world is. The grief associated with this knowledge is painful for the therapist. At times the intensity is too much and can lead a clinician to turn hard and cynical. Neither "bleeding" with clients or turning to stone are effective therapeutic stances. It is in the best interest of both the therapist and the client to come to a therapeutic world view which allows for reality, both positive and negative.

Supervision and case consultation are mandatory when working with this population. It is necessary for the therapist to discuss the countertransference issues she or he is having. It is impossible to stay clear and positively and effectively use all of the therapeutic opportunities which are present without ongoing consultation. A process of case management which only addresses the clients needs is not adequate. Rather, the supervision or consultation needs to include a processing of how the therapist feels and how she or he is interpreting the actions of the client. Separating countertransference issues from internal diagnostic reactions is important. When the therapist is feeling unsafe and scared, it is likely that one or more of the clients is overtly or covertly acting out perpetration. It often takes feedback from non-involved professionals to clearly see what is occurring, and respond appropriately.

Therapists also need to be able to leave their clients' problems at work. Firmly closing the clients' file, washing one's hands, verbally processing with a co-worker before leaving for the day and noting for supervision any obsessive tendencies toward a particular client, can all be effective strategies to help the therapist leave work at work.

RECOMMENDATIONS

1. Be a part of a supervision or case consultation group which allows for processing transference and countertransference issues, with specific attention to ethics and professional boundaries.

2. Be clear with clients about what the boundaries of the relationship include, and what they don't include. Have these written as well as explain them verbally.

3. Respectfully give clients feedback about the impact of their behavior on the therapeutic relationship.

4. Process group dynamics with specific attention to boundary issues in the group, and with attention to both victim and victimizer behavior.

5. Ideally co-facilitate groups when a large percentage of the members are from abusive systems.

6. Pay attention to your emotional response to a client at any given time. If you feel scared or "icky" about that client, get con-

sultation to determine how the client is acting-out perpetrator behavior.

7. Increase effectiveness at identifying current and past abusive patterns.

8. Monitor your own levels of spiritual despair and depression. If they are increasing, assess what you can do to take better care of yourself.

9. Get adequate support for yourself when your own "victim" issues get triggered.

CONCLUSION

In conclusion, professional boundaries and ethics take on a special meaning when working with boundary restructuring in therapy. While each therapist will have their own ideas of how to best address an issue with a client, the process remains one of constant assessment and consultation. It is impossible when doing this type of work to remain clear, courageous and ethical if operating within the isolation of the therapist/client relationship.

Therapeutically attending to the existing professional boundary issues within this type of therapy offers rich opportunities to provide the client with corrective and healing experiences.

REFERENCES

Coleman, E. & Colgan, P. (1986). Boundary Inadequacy in Drug Dependent Families. *Journal of Psychoactive Drugs*, 18(1), 21-30.

Coleman, E. & Schaefer, S. (1986). Boundaries of Sex and Intimacy Between Client and Counselor. *Journal of Counseling and Development*, 64, 341-344.

Ellis, G. (1987). Discussion on Transference and Countertransference, Unpublished paper.

Evans, S. & Schaefer, S. (1987). Incest and Chemically Dependent Women: Treatment Considerations. *Journal of Chemical Dependency Treatment*, 1(1).

Evans, S. (1987). Shame, Boundaries and Dissociation in Chemically Dependent, Abusive and Incestuous Families. *Alcoholism Treatment Quarterly*, 4(2), 157-159.

Kenworthy, K., Koufacos, C., & Sherman, J. (1976). Women and Therapy: A Survey on Internship Programs. *Psychology of Women Quarterly*, 1(2) Winter.

Nielsen, L. (1984). Sexual Abuse and Chemical Dependency: Assessing the Risk For Adult Children. *Focus on Family*, Nov/Dec.

Nielsen, L., Peterson, M., Shapiro, M., & Thompson, P. (1986). Supervision Approaches in Cases of Boundary Violations and Sexual Victimization by Therapists. Minnesota Task Force on Sexual Exploitation by Counselors and Therapists Manual.

Peterson, M. (1986). Boundary Issues in Psychotherapy, Unpublished Paper.

Shapiro, R. (1977). A Family Therapy Approach to Alcoholism. *Journal of Marriage and Family Counseling*, October.

Shoener, G. Paper available through Walk-In Counseling Center, Minneapolis, MN.

Thompson, P., Shapiro, M., Nielsen, L. & Peterson, M. (1986). Supervision Strategies To Prevent Sexual Abuse Of Clients By Therapists and Counselors. Minnesota Task Force on Sexual Exploitation by Counselors and Therapists Manual.

White, W. (1986). Incest in the Organizational Family, The Ecology of Burnout in Closed Systems. A Lighthouse Training Institute Publication.